SELECTED POEMS

FROM THE

DĪVĀNI SHAMSI TABRĪZ.

SELECTED POEMS

FROM THE

DĪVĀNI SHAMSI TABRĪZ

EDITED AND TRANSLATED

WITH AN INTRODUCTION, NOTES, AND APPENDICES

BY

REYNOLD A. NICHOLSON, M.A.

*formerly Sir Thomas Adams's Professor of Arabic
in the University of Cambridge*

KITAB BHAVAN
New Delhi-110002

Kitab Bhavan
Publishers, Distributors, Exporters & Importers
1784, Kalan Mahal, Darya Ganj
New Delhi-110002 (India)

Phone   :   (91-11) 3277392/93, 3274686
Web Site :   www.kitabbhavan.com
E-mail   :   nasri@vsnl.com
Fax   :   (91-11) 3263383

ISBN   :   81-7151-197-X
Book Code :   S00088

Ist Published in India   1898
IInd Edition   1994
IIIrd Edition   2000

Published in India by:
Nusrat Ali Nasri for Kitab Bhavan
1784, Kalan Mahal, Darya Ganj
New Delhi-110002 [India]

Printed in India at:
Lahooti Fine Art Press
1711, Sui Walan, Darya Ganj
New Delhi-110002 (India)

ἡ σπουδὴ οὐκ ἔξω ἁμαρτίας εἶναι, ἀλλὰ θεὸν εἶναι.   PLOTINUS.

This is that mystic religion which, though it has nothing in it but that same spirit, that same truth, and that same life, which always was and always must be the religion of all God's holy angels and saints in heaven, is by the wisdom of this world accounted to be madness. LAW.

But I'll pour floods of love and hide myself.
BROWNING.

PREFACE.

ABOUT six years ago, when I consulted Professor
Robertson Smith, whose kindness and heroic un-
selfishness none of his pupils can ever forget, as to what I
should make the subject of the dissertation expected from
candidates for a Trinity Fellowship, he suggested the
Dívāni Shamsi Tabrīz, in other words, the lyrical poetry of
Jalālu'ddīn Rūmī. I was the more ready to follow his
advice as the Ṣūfī doctrines had even then begun to inspire
me with the strange and irresistible fascination which a
religion of love and beauty exercises over certain minds.
Accordingly, Mr E. G. Browne having lent me his copy of
the Tabrīz Edition of the Dívān, I worked through it page
by page, selecting the poems that pleased me best and
translating them in prose or verse. The present volume is
an outcome of that experiment. It is not, however, merely
a réchauffé. My original dissertation was based upon a
single text and left many difficulties unsolved. In 1894 I
collated a splendid manuscript of the Dívān preserved in
the Vienna Hofbibliothek, and on my return I examined
one of equal importance, which the authorities of the
Leyden University Library generously placed at my
disposal. The texts thus obtained I have corrected and

supplemented by reference to MSS. in the British Museum
and elsewhere. As regards interpretation also much has
been gained. In a wider knowledge of Ṣūfī literature, and
especially of the *Maṣnavī*, I found the key to passages
which seemed hopelessly obscure. The comparative method
may be abused; its value is beyond dispute. Ṣūfiism has
few ideas, but an inexhaustible wealth and variety of
illustration. Among a thousand fluttering masks the
interpreter is required to identify each old familiar face.
Now one mask reveals more than another, and when that
has been penetrated, its neighbour can no longer dissemble
the likeness which hitherto remained unrecognised. I do
not, of course, pretend to have understood everything:
Ṣūfiism is neither an exact science nor a popular history of
the Creation. This enigmatic and ambiguous style, of
which the Dīvān is a masterpiece, will always leave ample
room for conjecture, even though its chief characters are
easily deciphered. I trust that my explanatory notes, if
occasionally they prove to be beside the mark, may nevertheless contribute to a better appreciation of the greatest
mystical poet of any age.

While the *Maṣnavī* is accessible in the scholarly abstract
of Mr Whinfield and the laborious but amazingly unpoetical
version of Bk. I. by Sir James Redhouse, the Dīvān, scarcely
inferior in merit or fame, has been less fortunate. There
is no English edition; Austria has given us Rosenzweig's
Auswahl (1838), and the clumsy translations of Von
Hammer in his *Schöne Redekünste Persiens*. For a notice
of both the reader is referred to the Introduction. I have
included three odes which appear in the *Auswahl*; the rest
are now published in Europe for the first time. The task

of selection was not a simple one, and I have necessarily relied on my own taste and feeling. If my book were not addressed to students of Persian rather than to lovers of literature, I should have been tempted to imitate Abū Tammām, whose *Ḥamāsa* is a compilation of verses torn from their context. Such a plan is peculiarly favoured by the loose structure of the ghazal, where couplets complete in themselves are strung together in the slightest fashion. But as no writer can fairly be judged by fragments, however fine, I have endeavoured to make this anthology a true and sufficient reflexion of the whole Dīvān.

My translation seeks to reconcile the claims of accuracy and art : it is therefore in prose. Obviously English verse cannot convey the full verbal sense of oriental poetry without lapsing into grotesque doggerel ; the translator must either profess a general adherence to his author's meaning (see Appendix II.) or, rising above the letter, he must catch the elusive spirit of his original and reproduce it in a worthy form. Of this, the highest and rarest kind of translation, Fitzgerald's 'Omar Khayyām is a classic example. I have done my best to avoid gratuitous banalities, when no misapprehension was possible. Thus I have not rendered *ṣaffi niʿāl* by 'shoe-rack,' nor have I described a burning heart as 'roast-meat.' Although some Persian compounds can hardly be englished except by coining equivalent terms, I have taken warning from the sad fate of more than one inventor. 'Nubiquity' and 'nulliquity' are terrible epitaphs.

Finally, my warmest thanks are due to Professor Cowell, who lent me his two manuscripts of the Dīvān ; to Mr E. G. Browne, who since I began to study Persian has never grudged me the benefit of his unrivalled knowledge and experience; to Mr G. Lowes Dickinson, who permitted me to make use of an unpublished dissertation on Plotinus; and above all to Professor Bevan, who not only read the proof-sheets throughout but assisted me with many ingenious and important suggestions.

I would also declare my obligation to the staff of the Cambridge University Press for the admirable way in which they have printed a very troublesome text.

TRINITY COLLEGE,
   July, 1898.

TABLE OF CONTENTS.

		PAGES
PREFACE	. . . .	vii—x
INTRODUCTION	. . . .	xv—li
§ 1.	Authorship of the Dīvān . . .	xv
§ 2.	Jalālu 'ddīn Rūmī	xvi
§ 3.	Shamsi Tabrīz	xviii
§ 4.	The Spiritual Director	xx
§ 5.	Jalālu 'ddīn and Shamsi Tabrīz . .	xxii
§ 6.	Ṣūfiism in Persian poetry. Development of Ṣūfiism	xxv
§ 7.	The doctrines of Jalālu 'ddīn and Plotinus	xxx
§ 8.	Criticism of the Dīvān	xxxvi
§ 9.	Editions and Manuscripts of the Dīvān	xlvii
ADDENDA AND CORRIGENDA	. . . . .	liii—lv
SELECTED POEMS	. . . .	2—195
NOTES	. . . .	197—318
ADDITIONAL NOTES	. . . . . .	319—330
APPENDICES	. . . .	331—350
I.	Illustrative passages from the Dīvān with a list of the historical and autobiographical allusions	331
II.	Translations in verse	342
III.	Table showing where the Selected Poems occur in other editions of the Dīvān .	347
IV.	Comparative Table of passages quoted from the Maṣnavī	349
INDICES	. . . .	351—367
I.	Persian and Arabic	351
II.	English	362

LIST OF ABBREVIATIONS.

For the MSS. denoted by the letters BB²B³CC²LV see the
Introduction, § 9.

References to the Tabrīz Edition of the Dīvān are by page
and beyt ; those to the Preface of that Edition are by page and
line. Small 'a' affixed to a number denotes that the corresponding line or beyt belongs to the marginal text.

LIST OF AUTHORS AND EDITIONS REFERRED TO IN THE NOTES.

(This list includes only those editions which have not been specified.)

Akhlāqi Jalālī (Lucknow, 1889).

Ardā Vīrāf, the Book of, ed. and translated by M. Haug and E. W. West (Stuttgart, 1872).

'Attār, *Mantiqu 'ttair*, ed. and translated by Garcin de Tassy (Paris, 1864).

'Attār, *Pendnameh*, ed. and translated by Silvestre de Sacy (Paris, 1819).

Bahāri 'Ajam, a Persian Dictionary (Lucknow, 1847 ; Delhi, 1853).

Burhāni Qāṭi', a Dictionary of the Persian Language (Calcutta, 1818).

Dabistān, translated by Shea and Troyer (Paris, 1843).

Deutsche Mystiker, ed. by Franz Pfeiffer (Leipzig, 1857).

Firdausī, *Shāhnāma*, ed. by Vullers (Lugduni Batavorum, 1877, etc.).

Freytag, G. W., *Arabum Proverbia* (Bonnae ad Rhenum, 1838, etc.).

Ghiyāṣu 'llughāt, a Persian Dictionary (Lucknow, 1849).

Gulshani Rāz, ed. and translated by E. H. Whinfield (London, 1880).

Ḥāfiz, the *Dīvān* of, ed. and translated by Vincenz Ritter v. Rosenzweig-Schwannau (Wien, 1858, etc.).

Ḥarīrī, les *Séances* de, publiées en Arabe avec un commentaire choisi par Silvestre de Sacy (Paris, 1847, etc.).

Ibnu 'l Fāriḍ, *Tā 'iyya*, ed. and translated by Hammer-Purgstall (Wien, 1854).

Ibn Khallikān, *Biographical Dictionary*, translated by De Slane (Paris, 1842, etc.).

Jāmī, *Bahāristān*, ed. and translated by Freiherr v. Schlechta-Wssehrd (Wien, 1846).

Jāmī, *Nafaḥātu 'l Uns*, with a biographical sketch of the author by W. Nassau Lees (Calcutta, 1859).

Jāmī, *Yūsuf ū Zulaikhā*, ed. and translated by Vincenz v. Rosenzweig (Wien, 1824).

Juan de la Cruz, in the *Biblioteca de autores Españoles*, Vol. 27 (Madrid, 1853).

Jurjānī, *Kitābu 'tta'rīfāt*, ed. by G. Flügel (Lipsiae, 1845).

Lane, E. W., an *Arabic-English Lexicon* (London, 1863, etc.).

„   , the *Thousand and One Nights* (London, 1841).

„   , an *Account of the Manners and Customs of the Modern Egyptians* (London, 1871).

Law, W., *The Spirit of Love* (London, 1893).

Maṣnavī, by Jalālu 'ddīn Rūmī. See Appendix IV.

Niẓāmī, *Iskandar-nāma* (Calcutta, 1812).

'Omar Khayyām, ed. and translated by E. H. Whinfield (London, 1883).

Sa'dī, *Būstān*, ed. by Ch. H. Graf (Vienna, 1858).

„   , *Gulistān*, ed. by Platts (London, 1874).

Ṭabarī, ed. by M. J. De Goeje and others (Lugduni Batavorum, 1879, etc.).

Tholuck, F. A. D., *Ssufismus* (Berolini, 1821).

Vaughan, R. A., *Hours with the Mystics* (London, 1860).

Vullers, J. A., *Lexicon Persico-Latinum* (Bonnae ad Rhenum, 1855, etc.).

INTRODUCTION.

§ 1. THE Dīvāni Shamsi Tabrīz acquaints us with a striking literary phenomenon[1]. It is true that books have been ascribed by ambition or malice to those who had no hand in producing them. It is true, again, that while the fashion of pseudonymous authorship is everywhere understood and practised, in Persia the poet à la mode cannot dispense with a takhallus, which instead of exciting curiosity and sparing modesty a blush serves to gratify the generous patron, to immortalise a place or event, to unfold some characteristic, and in fine to secure that its owner shall not for all time lie buried under one of those cumbrous family trees that betray alike the poverty and confusion of Mohammedan nomenclature. But here is no question of takhallus[2], forgery, or composition holding up to ridicule the imagined author. The Dīvān was never attributed to Shamsi Tabrīz, who probably died before it was complete. Why then does his name appear on the title-page and at the end of most of the odes? Who was he, and in what

[1] The case of Plato and Socrates is similar in kind, not in degree.
[2] In a certain mystical sense Shamsi Tabrīz may be regarded as a takhallus. Jalālu 'ddīn asserts the identity of subject and object: to him Shamsi Tabrīz represents the divine Beloved, the one Being in whom all individual names are manifested and ultimately merged.

relation did he stand to Jalālu 'ddīn Rūmī? Why should
a poet who ranks with Firdausī and Hāfiz lay on the brow
of an unknown dervish his wreath of imperishable lyric
song?

§ 2. Jalālu 'ddīn Rūmī was born at Balkh on the 6th
of Rabī'u 'l Awwal, 604 A. H. (30th September, 1207)[1].
We may pass lightly over the apocryphal genealogy which
connects him with Abū Bekr, the first Caliph. His descent,
on the mother's side, from the royal house of Khwārazm is
well established. Jalālu 'ddīn Husain Al-Khāṭibī married
a daughter of 'Alā 'u 'ddīn Muhammad Khwārazm-Shāh.
Their son, Bahā 'u 'ddīn Walad, is the poet's father.

Bahā 'u 'ddīn was a man of great learning and piety, an
eloquent preacher and distinguished professor. Unfortunately, not content with 'declaiming against the philosophers
and rationalists of the day,' he seems to have indulged in
political diatribes. According to Aflākī, he attacked the
'innovations' of the reigning monarch, Muhammad Ḳuṭbu
'ddīn Khwārazm-Shāh, surnamed Takash, who held sway
in the north-east of Persia and in Transoxania. Another
account depicts the king as jealous of his growing influence
and popularity. Whatever may have been the cause, he
found it convenient to quit Balkh with his family and a

---

[1] The fullest biography is that contained in the *Manāqibu 'l 'Ārifīn*,
written by Aflākī, a pupil of Jalālu 'ddīn's grandson, 'Ārif, between
710 and 754 A.H., but this work, rich in anecdote and valuable as a
thaumaturgic record, is not to be trusted in matters of fact. Copious
extracts are given by Redhouse in his translation of Bk. I. of the
Masnavi. I have also consulted Daulat Shāh (*Tadhkiratu 'l Shu'arā*,
p. 85, Bombay Ed.), who is agreeably sober and methodical, Jāmī's
Nafaḥātu 'l Uns, p. 530, and the Preface to the Tabrīz Edition of
the Dīvān (T).

few friends (about 607 A.H.). At Nīshāpūr the travellers were met by the famous Ṣūfī, Farīdu 'ddīn 'Aṭṭār[1], who gave Jalāl, at this time a mere child, his *Asrār-nāma* (Book of Mysteries), and prophesied that he would attain the highest pitch of spiritual eminence. From Nīshāpūr they went to Baghdād, where they received news of the destruction of Balkh by Jingīz Khān (608 A.H.); then to Mecca, Damascus, and Malaṭiya (Melitene). Four years were spent at Arzanjān in Armenia, and seven at Laranda. Here Jalālu 'ddīn married Jauhar Khātūn[2], daughter of the Lālā Sharafu 'ddīn of Samarcand (623 A.H.). Soon afterwards the family settled in Qōniya (Iconium), the capital of the Seljūq prince, 'Alā 'u 'ddīn Kaiḳubād, and Bahā 'u 'ddīn resumed his professorial activity under the royal patronage.

If we can believe the stories which are told of him, the poet must indeed have been a 'marvellous boy.' When he was six years old, he saw visions, imbued his playmates with philosophy, and performed extraordinary feats of fasting. He was educated first by his father and then by Burhānu 'ddīn Muḥaqqiq Tirmidhī, who was a pupil of Bahā 'u 'ddīn at Balkh. On his father's death (628 A.H.) Jalāl succeeded to the vacant chair[3]. Although the fame

---

[1] 'Aṭṭār was born in 513 A.H. The dramatic fitness of this encounter leads one to suspect that it is only ben trovato.

[2] She seems to have died young. Jalāl took a second wife, Kirā Khātūn, who survived him.

[3] بر مسند پدر نشست (T. 4. 10). Aflākī states that he had previously visited Aleppo and Damascus, and that on his return to Qōniya he devoted nine years to the study of theosophy with Burhānu 'ddīn.

of his erudition and the brilliancy of his eloquence brought
eager disciples from every quarter to his feet—he had a
class of 400—the positive sciences could not, he felt,
satisfy the soul's infinite longing for freedom and rest.
He embraced accordingly the pantheistic doctrines which
had early taken root in the barren soil of Islām, and sown
broadcast over the Mohammedan empire by a long series
of wandering saints, sprang up and blossomed with oriental
luxuriance.

§ 3. On the 26th of Jumādā 'l Ākhir, 642 A. H. (28th
November, 1244)[1] Shamsi Tabrīz[2], during his travels[3],
arrived in Qōniya. It will be proper to set down here the
few facts preserved by tradition concerning this weird
figure, wrapped in coarse black felt, who flits across the
stage for a moment and disappears tragically enough.

---

[1] So Aflākī and Jāmī. But Riẓā Ḳulī asserts (T. 4. 10) that
Jalāl was 62 years of age when Shamsi Tabrīz first came to Qōniya.
This date (666 A.H.) is apparently confirmed by a passage in the
Dīvān (T. 244. 1):

> Forty years did Reason plunge me in care;
> At three score and two I was made a prey and eschewed
> (worldly) meditation.

[See the original in Appendix I. F (c).] On the other hand Shamsi
Tabrīz is addressed in Bk. I. of the *Maṣnavī*, and we know that
Bk. II. was commenced in 662 A.H.

[2] See p. xvi, note. The tedious account in the *Jawāhiru 'l Asrār*
(a commentary on the first three books of the Maṣnavī by Kamālu
'ddīn Ḥusain of Khwārazm) adds little to our knowledge, and the same
remark applies to the *Majālisu 'l 'Ushshāq* (Ouseley, *Notices of Persian
Poets*, p. 247).

[3] در أثناي مسافرت (*Nafaḥātu 'l Uns*, p. 537, l. 3). He had
been sent by his spiritual teacher, Ruknu 'ddīn Sanjāsī, to seek Jalāl
in the land of Rūm (Daulat Shāh). Aflākī's description of their
meeting agrees in the main with that of Jāmī. Daulat Shāh gives
a somewhat different version.

Even his parentage is uncertain. Some declare that his father, Khāwand 'Alā 'u 'ddīn[1], claimed descent from Kiyā Buzurgumīd[2]. 'Alā 'u 'ddīn abandoned his ancestral sect (the Ismā'īlīs), burned their books and tracts, preached Islām in the strongholds of heresy[3], and privily sent Shamsu 'ddīn, a youth of rare beauty[4], to receive his education at Tabrīz. According to others he was born in Tabrīz, where his father carried on the trade of a cloth-merchant (بزّاز)[5]. He is said to have studied under Bābā Kamāl Jundī, Abū Bakr Sila-bāf, and Ruknu 'ddīn Sanjāsī[6]. He had travelled

---

[1] Some MSS. of Daulat Shāh read جلال ٱلدين.

[2] Successor of Ḥasan Ṣabbāḥ (see Von Hammer, *Geschichte der Assassinen*, p. 114 seqq.). The Assassins are a branch of the اسمٰعيليّه or باطنيّه (cf. Guyard, *Fragments relatifs à la doctrine des Ismaélis*, p. 8 seqq.).

[3] Hence he got the nickname, Nau Musalmān or Bū Musalmān (the MSS. vary).

[4] He was brought up, says Daulat Shāh, among the women, كه چشمِ نااهلى و نامحرمى بر وَى نَيُفتد. From them he learned the art of embroidering in gold, for which reason he is known as زردوز.

[5] Jāmī, who gives the full name of Shamsi Tabrīz as شمس ٱلدين محمّد بن على بن ملكداد تبريزى, has followed this tradition.

[6] On the authority of Daulat Shāh Shamsu 'ddīn's spiritual pedigree is:

> Ruknu 'ddīn Sanjāsī.
> Ẓiyā 'u 'ddīn Abū 'l Najīb Suhravardī.
> Aḥmad Ghazzālī.
> Abū Bakr Nassāj.
> Abū 'l Qāsim Gurgānī.
> Abū 'Usmān Maghribī.
> Abū 'Alī Kātib.

much; whence he obtained the sobriquet, Paranda (the Flier). His character was despotic and overbearing; he was extremely bitter in his sermons, and likened his learned auditors to oxen and asses. Perhaps this may be the cause why Dr Sprenger calls him 'a most disgusting cynic[1].' He was comparatively illiterate[2], but his tremendous spiritual enthusiasm, based on the conviction that he was a chosen organ and mouth-piece of Deity, cast a spell over all who entered the enchanted circle of his power. In this respect, as in many others, for example, in his strong passions, his poverty, and his violent death, Shamsi Tabríz curiously resembles Socrates; both imposed themselves upon men of genius, who gave their crude ideas artistic expression; both proclaim the futility of external knowledge, the need of illumination, the value of love; but wild raptures and arrogant defiance of every human law can ill atone for the lack of that 'sweet reasonableness' and moral grandeur which distinguish the sage from the devotee.

§ 4.   It has been observed that the Neoplatonic deity—the Absolute One of Plotinus—owing to its all but in-

> Abū 'Alī Rūdbārī.
> Abū 'l Qāsim Junaid.
> Siŋ ī Saqatī.
> Abū Maḥfūẓ (Maʻrūf Karkhī).

The Imām ʻAlī ibn Mūsā 'l Riẓā.   Abū Sulaimān Dā'ūd Ṭā'ī.
Ḥaẓraṭi Risālat (the Prophet).   Ḥabīb, the Persian.
                                    Ḥasan of Baṣra.
                                    ʻAlī ibn Abī Ṭālib.

---

[1] *Catalogue of Oudh Manuscripts*, p. 490.

[2] Cf. the anecdote related by Jāmī, *Nafaḥātu 'l Uns*, p. 536, l. 12 seqq.

accessible isolation was quickly overshadowed, if not dethroned, in the hearts of its worshippers, by the dei minores (daemons, angels, heroes and the like) forming a luminous staircase between earth and Heaven. These subordinate hierarchies, more or less remote from the divine Essence, seemed to offer a practicable hope, even a measure of responsive sympathy: anything was better than blank infinite negation. So with the Ṣūfīs. Professing to adore a universal abstraction, they make individual men the objects of their real worship. 'Among the religious-philosophical sects of the period in which our poet lived the doctrine was generally held, that Man, if he be left to his own devices, will inevitably go astray : therefore he must choose a Master to guide him in the right path[1].' The Master (پیر) is God's representative, his actions are God's actions, in spirit he is one with God. His blasphemies and immoralities, nay, his very crimes, are not only con-doned but glorified: darkness cannot proceed from the sun, nor evil from God. What we call evil is intrinsically good, though it seems imperfect in relation to ourselves. The mischievous effect of such theories on vulgar and uneducated minds need hardly be pointed out. 'Alī, Ja'far Ṣādiq, Abū Muslim, and innumerable others, were regarded as incarnations of the Godhead. Ḥasan Ṣabbāḥ was flattered by his adherents with divine honours and a fanatical devotion that braved the worst tortures of impotent revenge. While we readily acquit Jalālu 'ddīn of sharing this extravagant materialism, which indeed he is at pains to discountenance, we must confess that his

---

[1] Rosen's *Maṣnavi*, **Note 159.**

language is sometimes ambiguous. For instance, in the
last beyt of one of his ghazals he says, referring to Shamsi
Tabrīz:

$$ \text{آن پادشاهِ اعظم در بسته بود مُحکَم} $$

(T. 180. 2) $ \text{پوشیده دلقِ آدمِ امروز بر در آمد} $

That monarch supreme had shut the door fast;
To-day he has come to the door, clothed in the garment
of mortality.

The pretensions of Shamsi Tabrīz himself may be judged
by an anecdote in the *Manāqibu 'l 'Arifīn*. One day a
person met him in the market-place and exclaimed, "There
is no god save God; Shamsu 'ddīn is the apostle of God."
The people, on hearing this, raised a great hubbub, and
wished to kill him, but Shams intervened and led him
away, remarking: "My good friend, my name is Muḥammad.
Thou shouldst have shouted, 'Muḥammad is the apostle of
God.' The rabble will not take gold that is not coined[1]."

§ 5.   How utter was Jalāl's self-abandonment, how
complete his submission to the glowing faith and imperious
will of his new friend, Aflākī informs us: Shamsu 'ddīn
demanded and received the obedience due to a sultan from
the meanest of his slaves.   To quote the vivid words of
Riẓā Ḳulī, 'he (Jalāl) was so transported and smitten[2],
that for a time he was thought insane.'   He renounced his
teaching, and retired with Shams to solitary and desert

---

[1] Aflākī in Redhouse's *Maṣnavi*, p. 105. The theory that all
prophets are identical with each other and with God is expounded
in the *Maṣnavi* (Būlāq Ed.), Vol. I. p. 68, l. 15 seqq.

[2] $ \text{مجذوب و مطعون} $ (T. 4. 11—12).

places, where in close communion they discussed the deepest arcana of mystical philosophy.

Bitterly resenting what they conceived to be an insidious attempt to seduce their beloved Master from the true religion, Jalāl's scholars and disciples assailed the unwelcome visitor with abuse, if not with actual violence. Shams fled to Tabrīz. Thither he was followed by his convert, who brought him back in triumph, but soon a fresh outbreak of persecution caused him to undertake a journey to Damascus[1], where he stayed for two years. He was passionately regretted by Jalāl, who bade the musicians chant songs of love and engaged, day and night, in the samā'. Most of his ghazals were composed during this period of separation. Here the course of events becomes obscure. Apparently Jalāl, unable to forego the society of his dearest friend, sent his son, Sultān Walad, to Damascus, charged with the task of finding Shams and recalling him to Qōniya. Soon after his return he vanished mysteriously. Most authorities agree that he was put to death: only the cause and manner of it are disputed[2].

[1] Cf   رسید مُژده بشام است شمسِ تبریزی

چه صُبحها که نماید اگر بشام بُوَد (T. 161. 13).

The news has come! Shamsi Tabrīz is in Damascus.
If he is in Damascus, what mornings will appear!

(I have not tried to reproduce the play on شمس and on the double sense of شام).

[2] Aflākī says that he was put to death 'without inquiry or formality' by the Sultan's police (Redhouse's *Maṣnavi*, p. 108), but the motive alleged is absurdly inadequate. Daulat Shāh mentions another story, that one of Jalālu 'ddīn's disciples (فرزند از فرزندانِ

مولانا) 'threw down a wall on his head,' adding, however, that this

That any of the extant versions is founded on knowledge
seems highly improbable; they may be described as legends
begotten by the credulous imagination of the dervish,
stamped on the floating currency of popular superstition,
and accepted by the biographer without scruple. The
following is Jámí's account : ' One evening Shaikh Shamsu
'ddín and Maulāná (Jalālu 'ddín) were sitting in private,
when somebody outside desired the Shaikh to come forth
immediately. He rose, saying to Maulāná, " I am called
to my death." After a long pause, "*Verily*," said Maulāná,
" *His is the whole creation and the empire thereof.* *Blessed
be God, the lord of all creatures !*[1]" Seven conspirators
were lying in ambush and fell upon him with knives, but
the Shaikh uttered so terrible a cry that they all were
dumbfoundered. One of them was 'Alā 'u 'ddín, Maulāná's
son, who bore the brand of " *He is not of thy people*[2]."
When they recovered their senses, they saw nothing except
a few drops of blood. From that day to the present time
no trace of that spiritual monarch has appeared. This
happened in the year 645. Each of the aforementioned
villains was speedily involved in calamity and perished.
'Alā 'u 'ddín Muhammad was overtaken by a strange
disease and died ere the murder was many days old.
Maulāná did not attend his funeral. Some say that
Shaikh Shamsu 'ddín is buried beside Maulāná Bahā 'u
'ddín Walad, but according to another report these villains
threw his blessed body into a well. One night Sulṭān
Walad dreamed that Shaikh Shamsu 'ddín signified to him

is only the talk of dervishes and travellers, and is not supported by
any trustworthy MS.

[1] Kor. VII. 52. [2] Kor. XI. 48.

that he was asleep in this well. When midnight came, he gathered his intimate friends, and they interred Shams in Maulānā's college by the side of the founder, Amīr Badru 'ddīn. And God knoweth best[1].'

In memory of his teacher Jalāl is said to have instituted the order of Maulavī dervishes 'with their special dress, the Indian garb of mourning,' and their whirling dance (سماع). Riẓā Kulī implies that the Dīvān itself was written *in memoriam*[2]. The *Maṣnavī* was commenced later at the instigation of Chelebī Ḥusāmu 'ddīn[3]. Jalāl is also the author of a treatise in prose, entitled *Fīhi mā fīhi*, 'which runs to three thousand beyts and is addressed for the most part to Muʿīnu 'ddīn[4], the Parwāna of Rūm. Manuscripts of this work are rare[5].'

Jalāl died at Qōniya on the 5th of Jumādā 'l Ākhir, 672 A.H. (16th December, 1273).

§ 6. The great poets of Persia, with few exceptions, have borrowed the ideas and speak the language of Ṣūfiism. These again fall into two classes. Some, like Ḥāfiz, make

---

[1] *Nafaḥātu 'l Uns*, p. 539, ll. 4—22.

[2] This may be inferred from the sequence of his narrative (T. 4. 13—14). We have seen that part of the Dīvān was composed while Shamsi Tabrīz was still living, but probably the bulk of it belongs to a later period, and not, as Daulat Shāh asserts, to the two years when Shamsu 'ddīn was staying at Damascus.

[3] Aflākī in Redhouse's *Maṣnavi*, p. 88; *Nafaḥātu 'l Uns*, p. 540, l. 22 seqq.

[4] 'Ainu 'ddīn (T). He is the 'Muʿīnu 'ddīn Sulaimān ibn 'Alī, potentissimus minister Seljukidarum, Ruknu 'ddīn Kilij Arslān IV. and Ghiyāṣu 'ddīn Kai Khosrau III.,' mentioned in the Leyden *Catalogue of Oriental Manuscripts*, Vol. II. p. 51.

[5] T. 4. 18ᵃ seqq. I have not been able to find any further notice of this brochure.

the mystic terminology, 'adopté par une secte pour cacher aux profanes la connaissance de ses dogmes,' serve the function of a mask or a lady's fan in the last century. By tantalising the reader, by keeping him, as it were, suspended between matter and spirit, they pique his ingenuity and double his pleasure. Nearly every line is a play of wit. Love, Wine, and Beauty are painted in the warmest, the most alluring colours, but with such nicety of phrase that often the same ode will entrance the sinner and evoke sublime raptures in the saint. The majority, however, are themselves Ṣūfīs by profession or conviction. 'The real basis of their poetry is a loftily inculcated ethical system, which recognises in purity of heart, charity, self-renunciation, and bridling of the passions, the necessary conditions of eternal happiness. Attached to this we find a pantheistic theory of the emanation of all things from God, and their ultimate reunion with Him. Although on the surface Islām is not directly assailed, it sustains many indirect attacks, and frequently the thought flashes out, that all religions and revelations are only the rays of a single eternal Sun; that all Prophets have only delivered and proclaimed in different tongues the same principles of eternal goodness and eternal truth which flow from the divine Soul of the world[1].'

---

[1] A. von Kremer, *Geschichte der herrschenden Ideen des Islāms*, p. 257. The advanced and uncompromising Ṣūfīism taught by Jalālu 'ddīn makes ethics subservient to philosophy. Virtue, as he conceives it, is not an end, but a means: the end is union with God through Love. Thus his poetry is based on a transcendental pantheism, which however he works out from the moral, not the metaphysical, standpoint.

Among these, the genuine Ṣūfī poets, Jalālu 'ddīn Rūmī
is without a rival.

While the vexed problem as to the origin of Ṣūfiism
does not call for discussion here, a few remarks concerning
its historical development and the various elements of
which it is composed may be helpful to the student,
who will find an admirable summary of the doctrine in
Whinfield's editions of the *Maṣnavī* and *Gulshani Rāz*[1].

The early Ṣūfīs—they were not yet distinguished by
this name—showed, perhaps under Jewish and Christian
influence, a strong tendency to asceticism. Self-control,
self-sacrifice, patience, boundless trust in God, all the
virtues of a Bernard and a Thomas à Kempis, animate
their zealous and devout, if somewhat narrow and practical,
aspiration. They were not in opposition to Islām, but
formed an extreme wing of the orthodox party. The
pantheistic extravagances in which full-blown Ṣūfiism
delights are foreign or at least unfamiliar to them. With
Rābi‘a, a pious woman who died at Jerusalem (135 A. H.),
Love, the unquenchable flame smouldering in the ashes of
ceremonial religion and kindling the torch of mysticism
through the darkest ages, began its conquest of Mohammedan hearts. The first who bore the *name* of Ṣūfī was
Abū Hāshim (ob. 150 A. H.), and in his lifetime or soon
afterwards the first convent for Ṣūfīs (خانقاه) was founded
at Ramla, in Palestine, by a Christian Amīr.

This ascetic type belongs especially to the Arab race.

---

[1] Broadly speaking, the views expressed in the following paragraphs
are those of A. von Kremer (see note above), who has drawn his
materials almost exclusively from Arabic sources. For insight and
suggestiveness his account of Ṣūfiism remains unsurpassed.

Hand in hand with the Persian revival under the 'Abbāsids came a new current of ideas. Speculation takes a bolder flight and essays to reconcile the creature with his Creator, to bridge the chasm between the finite and the Infinite. Dhū 'l Nūn (ob. 245 A.H.) is said to have introduced the doctrine of ecstasies (احوال) and mystical stages (مقامات), and Sirrī Saqaṭī (ob. 253 A.H.) that of unification (توحيد). According to Jāmī (*Nafaḥātu 'l Uns*, p. 36, ll. 2—6): 'Dhū 'l Nūn is the head of this sect; they all are derived from, and connected with, him[1]. There were eminent spiritualists before him, but he was the first to interpret symbolic expressions (اشارت با عبارت آورد) and to discourse on Ṣūfiism. Junaid (ob. 297 A.H.) systematised and developed this knowledge, and composed writings on the subject. Shiblī (ob. 334 A.H.) carried it to the pulpit and proclaimed it openly.' In 309 A.H. Manṣūr Ḥallāj was executed for asserting his identity with God[2]. But the word had been spoken. Henceforth Ṣūfiism is frankly pantheistic. The terms زُهد and تَصَوُّف have now scarce anything in common; the عابد is succeeded by the عارِف. There survives, indeed, a small group of moderates who, in

---

[1] Qazwīnī (*Kosmographie*, Ed. Wüstenfeld, Part II. p. 241, under خاوران) says of Abū Saʿīd ibn Abī 'l Khair: وَهُوَ ٱلَّذِى وَضَعَ طَرِيقَةَ ٱلتَّصَوُّفِ وَآدَابُ ٱلصُّوفِيَّةِ كُلُّهَا مَنْسُوبَةٌ إِلَيْهِ وَكَذَا ٱلِانْقِطَاعُ عَنِ ٱلدُّنْيَا. As Abū Saʿīd lived to 440 A.H., these statements cannot be accepted without reserve.

[2] See XVII. ١, note.

outward conformity with Islām, are none the less effectually
undermining its foundations.   The main body, grasping at
a glorious phantom, follow their principles to the logical
issue.   For these free-thinkers Islām, however they might
lean upon it, was a broken reed.   Scorning the barren
virtues of the cloister, ' the base degrees by which they did
ascend,' admitting no guidance but the pole-star of divine
illumination, they press in wild career to the very brink of
madness.   As citizens they are undeniably a grave scandal
and a useless burden to the state ; they sap the national
prosperity[1] and demoralise the national character; but if
a country's literature is rightly reckoned among its noblest
heirlooms, the debt which Persia owes to the Ṣūfīs may
balance, and perhaps overpay, these injuries.

Ṣūfiism, then, is no exotic growth, but shoots up like a
tender plant in the desert.   It is a child of the soil, called
into being by the deeper and truer religious spirit which
the dry monotheism and stubborn dogmas of the Kor'ān
had stifled.   We have seen how in the 3rd century it
began to take a wider range.   The rapid expansion of the
Mohammedan empire brought about a corresponding dif-
fusion of culture.   Greek philosophy was introduced[2];
Aristotle, coloured by Alexandrian commentators, appeared
in Arabic.   Ṣūfiism, moreover, had its organised mendi-
cants, who travelled to every part of the eastern world.
Often these wanderers were men of active and ingenious
minds.   They gathered much besides their daily alms :

---

[1] ' For when a man bids adieu to the world, the king's money is
cut off ' (*Nafaḥātu 'l Uns*, p. 399, l. 17).

[2] See Wenrich, *De auctorum Graecorum versionibus et commentariis
Syriacis, Arabicis, Armeniacis, Persicisque Commentatio*, Lipsiae, 1842.

their mysterious lore would be eagerly communicated and in due course would swell the public stock of unrecorded tradition. In this way Zoroastrian, Buddhistic, Christian, and other elements may have gained entrance. Probably the Shi'ite sects, e.g. the Ismā'īlīs, with their fantastic notions of a hidden Imām, their theories of incarnation and emanation, and their abuse of allegory, contributed something in return for what they borrowed. Ṣūfiism, pure in its origin, became eclectic ere reaching its prime.

§ 7. Our data are not yet sufficient to let us trace with certainty the derivation of Ṣūfī doctrine. Such an attempt would in any case be accompanied by almost insuperable difficulties. The identity of two beliefs does not .prove that one is generated by the other : they may be results of a like cause. Even where connexion is assured, it may be impossible to show which is the ancestor and which the descendant. Moreover, since all manifestations of the mystical spirit are fundamentally the same, in so far as each is not modified by its peculiar environment and by the positive religion to which it clings for support, we shall not be astonished to encounter in remote lands and different ages of the world 'one set of principles variously combined.' I propose to illustrate this parallelism with regard to the chief doctrines of Jalālu 'ddīn and Plotinus. Although the name of Plotinus was unknown in the East[1], his philosophy, made popular by his immediate successors and reflected in Aristotelian commentaries, had considerable influence upon the kindred oriental system. The idea of emanation, or rather the particular form of it

---

[1] See Renan, *Averroès et l'Averroïsme*, p. 71, note 1.

exhibited in Ṣūfiism, proceeded, if we are not mistaken, from the Neoplatonic mint. Ṣūfī metaphysics—naturally the product of mature speculation—are cast throughout in the mould which Alexandria aptly contrived to satisfy at once the despairing credulity and devotional enthusiasm of the time. This resemblance, extending also to practical ethics, would be still more striking, were it not disguised by a total contrast of expression. What Plotinus states tersely and baldly Jalālu 'ddīn throws into an obscure allegory : he 'implies things,' but seldom utters them. It has already been remarked that Jalālu 'ddīn approaches his subject on the moral side, and while he makes no pretence to logical and coherent exposition, in his brief metaphysical flights he is so vague, fanciful, and allusive, that the depth of his acquaintance with Greek and Arabian philosophy cannot be definitely fixed. Nevertheless, if we fairly interpret these oracular deliverances in the light afforded by Ṣūfī authors and commentators, the following sketch of Neoplatonism will be found to contain little or nothing that Jalālu 'ddīn has not presented, after his own fashion, to readers of the Maṣnavī and Dīvān[1].

The aim of Plotinus is to achieve perfect union with God. Assuming the reality of a supernatural over against

---

[1] It is stated in the *Dabistān* (Vol. iii. p. 281) that the belief of the pure Ṣūfīs is the same as that of the Platonists (اَلْاِشْرَاقِيُّون).
In this connexion the words of Tholuck, referring to Ṣūfiism and the Cabbala, deserve to be quoted : Mirabilis profecto utriusque dogmatis concentus ; nec tamen vel in hac quanta cogitari potest maxima opinionum similitudine nos ii sumus, qui statim de nexu historico cogitemus. Malumus vel hanc tantam sententiarum concordiam Orientali dare ingenio poeticaeque indoli (*Ssufismus*, p. 164).

the material world, he has to show (*a*) the relation existing
between them, (*b*) the means whereby he may ascend.

(*a*) 'The one watchword in the new Platonic philosophy
is *continuity*[1].' There shall be no impassable gulf dividing
God from Man, spirit from matter: they shall be the first
and last links of a single chain.

Thus we have, according to Plotinus,

(1) Absolute Unity (τὸ ἕν)[2], the ground of all being,
the highest Thought, the highest Good, the highest Beauty.
Nay, it is something above all these. It is inconceivable,
and therefore ineffable; it can only be expressed by
negation[3].

(2) Universal Mind (νοῦς)[4], the eldest offspring of the
One, which it eternally contemplates. It is inferior to the
One, for thought involves duality. It is the home of the
Ideas[5] and the true archetype of the phenomenal world[6].

(3) Universal Soul (ψυχή)[7], begotten by νοῦς and
connecting it with the world of sense. She has thus a

---

[1] Bussell, *The School of Plato*, p. 327.

[2] The Ṣūfī قدم. Jalālu 'ddīn has no special term to denote the
highest hypostasis. His favourite metaphors, referring to Absolute
Being, are Sea, Light, Love, Wine, Beauty, and Truth.

[3] Cf. xxxi. ١—٦; Whinfield's *Maṣnavi*, pp. 5. 31, 263.

[4] عقل كلّ (ix, ٥, note). Jalālu 'ddīn calls it the First
Soul (Whinfield's *Maṣnavi*, p. 148).

[5] اعیان علمیّه. The same Ideas manifested in the phenomenal
world are called اعیان ثابته.

[6] Whinfield's *Maṣnavi*, p. 214; *Ssufismus*, p. 219.

[7] جانِ كلّ or نفسِ كلّ.

double nature. As the heavenly Aphrodite[1], she receives the overflowing radiance of νοῦς, which, as an earthly goddess, she communicates to the region below.

This region is the material world. Matter (ὕλη) is absence of Form (εἶδος)[2], mere defect and privation (στέρησις)[3]. Nothing in itself, it is yet the mirror of all things[4]. It is also Evil, being utterly devoid of the Good (ἔλλειψις τοῦ ἀγαθοῦ)[5].

But why, we may ask, should plurality issue from the inmost seclusion of the One? Plotinus answers that every perfect being desires to create another[6]. The One remains, indeed, unmoved and undiminished: its substance suffers no change, but its redundant energy streams over (οἶον

---

[1] Zuhra (v. ٦, note).

[2] صورت, which is the manifestation of soul. See xxv. ١٣ (first miṣrā‘) and note.

[3] عدم. Tholuck (Ssufismus, p. 184) distinguishes عدم from τὸ μὴ ὄν, but his reasons appear to me inadequate.

[4] iv. ٣, note; Whinfield's Maṣnavi, p. 48. The full significance of this figure is discussed by Zeller, iii.², p. 494 seq.

[5] The views of Plotinus concerning Evil coincide to an amazing degree with those expressed by Jalālu 'ddīn. Cf. Whinfield's Maṣnavi, p. xx seq., Zeller, iii.², p. 502 seqq.

[6] The Ṣūfīs, like the Neoplatonists, invoke a deus ex machina, in the shape of metaphor, to solve the mystery of creation (cf. notes on iv. ٦, xxiii. ٧; Browne, The New History of the Bāb, p. 328; Gulshani Rāz, 134 seqq.; Ssufismus, p. 158 seqq.; Dabistān, Vol. iii. p. 226). Zeller's remark (iii.², p. 443) is very much to the point: Dieses Bedürfniss des bildlichen Ausdrucks weist immer auf eine Unklarheit des Gedankens, es zeigt dass der Sprechende seine Idee eben nur in und an dem Bilde, daher mehr oder weniger unbestimmt ergriffen hat, und diess wird in neun Fällen unter zehen darin seinen Grund haben, dass die Unbestimmtheit das einzige Mittel ist, einen Widerspruch zu verdecken.

$\dot{v}\pi\epsilon\rho\rho\dot{v}\eta$). He compares this process to the sap coursing through a tree, or to the sunbeams which illumine the atmosphere[1]. Thus all things partake of God in proportion as they approximate to the divine centre; all strive upward to that Unity without which they would not exist[2], and of this strife the Universe is born[3].

(b) The soul in her primeval state belongs to the World-Soul[4]. Going forth from Eternity and passing the frontiers of the Intelligible, she enters the realm of Matter, not by an act of will, but in obedience to an instinctive necessity[5]. As embodied she is a part of Nature, as

[1]

خَورشیدِ رُخت چو کُشت پَیدا

ذَراتِ دو کَون شُد هُوَیدا

مِهرِ رُخِ تو چو سایه افتِند

ز آن سایه بدید کُشت اشیا   (T. 113. 8ᵃ).

Cf. ix. ٢٠, note; *Ssufismus*, pp. 167, 168.

[2] Cf. notes on xviii. ٦, xx. ١; Appendix I. (E).

[3] Accordingly, the phenomenal world is a dream of the soul, a subjective entity (امرِ اعتباری). Cf. T. 25. 13:

آسمان گِردِ عشق میگَردد

بهرِ عشق است کُنبِد دوّار

[4] xvii. ١, note.

[5] ἀρχὴ μὲν οὖν αὐταῖς τοῦ κακοῦ ἡ τόλμα καὶ ἡ γένεσις καὶ ἡ πρώτη ἑτερότης καὶ τὸ βουληθῆναι δὲ ἑαυτῶν εἶναι (*Enneades*, v. 1. 1). The soul, like Narcissus, made of herself an idol and desired to embrace it (cf. 'Attār's fable of the fox, *Ssufismus*, p. 119). Egoism no less than Fate is the cause of her fall. Plotinus agrees with Jalālu 'ddīn that Man has freewill, though his freedom is subordinate to eternal law. In so far as he yields to the sensual he is not free: his freedom

spiritual she still firmly plants her foot in the ideal world[1]. She is fallen, but not irretrievably : 'the ancient track' lies open, if she will tread it. Return (ἐπιστροφή) sums up the whole duty of Man.

As the imperfection of the soul is due to nothing except the contaminating influence of the body, it follows that she again becomes perfect when this tie is dissolved. By purifying herself from lusts, passions, and worldly imaginations, from whatever is alien to the divine element, she wins back the Paradise that she had lost awhile. Yet even the sensible may serve as a bridge to the spiritual, and love of earthly beauty kindle a holier flame[2], for what is love but a yearning to the Good and Fair?[3] The soul travels homeward by a series of ascending stages, which correspond to those of descent[4]. In the last stage she rises beyond reason and knowledge to a state of unconscious rapture

consists in following reason instead of passion. He sins under compulsion, but surrender to this compulsion is the original sin. Cf. notes on xi. ٨, xiii. ٣; Whinfield's *Maṣnavi*, p. xxi.

[1] Cf. Add. Notes on xxii. ٧.

[2] xxxiv. ١, note; Add. Notes, ibid.

[3] Whinfield's *Maṣnavi*, p. 1, note. Mr Whinfield asserts the identity of عشق with the ἀγάπη of the New Testament. We know how the Christians of Syria 'loved one another'; if the Ṣūfīs borrowed from them, it was '*lucus a non lucendo.*' The fact that Rābi'a (see above, § 6) passed her life at Jerusalem may seem to favour the conjecture. But, after all, is it likely that a feeling so spontaneous and universal was either imitated or imported? Was the Kor'ānic idea of Allah too mild and tender to provoke rebellion? Mr Whinfield, as I think, greatly exaggerates the debt of Ṣūfiism to Christianity.

[4] Cf. *Gulshani Rāz*, 316. For the Ṣūfī stages (مقامات) see Ethé, *Morgenländische Studien*, p. 99 seqq.

($\xi\kappa\sigma\tau\alpha\sigma\iota\varsigma$)[1], where seer and Seen are no more distinct, seeker is one with Sought, lover with Beloved. Putting off her humanity, she 'assumes the god[2].'

§ 8. Before considering the general character of Jalāl's lyric poetry, what traces can we discover, either in his writings or in the biographies and traditions concerning him, of any external influences that may have helped to form his style?

(1) When Jalāl was passing through Nīshāpūr on the way from Balkh, he met Farīdu 'ddīn 'Aṭṭār, who gave him the *Asrār-nāma*[3].

(2) He was well acquainted with the poems of Sanā'ī[4], to whom he pays a tribute in one of his odes (XXII. in this selection).

(3) His meeting with Saʿdī is mentioned by Aflākī (Redhouse, *Masnavi*, p. 29) and Riẓā Ḳulī (T. 4. 13ᵃ).

(4) Niẓāmī is referred to (x. ١٠, in this selection).

(5) We find what seem to be echoes of 'Omar Khayyām[5].

---

[1] حال or فنا (i. ٤, note).

[2] παυσάμενος δὲ τοῦ ἄνθρωπος εἶναι μετεωροπολεῖ καὶ πάντα τὸν κόσμον διοικεῖ· γενόμενος γὰρ τοῦ ὅλου τὸ ὅλον ποιεῖ (*Enneades*, v. 8. 7). Cf. Appendix I. (A).

[3] See above, § 2.

[4] Jalāl is reported to have said, 'The Word of God (Kor'ān) is but milk of which the Ilāhī-nāma is the cream and the butter' (Aflākī in Redhouse's *Masnavi*, p. 65). The Ilāhī-nāma is another name for the Ḥadīqa. Cf. *Masnavi* (Teherān Ed. 1307 A.H.), p. 391, l. 27, with gloss ad loc. Jāmī mentions the Ilāhī-nāma and Manṭiqu 'ṭṭair together (*Nafaḥātu 'l Uns*, p. 540, last line).

[5] These perhaps are only coincidences. The miṣrāʿ

نی مستِ شرابیم و کبابیم و ربابیم '(T. 265. 11ᵃ)

recalls

Compare

(T. 161. 2ᵃ) آن چیز که دارد او او داند و او داند

with

(Quatrain 401) او داند او داند او داند او

and

(T. 289. 8) چون فاخته او پرّان فریاد کُنان کو کو

with

دیدیم که بر کُنگُرهاش فاختهٔ

آواز همیداد که کو کو کو کو

(Quatrain 392).

We shall be safe in asserting that none of the last three made a deep impression on his mind. Sa'dī with his practical morality, his heart-felt piety, and half-hearted mysticism, could never have appealed to a sensitive God-intoxicated nature like Jalāl's. The distinction comes out plainly enough in their writings. 'The ghazals of Sa'dī,' says the Tabrīz editor (T. 3. 11ᵃ), 'are extremely elegant and exceedingly beautiful, but the thoughts will prove to be mostly profane (مجاز)[1] and the diction full of amatory conceits (ناز و نیاز): no revelation of the Truth or explanation of the mystic Path will be found there; the discerning critic and intelligent reader knows that in the utterances of Janābi Maulavī Ma'navī 'tis another story.'

Nor can he have been attracted by the extant com-

در مجلسِ احرار سه چیز است و دِگر نه

وآن هر سه کبابست و ربابست و شرابست

(Minuchihrī, Ed. Kazimirski, p. 14).

[1] For this word see XIII. o, note.

positions of Niẓāmī except, possibly, the *Makhzanu'l Asrār*,
while 'Omar Khayyām's negation and instability were even
less calculated to lay hold of him.

With 'Aṭṭār and Sanā'ī, on the contrary, he was in
full accord. We may conjecture that the first impulse in
his mind towards Ṣufiism arose from the perusal of their
celebrated poems, the *Manṭiqu 'ṭṭair* and the *Ḥadīqa*.
They were always his leaders, the soul and eyes of
Taṣawwuf :

عطّار روح بود و سنائی دو چشمِ او

'ما از پَی سنائی و عطّار آمدیم

We have seen that Ṣūfīistic theosophy is the fountain-
head of Jalāl's inspiration. From this the Maṣnavī and
Dīvān descend by separate channels. The one is a majestic
river, calm and deep, meandering through many a rich and
varied landscape to the immeasurable ocean ; the other a
foaming torrent that leaps and plunges in the ethereal
solitude of the hills. It may be doubted whether the vast
reputation of the Maṣnavī has not injured the poet's fame.
He has even been denied a place in 'the notable succession
of Oriental singers about whom the world is willing to
hear[2].' And perhaps this estimate is not altogether sur-
prising. Had Wordsworth never written anything besides
the *Excursion*, he would still be read by Wordsworthians
and neglected by his countrymen. The Maṣnavī contains
a wealth of delightful poetry. But its readers must pick

---

[1] The poem from which this beyt is quoted does not occur in the
Tabrīz or Lakhnau editions of the Dīvān.

[2] *Quarterly Review*, January, 1892, p. 34.

their way through apologues, dialogues, interpretations of Kor'ānic texts, metaphysical subtleties and moral exhortations, ere all at once they chance upon a passage of pure and exquisite song.

Now in the Dīvān we have the poet with his singing-robes about him. Thus equipped he can hardly fail to be recognised.

That his odes should exhibit a certain monotony of ideas is inevitable. To the mystic all apparent difference is the evidence and manifestation of an underlying unity, or rather it *is* unity :

> What was that mass of waters? Nought but the wave.
> What was that wave? Nought but the Sea[1].

For him the world is non-existent, and he will not study the unreal ; like the compass he circles ever round a point, on which his thoughts, actions, and very being depend : he cannot stray from his course any more than a star can leave its orbit. Hence all mystical writings are the record of one spiritual experience and are pervaded by a single overpowering emotion. The language of all mystics is the same. How often do Law, Emerson, and Shelley remind us of the Maṣnavī ! Juan de la Cruz has indited lyrics which it would be easy to mistake for translations from the Dīvān.

To continue our criticism, the marks of haste and occasional roughnesses, that cannot escape any one accustomed

آن لُبّه چه بود عَینِ آن مَوج

آن مَوج چه بود عَینِ دریا (٢. 113. 12ª).

to the elaborate technique of Hāfiz and Jāmī, are doubtless due to the circumstances in which the Dīvān was composed. 'For the most part,' says Riẓā Ḳulī (T. 3. 1), 'they are poems inspired in divers states of reason and love and ecstasy and intoxication and effacement and mystic dance. Consequently they will not be to all classes dear nor acceptable to every ear, as a famous one hath said, "We are known by those of our own kind, but other men deny us."' According to Daulat Shāh, 'There was a pillar in the Maulavī's house, and when he was drowned in the ocean of love he used to take hold of that pillar and set himself turning round it. Meanwhile he versified and dictated and people wrote down the verses.'

Again, we have certain words and phrases run to death, as the saying goes. To some extent this fault is common to all Persian poetry. They did not cultivate 'the art to blot' at Shīrāz and Bokhārā, whose laureate, Rūdagī, is credited with nearly three million lines. Naturally an improvisateur, pouring forth his thoughts as fast as they come to his lips and wrought by sphere-music to a pitch of transport where all conscious sense of polish and style has long ago been annihilated—naturally such a one will offend in this point more conspicuously than self-contained and soberer spirits.

The beauty and purity of his diction need not be illustrated at length. I will quote one passage in his noblest manner :

این خواجه‌را در کویِ ما در کُل فرو رفته است پا

با تو بگویمِ حالِ او بر خوان إِذَا جَاءَ ٱلْقَضَا

جبّاروار و زفت او دامن کشان میرفت او

تسخر کُنان بر عاشقان بازیچه دید عشق‌را

ای خواجه سرمستک شُدی بر عاشقان خُنبک زدی

مستِ خُداوندِ خَودی کُشتی گِرفتی با خُدا

بس مُرغ پرّان درِ هوا از دامها فرد و جُدا

میآید از چرخِ قضا بر سینه اش تیرِ بلا

(T. 15. 1).

Hard by a master dwells, his feet in mire
Deep-sunken ; of his state I prophesy.
Recite the boding verse, " *When doom shall fall*[2]."

Tyrannous he and mighty, and oft he swept
Along in proud magnificence to mock
At lovers, love he deemed an idle play.

Lo, a besotted fool like thee to scorn
The votaries of love ! God's wine has drowned
Thy wits and bidden thee wrestle with thy Lord.

As when a bird his airy flight resumes
Exultingly, nor dreads the distant lure :
Fate to his bosom speeds the shaft of woe.

The style throughout is simple and unaffected. Passages
like the following, which recalls the decadent euphuism of

---

[1] V. بامها (T).

[2] These words are not found in the Kor'ān. Possibly there is an
allusion to LXIII. 11: 'And God will by no means grant further
respite to a soul, when its time shall come' (إِذَا جَآءَ أَجَلُهَا).

the Anvāri Suhailī *et hoc genus omne*, are comparatively rare :

بیجا شَو و در وَحدت در عَینِ بقا جا کُن

هر سر که دوئی دارد در گُردنِ ترسا کُن

اندر قفسِ هستی این طوطیِ قُدسیرا

زآن پیش که بر پرّد شُکرانه شَکَرها کُن

چون مستِ ابد کُشتی شمشیرِ ازل بِستان

هندویَک هستیرا تُرکانه تو یَغما کُن

(T. 280. 2ᵃ).

Go forth from Place, and settle in Unity, in absolute
    Everlastingness ;
Plant every head that is dual on the Christian's
    neck.
To this holy parrot in the cage of existence
Thankfully give sugar to peck, ere it soars aloft.
When thou art grown drunk with eternity future,
    take the sword of eternity past ;
Plunder, like a Turk, the wretched Hindoo, Life.

A glance at these impassioned hymns will inform the
reader that the weapon of allegory is seldom out of the
poet's hand. But Jalālu 'ddīn does not balance literal
and spiritual meanings so equally as to leave the choice
uncertain. His words will always bear the profoundest
interpretation. He is no juggler with mysteries. Although
his metaphors are drawn from every field of Nature and
Art, neither Art nor Nature is the subject which they
adorn.

مَی و ساقی چه باشد نیست جُز حقّ

خُدا داند که این عشق از چه بابست

(T. 143. 10ª).

God is the Sākī and the Wine :
He knows what manner of Love is mine.

While these figures are sometimes to our taste grotesque
and inappropriate in a 'Buch der Lieder,' they more often
display a daring and felicitous originality.

اگر زمین بسراسر بروید از تَوبه

بیَک دم از آن همهرا عشق بدرَوَد چو کِیا

ازآنکه تَوبه ¹هُجُور است ²و بند نپذیرد

غُلِّ مَوج چو کُهسار ³و غُرِّش دریا

(T. 9. 11).

Tho' Penitence spring up and grow apace,
Love will uproot it in a moment's space.
Let vows bind all, ye cannot bind the free
And mountain-surging thunder of the Sea.

شرابِ لُطفِ خُداوَندرا کرانی نیست

و گر کرانش نماید قُصورِ جامِ بُوَد

(T. 161. 8).

The wine of God's grace hath no brim :
If it appear to have a brim, 'tis the fault of the cup.

---

¹ هُجُور (C²). ز بندست (T). حور است (T). is the act of binding
a camel with the rope called هِجار.　Cf. xxxvii. ۱۳ (note on عقیله).

² و om. (T).

³ و om. (T). غرّهٔ (T). غُرِّش (C²).

این همه کاسهٔ زرّین زَبَرِ خوانِ فلك

بهرِ آنست که یکروز صلائی برسد

(T. 192. 12).

All these 'patines of bright gold' on the table of heaven
Are in order that one day we may be bidden to the feast.

برف بُدم کُداختم تا که زمین مرا بخَورد

تا همه دودِ دل شُدم تا سویِ آسمان شُدم

(T. 236. 2ᵃ).

I was snow and melted away, so that the earth drank
me up,
Till I became one mist of soul and mounted to the sky.

Jalālu 'ddīn is especially partial to metaphors of light
and sound. The conception of God as a radiant Sun[1],
whose shadow is the world, recurs continually with reference to Shamsi Tabrīz. Love is a fierce-sparkling fire
(آتشِ عظیمِشرار), the lover

Shineth among his fellows as in heaven
The brilliant moon among the host of stars[2].

The soul is a flashing mirror, wherein God reveals his
beauty; in the hour of separation it becomes a glowing
furnace. Now it is a falcon summoned by the fowler's
whistle to perch again upon his wrist[3], now a lonely dove

---

[1] This may have come from Maǵianism. See Von Kremer,
Geschichte der herrschenden Ideen des Islāms, p. 95.

[2]
میانِ صد کس عاشق چنان بدید آید

که بر فلك مِه تابان میانِ کوکبها

[3] XVI. ۳, note.　　　　　　　(T. 118. 13).

that seeks her mate and ceases not to moan[1]. The poet likens it also to a lute thrilling at the lightest touch of the musician[2], or to a voice that echoes on the hillside[3]. To Nature he never appeals in vain[4]. The stork's cry bids him think on God, 'to whom is the kingdom and the glory[5]'; in autumn the pale vine-leaves mourn the loss of his Beloved[6].

To conclude this somewhat desultory review, let me state briefly the merits and defects of the Dīvān.

[1] Cf.

ای مُطرِبِ خَوشقاقا تو قی قی و من قو قو

تو دق دق و من حق حق تو هَی هَی و من هو هو

ای شاخِ درختِ کُل ای ناطقِ امرِ قُل

تو کبکصِفَت بو بو من فاخته‌سان کو کو

(T. 296. 8).

The first couplet is an orchestra in itself.

[2] xvi. ٢٢, note.

[3]

اصلِ نِدا از دل بُوَد در کوهِ تن اُفتد صدا

خاموش رو در اصل کُن ای در صدا آویخته

(T. 57. 10ᵃ).

[4] Nature's sympathy with the mystic is finely expressed by Sa'dī (Būstān, p. 221, l. 289 seqq.).

[5]

عارِف مُرغانئست لكلك لكلكش دانی که چیست

مُلك لَك وَالأَمُر لَك وَالْحَمْدُ لَك یَا مُسْتَعَانْ

(T. 54. 5).

[6]

رفتم هنگامِ خزان سویِ رزان دست گُزان

نَوحه‌گرِ هجرِ تو شُد هر وَرَقِ زرد مرا

(T. 127. 8).

Jalālu 'ddīn lacks the colour and perfume of Hāfiz, who is by turns grave and gay, blasphemous and devout, serious and ironic; his music is rich and full, but for the most part he plays on one string; he has no sense of humour; his allegory is often grotesque and his execution careless.

In sublimity of thought and grandeur of expression he challenges the greatest masters of song; time after time he strikes a lofty note without effort; the clearness of his vision gives a wonderful exaltation to his verse, which beats against the sky; his odes throb with passion and rapture-enkindling power[1]; his diction is choice and unartificial; at intervals we meet with some splendidly imaginative figure,

> 'A bracelet of bright hair about the bone.'

As a mystic, he was too much in earnest to care for, even if he observed, the incongruities which draw upon him the censure of fastidious critics. As a poet, he sought to invest the Ṣūfī doctrine with every charm that his genius could inspire. The traces of this conflict are not wholly obliterated. *Apparet adhuc vetus inde cicatrix.* But in higher moments the opposing characters are swept away and overwhelmed in a flood of celestial harmony, for of Jalālu 'ddīn as of Shelley it may be truly said: 'This is not poetry borrowing the forms of pantheistic speculation, but pantheism assuming to itself the faith and passion which transmutes speculative thought into religion[2].'

---

[1] چون غـزلیّاتِ مَولانا در عجم نظمی وجدانگیز و
عشق‌آمیز نـدیـده امـ (T. 3. 14).

[2] J. A. Symonds, *Essays*, Vol. ii. p. 120.

§ 9.　There are three editions of the Dīvān.

(1)　Tabrīz Ed. (T), published in 1280 A.H., 378 pp., divided as follows : Preface, 2—5 ; first Dīvān, entitled
ديوانِ شمس الّحقايق من مصنّفاتِ جنابِ مولوى معنوى
عليه الّرحمة, 6—110 ; second Dīvān, with the heading
هذا كتاب الغزليّاتِ مولانا قّدس سّره, 112—361 ; rubāʿīs,
361—376 ; note by the editor, 376—378.

This edition does not pretend to completeness[1]. It contains about 9000 beyts, exclusive of rubāʿīs, and the text is remarkably good. The editor, Riẓā Ḳulī Khān, with the *nom de plume* Hidāyat, is an authority on Persian history and literature. He wrote a supplement to Mīr-khwānd's *Rauẓatu'ṣṣafā*, bringing it down to his own time (see Browne, *Episode of the Bāb*, Vol. II. p. 188).

(2)　Lakhnau Ed. (Lakh.), published in 1295 A.H., 378 pp, containing over 12,000 beyts. Like most Persian texts printed in India, it is disfigured by numerous errors, while the readings are often inferior. Its value depends on the large quantity of new matter which it embodies.

(3)　Rosenzweig's *Auswahl* (R)[2], published at Vienna

---

[1] 'Although this Dīvān contains many thousands of agreeable verses and much excellent poetry, yet the whole of it is not suited to the taste of an audience. Perceiving, however, that a number of the sincere and candid (جمعى از اربابِ وفا و اصحابِ صفا) were very eager to have it printed, I resolved to prepare a selection of the qaṣīda-like love-poems, the tarjīʿs sweeter than sugar, the delightful ghazals, and the priceless quatrains included in the Dīvān' (T. 4. 26ᵃ seqq.).

[2] The full title is : *Auswahl aus den Diwanen des grössten mystischen Dichters Persiens, Mewlana Dschelaleddin Rumi, aus dem Persischen mit beigefügtem Original-Texte und erläuternden Anmerkungen* von Vincenz v. Rosenzweig.

in 1838, 236 pp. The selected poems are 75 in number.
The author commands a flow of easy and musical verse: it
is his highest praise that we are occasionally reminded of
Rückert. On the other hand his scholarship is far from
exact and his knowledge of Persian prosody quite inadequate. E.g. on p. 88 (beyts 6—7) we read:

خنك آنرا که دستِ او ببوسید

بوقتِ مرك شیر شد دهانش

ز رویش شکر گویم باز خویش

که کفو او نمیبیند جهانش

which is thus rendered:

> Glückselig Jene die die Hand ihm küssen!
> Ihr Mund träuft Milch, ruft einst der Tod sie ab.
> Ich spreche zuckersüss von seinen Wangen,
> Ihm Gleiches wird die Welt wohl nimmer seh'n.

In the second line the metre requires شیرین for شیر,
and in the third شُكر, not شَكَر, as Rosenzweig has translated it. باز خویش is nonsense. What Jalālu 'ddīn wrote
was:

ز رویش شُكر گویم یا ز خویش

Shall I give thanks for his countenance or for his nature?

Blunders of this kind are too frequent. The 'eluci-
dating remarks' do not invite serious criticism: they fill
five pages and seem designed to spare the reader the
trouble of using his dictionary. Apart from the literary
merit of the translation, we cannot speak favourably of the
work as a whole, though perhaps it fairly represents the
level reached by oriental learning in Europe sixty years ago.

The renderings by Von Hammer in his *Schöne Rede-künste Persiens* (pp. 173—195) are superior to Rosenzweig's in point of accuracy, but 'they are so deficient in poetical feeling and beauty of form, that the reader is repelled rather than attracted[1].' Of the seventy pieces which he has translated only four occur in the present anthology[2].

I have consulted the following manuscripts :

(L) A MS. in the Leyden University Library, dated 851 A.H. and described in the *Catalogue of Oriental Manuscripts*, Vol. II. p. 110. It contains the *Maṣnavī* as well as the Dīvān.

(V) A MS. in the Hofbibliothek at Vienna, dated 4th Muḥarram, 845 A.H., and described in Flügel's *Handschriften der Wiener Hofbibliothek*, Vol. I. p. 522.

(B) A MS. in the British Museum (Or. 2866), dated 1st Jumādā 'l Ākhir, 774 A.H., and described in Rieu's *Supplement to the Persian Catalogue*, p. 163.

(B²) A MS. in the British Museum (Add. 16,779), apparently of the 16th century. It is described in Rieu's *Persian Catalogue*, p. 825.

(B³) A MS. in the British Museum (Or. 289), dated Dhū'l Qa'da, 824 A.H., and described in Rieu's *Persian Catalogue*, p. 593. This MS. contains ghazals from ل to ی only.

(C) A MS. in the possession of Professor E. B. Cowell, 523 pp., written partly in good Nasta'līq and partly in a very illegible modern hand.

(C²) A MS. belonging to Prof. Cowell, written in clear Nasta'līq, apparently in the 17th century. It consists of about 330 pp. The ghazals from ز to م are wanting.

There is no *textus receptus* of the Dīvān. The MSS. differ not only in the number and order of the beyts in

---

[1] Ethé, *Morgenländische Studien*, p. 111.

[2] VIII., XVII., XXXI., XLII.

each ghazal, but in the number and order of the ghazals themselves. Three of the finest poems in this selection (XII. XVII. and XXXI.) occur in a single manuscript. We can hardly doubt that several spurious pieces are included. According to Riẓā Ḳulī (T. 4. 24ᵃ seq.) the Dīvān consists of about 50,000 beyts. Sprenger mentions a copy in the Moty Maḥall at Lucknow, which contains ghazals, 1200 pp. of 34 beyts, tarjī'-bands, 46 pp., and about 4000 rubā'īs (nearly 60,000 beyts in all)[1].

Though I have collated the text of the selected poems in the various MSS., I have not exhibited the complete results of this collation, as it seemed undesirable to increase largely the bulk of a book already swollen beyond its original design. Moreover, little was to be gained by presenting to the reader a confused mass of discrepancies without any possibility of determining what the poet actually wrote. In preparing the text of each ghazal I have followed one MS., which is signified by the capital letter placed opposite the first line. All important deviations from this MS. are noted below, and a few trivial errors have been tacitly corrected. At the foot of each ghazal I give a list of the MSS. and editions in which it is found. Unfortunately, the references to L and V are somewhat defective, as a number of poems have been added to the text since I last had an opportunity of examining these valuable manuscripts. I have not, as a rule, resorted to B² except in difficult passages. Prof. Cowell's second MS. (C²) did not come into my hands until the greater portion of the book was in type.

A word as to the orthography. In the first place, there

---

[1] *Catalogue of Oudh Manuscripts*, p. 497.

are some inconsistencies of spelling mainly due to the plan,
which I have adopted, of compiling a text from separate
MSS. These are unimportant. Now and then I have
abandoned the MSS. spelling for metrical reasons : e.g.
my text gives أئينه (– – ◡), آينه (– ◡ ◡), معناي (– – ◡)[1],
معنَي (– ◡ ◡), while the MSS. have آينه and معنى in-
differently. As regards the vowel-points, which are very
seldom marked in the MSS., my intention was to insert
kasra and *ḍamma* throughout, but *fatḥa* only in doubtful
cases. This method, though not indefensible, is perhaps
too liberal in a work addressed to those who have mastered
more than the rudiments of Persian, and I do not regret
that my practice has fallen short of the principle. Were I
commencing anew, I should mark the *iẓāfat* and omit
everything else. The pointing, خَود (khvad) and خَوش
(khvash), is authorised by Salemann and Shukovski in
their *Persische Grammatik*. A few words have been
wrongly pointed, e.g. كافِر, which ought to be written كافَر,
as is shown by its occurrence in rhyme. Most of these, I
think, will be found in the list of Addenda and Corrigenda.

---

[1] I have represented MSS. معنى (– – ◡) by معنَّي, but معناي is
in accordance with usage, and should be preferred.

ADDENDA AND CORRIGENDA.

This list does not include errors of translation which have been corrected in the Notes.

p. 2, l. 1. For مخبون مقصور read مخبونِ مقصور.

p. 5, l. 2. For 'Adrā read 'Adhrā.

p. 14, beyt ٦. For سُلطان read سُلطانِ.

p. 22, beyt ٦. For کافران read کافرانِ. کافِر is required by the rhyme in T. 165. 1 (quoted in the note to XVI. ١٠), T. 35. 4ᵃ, etc.

p. 24, beyt ٩. For نگنجد read نگُنجد; also in XV. ٣.

p. 24, beyt ١٣. For معنی read معنای.

p. 24, beyt ١٤. For مُجَرّد read مُجَرَّد.

p. 26, beyt ٤. Cf. *Gulshani Rāz*, 450.

p. 34, beyt ٩. For قالب read قالَب; also in XXII. ٥, XXIX. ١١.

p. 38, l. 1. For مخبون مقصور read مخبونِ.

p. 42, l. 1. For مکفوف مقصور read مکفوفِ.

p. 44, beyt ١٣. For خوبی read خوبیّ.

p. 50, beyt ٤. For بسوی read بسویِ.

p. 50, beyt v. For خزان read خَزان ; also in xx. v, XLVIII. ١١.

p. 54, beyt ٣. For دعوَيّ read دعواي.

p. 58, beyt ٥. For تُرانست read تُرانست.

p. 60, beyt ١٦: در بيشهٔ شيران. Cf. Yāḳūt's *Mushtarik* (Ed. Wüstenfeld), p. 77, l. 4: الثانى بيشة موضع بالبادية من اوايل ارض اليمن تُنْسب اليها الأُسْدُ لانها كثيرة الشَعْر وهى قرب السُّرَيْرِ.

p. 64, beyt v. For نهنگمر read نَهنگمر.

p. 76, beyt ٢. For تجلّيّ read تجلّي.

p. 80, beyt ١: ولى مكش تو چو تيرش. Cf. the story of the Faqīr and the hidden treasure, Whinfield's *Maṣnavī*, p. 298 seq.

p. 84 (at the foot). After Lakh. add T.

p. 92, beyt v. For وَٱلضّحَى read وَٱلضّحَى.

p. 94, l. 1. For مُخبون read مُجتَتِ, and for مخبون مقصور read مخبونٍ مقصور.

p. 98, beyt ٢: جهى. The grammars give only جه as the Imperative of جُستن, but if I have rightly explained رخنه‌جه (XXXVI. ١١), the form جه must also be admitted, as in that passage the pointing with *kasra* is demanded by the rhyme.

p. 100, beyt ١٢: بر لبِ خندق. On bridges as stands for beggars see Mayor's *Juvenal*, IV. 116, note, and on blind beggars, cf. ibid. 117, note.

p. 112 (at the foot). After BCL add T.

p. 140. In my critical notes to this ghazal (XXXVI.) I find that I have unaccountably confused the MSS. B² and B³. The following corrections are necessary:

beyt ٢. Transpose B² and B³.

beyt ٣. For B³ read B².

beyt ٧. Delete B² after هر كوى and insert it after هر سوى.

beyt ٨. After آن كو read B² for B³.

beyt ١٠. After درجا read B² for B³. After لرزان لزان read B³ for B².

beyt ١٣. Add B² after ديك سياه.

beyt ١٤. After سوزائى read B² for B³.

beyt ١٦. Delete B²B³ after بر آسمان.

beyt ١٧. Delete B³ after بر آسمان.

p. 140, beyt ٢. For قطارها read قطّارها.

p. 148, last line. After خشكى آورى delete B.

p. 156, beyt ٨. For عد read عدّ.

p. 180, beyt ٧ (note on عقيده). Cf. De Sacy's *Chrestomathie Arabe* (2nd ed.), Vol. I. p. 280, where he attributes to عقده the meaning of gelée, suc épaissi.

p. 247 (second line from the foot). روحى refers properly to the spirit of Muḥammad, who is identified with عقل كلّ (see IX. ٥, note).

p. 333, B (a), beyt ٢: شخص عالم كبرى. Possibly the poet means Universal Reason, 'which bears the same relation to the great world (العالم الكبير) and its realities as the spirit of Man to the body and its faculties' (Jurjānī, *Kitābu 'tta'rīfāt*, p. 39, under الانسان الكامل). Cf. *Ssufismus*, p. 277.

DĪVĀNI SHAMSI TABRĪZ.

SELECTED POEMS.

١

Metre: مُجتَثِّ مُثَمَّنِ مخبون [ـ ـ ـ | ـ ـ ـ ـ | ـ ـ ـ ـ | ـ ـ ـ]

L.

١ اگر تو عاشقِ عشقی و عشق‌را جویا
بگیر خنجرِ تیز و ببُر گلویِ حیا

٢ بدان که سِدِّ عظیم است در رَوِش ناموس
حدیثِ بی غَرَضست این قبول کُن بصفا

٣ هزار گونه جُنون از چه کرد آن مجنون
هزار شَید بر آورد آن گُزینِ شَیدا

٤ گهی قبا بدرید و گهی بکوه دَوید
گهی ز زهر چشید و گهی گُزید فنا

٥ چو عنکبوت چنین صَیدهایِ زفت گِرِفت
به بین که تا چه کُند دامِ رَبِّیَ الْأَعْلَی

٦ چو عشقِ چهرهٔ لَیلَی همی بدین ارزید
چگونه باشد أُسْرَی بِعَبْدِهِ لَیْلَا

_____

BCL Lakh. TV

١ا قباش درید (LT).   (VT). حیا for هوا

٦ بدآن همه ارزید (B).

I.

If thou art Love's lover and seekest Love,

Take a keen poniard and cut the throat of bashfulness.

Know that reputation is a great hindrance in the path ;

This saying is disinterested : receive it with pure mind.

Wherefore did that madman work madness in a thousand
forms,

That chosen wild one display a thousand wiles ?

Now he rent robe, and now sped o'er mountain,

Now sipped poison, and now chose death.

Since the spider seized prey so large,

Behold what the snare of *My Lord the Supreme* will do !

Since the love of Laila's face had such value,

How will it be with "*He took His servant by night*" ?

٧   نَدیدهٔ تو دَواوینِ وَیسه و رامین

نخوانده‌ٔ تو حِکایاتِ وامِق و عَذرا

٨   تو جامه کُرد کُنی تا ز آب تر نشَود

هزار غَوطه تُرا خَوردنیست در دریا

٩   طریقِ عشق همه پستی آمد و مستی

که سَیل پست رَوَد کَی رَوَد بسویِ علا

١٠   میانِ حلقهٔ عُشّاق چون نِگِین باشی

اگر تو حلقه بگُوشِ نِگِینی ای مَولا

١١   چنانکه حلقه بگُوش است چرخ‌را این خاک

چنانکه حلقه بگُوش است روح‌را اعضا

١٢   بیا بگُو چه زیان کرد خاک ازین پَیوَند

چه لُطفها که نکردست عقل با اجزا

١٣   دُهُل بزیرِ گِلیمِ ای پسَر نشاید زد

عَلَم بزن چو دلیران میانهٔ صحرا

١٤   بگُوشِ جان بِشنَو از غریوِ مُشتاقان

هزار غُلغُله در جَوفِ کُنبَدِ خَضرا

---

٧ حِکایاتِ وَرقه و گُلشه for الخ دَواوین (L). مقامات (L).

١٠ چون نِگِین می باش (L). حِکایات for (L).

نِگِینی ای مَولا نِگِین کُنی (L). کمینی for نِگِینی (T).

١٤ عزیزِ مُشتاقان (L). جَوّ for جَوف (BCT).

Hast thou not seen the dīvāns of Waisa and Rāmin?

Hast thou not read the tales of Wāmiq and 'Adrā?

Thou gatherest up thy garment lest the water should wet it:

Needs must thou plunge a thousand times in the sea.

Love's way is all lowliness and drunkenness:

For the torrent runs down: how should it run upward?

Thou wilt be as the bezel in the ring of lovers

If thou art the bezel's thrall, O master.

Even as this earth to the sky is thrall,

Even as the body to the spirit is thrall.

Come, say, what did the earth lose by this connexion?

What kindnesses has not the reason done to the limbs?

It behoves not, son, to beat a drum under a quilt;

Plant, like brave men, thy banner in the midst of the desert.

Hark with the soul's ear to the sounds innumerable

In the hollow of the green dome, rising from lovers'
    passionate cry.

۱۵ چو بر کُشاید بندِ قبا ز مستيِ عشق

تو هاي و هويِ فَلَك بين و حَيرتِ جَوزا

۱۶ چه اِضطراب که بالا و زیر عالَمراست

ز عشق کوست مُنَزَّه ز زیر و از بالا

۱۷ چو آفتاب بر آید کُجا بماند شب

رسید عَیشِ عنایت کُجا بماند عَنا

۱۸ خَموش کردم ای جانِ جانِ جان تو بگو

که ذرّه ذرّه ز شَوقِ رُخِ تو شُد گویا

---

۱۵ جَوزا (BCT). حَورا for فَلَك and مَلَك and
(B²), عَین (LT), عَیش for جَیش ۱۷ نماید شب (L).
حُسن (CV).

When the strings of thy robe are loosed by the intoxi-
    cation of love,

Behold heaven's triumph and Orion's bewilderment!

How the world, high and low, is troubled

By love, which is purified from high and low!

When the sun goes up, where stayeth night?

When the joy of bounty came, where lagged affliction?

I am silent.　Speak thou, O soul of soul of soul,

From desire of whose face every atom grew articulate.

٣

Metre : مُتَقارِب مُثَمَّن محذوف [⏑–– | ⏑–– | ⏑–– | ⏑–]

۱	کِناری ندارد بیابانِ ما
V.	قراری ندارد دل و جانِ ما
۲	جهان در جهان نقشِ صورت گِرِفت
	کُدامست ازین نقشها آنِ ما
۳	چو در ره ببینی بُریده سری
	که غلطان رَوَد سوی مَیدانِ ما
۴	ازو پُرس ازو پُرس اسرارِ دل
	کزو بِشنَوی سِرِّ پنهانِ ما
۵	چه بودی که یك گُوش پَیدا شُدی
	حریفِ زبانهایِ مُرغانِ ما
۶	چه بودی که یك مُرغ پرّان شُدی
	برو طَوقِ سِرِّ سُلَیمانِ ما
۷	چه گُویم چه دانم که این داستان
	فُزونست از حدّ و اِمکانِ ما

BCL Lakh. TV

۵ شنودی for حریف (CT). ۷ چه دانم چه دانم (V).

II.

Our desert hath no bound,

Our hearts and souls have no rest.

World in world has ta'en Form's image;

Which of these images is ours?

When thou seest in the pathway a severed head,

Which is rolling toward our field,

Ask of it, ask of it, the secrets of the heart:

For of it thou wilt learn our hidden mystery.

How would it be, if an ear showed itself,

Familiar with the tongues of our songsters?

How would it be, if a bird took wing,

Bearing the collar of the secret of our Solomon?

What shall I say, what think? for this tale

Is too high for our limited and contingent being.

٨ چگونه زنم دم که هر دم بدم
پریشانتر است این پریشانِ ما

٩ چه کبکان چه بازان بهم می پرند
میانِ هوایِ کُهِستانِ ما

١٠ میانِ هوائی که هفتُم هواست
که در اوجِ آنست کَیوانِ ما

١١ نه هفت آسمان کآن ز عرش است زیر
از آن سویِ عرش است جَولانِ ما

١٢ چه جایِ هواهایِ عرش و فَلَک
بگُلزارِ وَصلست سَیرانِ ما

١٣ ازین داستان بِگُذَر از ما مپُرس
که در هم شِکستست دستانِ ما

١٤ صلاحُ الحق و دین نماید تُرا
جمالِ شهنشاهِ سُلطانِ ما

ستان می برند (B). شان می برند (V). که بازان ٩
بپُرس ١٣ (T). بهم می پرند (V). شنا می برند ;(CL)
(V). جمال for تجلّی ١٤ (LV).

How keep silence, when every moment

Our anguish grows more anguished?

Partridge and falcon alike are flying together

Mid the air of our mountain-land;

Mid an air which is the seventh atmosphere,

At the zenith whereof is our Saturn.

Are not the seven heavens below the empyrean?

Beyond the empyrean is our revolution.

What place here for aspirations toward the empyrean
     and the sky?

Our journey is to the rose-garden of union.

Leave this tale. Ask not of us,

For our tale is wholly interrupted.

Ṣalāḥu 'lḥaq ū dīn will declare to thee

The beauty of our Sultan, the King of kings.

~

Metre : رَمَل مُثَمَّن محذوف [−∪−−|−∪−−|−∪−−|−∪−×]

L. ۱ دوش من پَيغام كردم سوي تو اِستارهرا
كُفتمش خِدمت رسان از من تو آن مَهپارهرا

۲ سِجده كردم كُفتم آن خِدمت بدآن خُورشيد بر
كو بتابَش زر كُند مر سنگهاي خارهرا

۳ة. سينهٔ خَود باز كردم زخمها بنمودمش
كُفتمش از من خَبَر كُن دِلبرِ خونخوارهرا

۴ سو بسو گُشتم كه تا طِفلِ دلم ساكِن شَوَد
طِفل خُسپد چون بجُنباند كسى كهوارهرا

۵ طِفلِ دلرا شير دِه مارا ز گِريَهاش وا رهان
اى تو چاره كرده هر دم صد چو من بيچارهرا

۶ شهرِ وَصلت بوده است آخِر ز اوَّل حاي دل
چند دارى در غريبى اين دلِ آوارهرا

۷ من خَمُش كردم و ليكن از پَي دفع خُمار
ساقيا سرمست گُردان نرگِس خَمّارهرا

CL Lakh. TV

(V). ساقيِ عُشَّاق ۷ (LV). مارا ز گُردِش ۵

۸

III.

Yestereve I delivered to a star tidings for thee :

'Present,' I said, 'my service to that moon-like form.'

I bowed, I said : 'Bear that service to the sun

Who maketh hard rocks gold by his burning.'

I bared my breast, I showed it the wounds :

'Give news of me,' I said, 'to the Beloved whose drink
is blood.'

I rocked to and fro that the child, my heart, might
become still ;

A child sleeps when one sways the cradle.

Give my heart-babe milk, relieve us from its weeping,

O thou that helpest every moment a hundred helpless
like me.

The heart's home, first to last, is thy city of union :

How long wilt thou keep in exile this heart forlorn ?

I speak no more, but for the sake of averting headache,

O Cup-bearer, make drunken my languishing eye.

۴

Metre: رَجَزِ مُثَمَّن سالِم [ـ ∪ ـ ـ | ـ ـ ∪ ـ | ـ ـ ∪ ـ | ـ ـ ∪ ـ]

۱ L. داود کُفت ای پادشا چون بی نیازی تو ز ما
حِکمت چه بود آخِر بِگو در خِلقتِ هر دو سرا

۲ حق کُفتش ای مردِ زمان گَنجی بُدم من در نِهان
جُستِم که تا پَیدا شَوَد آن گَنجِ اِحسان و عطا

۳ آئینهٔ کردم عیان رویَش دل و پُشتش جهان
پُشتش شَوَد بِهتر ز رو گر تو ندانی رویِ‌را

۴ چون گاه جُفتِ گُل بُوَد آئینه کَی مُقبِل بُوَد
چون که جُدا کردی ز دِل آئینه گَردد با صفا

۵ شیره نَگردد مَی اگر در خُم نجوشد مُدّتی
خواهی که دل رَوشن شَوَد اندك عَمَل باید تُرا

۶ جانی که بیرون شُد ز تن گُوید بدو سُلطان من
زین سان که رفتی آمدی آثار کو ز آلّای ما

۷ مشهور آمد این که مِس از کیمیا زر میشَوَد
این کیمیایِ نادِره کردست مِسرا کیمیا

(V). پُشتِ دلش سویِ جهان ۳

IV.

David said : ' O Lord, since thou hast no need of us,
Say, then, what wisdom was there in creating the two
    worlds ? '
God said to him : ' O temporal man, I was a hidden
    treasure ;
I sought that that treasure of lovingkindness and bounty
    should be revealed.
I displayed a mirror—its face the heart, its back the
    world—
Its back is better than its face—if the face is unknown
    to thee.'
When straw is mixed with clay, how should the mirror
    be successful ?
When you part the straw from the clay, the mirror be-
    comes clear.
Grape-juice does not turn to wine, unless it ferment
    awhile in the jar ;
Would you have your heart grow bright, you must take
    a little trouble.
The soul which issued forth from the body—my king
    saith to it :
' Thou art come even as thou wentest : where are the
    traces of my benefactions ? '
'Tis notorious that copper by alchemy becomes gold :
Our copper has been transmuted by this rare alchemy.

۸ نه تاج خواهد نه قبا این آفتاب از فَیضِ حق
زو هست صد کَلرا کُلَه وَز بهرِ دَه عُریان قبا

۹ بهرِ تواضُع بر خری بِنشَست عیسَی ای پِسَر
وَرنه سواری کَی کُند بر پُشتِ خر بادِ صبا

۱۰ ای روح اندر جُست و جو سر ساز همچون آبِ جو
وَی عقل بهرِ آن بقا دائم بِرَو راهِ فنا

۱۱ چندان همی کُن یادِ حق کز خَود فراموشَت شَوَد
تا محو در مَدعُو شَوی بی رَیبِ داعی و دُعا

(V). او هست ۸   (V). ۱۰ سر ساز پا چون آبِ جو

From God's grace this sun wants no crown or robe :
He is cap to a hundred bald men and cloak to ten naked.
Child, Jesus sate on an ass for humility's sake :
How else should the zephyr ride on the back of an ass ?
O spirit, make thy head in search and seeking like the
    water of a stream,
And O reason, to gain eternal life tread everlastingly the
    way of death.
Keep God in remembrance till self is forgotten,
That you may be lost in the Called, without distraction
    of caller and call.

٥

Metre : رَمَلِ مُثَمَّنِ مشكول [∪∪−∪ | −∪−− | ∪∪−∪ | −∪−×]

L.

۱ چَمَنی که تا قیامت گُل او بِبار بادا

صَنَمی که بر جمالش دو جهان نِثار بادا

۲ ز پگاه میرِ خوبان بشِكار می خرامد

که بتیرِ غمزهٔ او دلِ ما شِكار بادا

۳ بدو چشمِ من ز چشمش چه پیامهاست هر دم

که دو چشمِ از پیامش خَوش و پُر خُمار بادا

۴ درِ زاهدی شِكستم بِدُعا نمود نِفرین

که بِرو که روزگارت همه بیقرار بادا

۵ نه قرار ماند نه دل بدُعایِ او ز یاری

که بِخونِ ماست تِشنه که خُداش یار بادا

۶ تنِ من بِماه ماندَ که ز عشق می گُدازد

دلِ من چو چنگِ زُهره که گُسته‌تار بادا

۷ بِگُداز ماه منگر بِگُسِستثیّ زُهره

تو حلاوتِ غمش بین که یکی هزار بادا

CL Lakh. T

۳ که چشمش (L.). ۷ که دو چشمِ (L.). بِگُذار ماه (C).

V.

A garden—may its rose be in flower to Resurrection!
An idol—may the two worlds be scattered o'er his beauty!
The prince of the fair goes proudly forth to the chase
    at morning;
May our hearts fall a prey to the arrow of his glance!
From his eye what messages are passing continually to
    mine!
May my eyes be gladdened and filled with intoxication
    by his message!
I broke an ascetic's door: with a prayer he banned me,
Saying, 'Go, may all thy life be without peace!'
No peace, no heart is left me, on account of his prayer,
    by the Friend
Who thirsts for our blood—may God befriend him!
My body is like the moon which is melting for love,
My heart like Zuhra's lute—may its strings be broken!
Look not on the moon's waning nor on Zuhra's broken
    state;
Behold the sweetness of his affliction—may it wax a
    thousandfold!

٨   چه عروسیست در جان که جهان ز عکس رویش

چو دو دستِ نَوعروسان تر و پُرٰ نِگار بادا

٩   بعذارِ جِسم منگر که بپوسد و بریزد

بعذارِ جان نِگر که خَوش و خَوشگُوار بادا

١٠   تنِ تیره همچو زاغی و جهانِ تن زَمستان

که برغمِ این دو ناخَوش ابدًا بهار بادا

١١   که قوامِ این دو ناخَوش بچهار عُنصُر آمد

که قوامِ بندگانت بجُز این چهار بادا

خَوشعِذار (L).   ٩ بعِذار چشمِ (L).   ٨ پُرٰ خُمار

for (L).   خَوشگُوار ١٠ زاغ (L).

What a bride is in the soul! By the reflection of her
    face

May the world be freshened and coloured like the hands
    of the newly-married!

Look not on the fleshly cheek which corrupts and decays;

Look on the spiritual cheek—may it be sweet and
    agreeable!

The dark body resembles a raven, and the body's world
    winter;

Oh, in spite of these two unpleasants may there be
    eternal spring!

For these two unpleasants subsist by the four elements:

May the subsistence of thy servants depend on some-
    thing other than these four!

٦

[– ᴗ –|– ᴗ ᴗ –‖– ᴗ –|– ᴗ ᴗ –] مُنسَرِح مُثَمَّنِ مَطوِی : Metre

V.

١ ای که بهنگامِ دردِ راحتِ جانی مرا

ای که بتلخیّ فقر گُنجِ روانی مرا

٢ آنچه نبُردست وَهم آنچه ندیدست فَهم

از تو بجان میرسد قبله از آنی مرا

٣ از کَرمت من بناز می نِگْرم در بقا

گر نفریبد شها دَولتِ فانی مرا

٤ نعمتِ آنکس که او مُژدهٔ تو آرد او

گرچه نخوانی بُوَد به ز اغانی مرا

٥ در رَکعاتِ نماز هست خیالِ تو شه

واجب و لازمِ چنانک سبع مثانی مرا

٦ در گُنهِ کافران رحم و شفاعت تُراست

مِهتری و سرورِ سنگدِلانی مرا

٧ گر کَرمِ لایَزال عرضه کُند مُلکها

پیش نِهد هرچه هست گُنجِ نِهانی مرا

TV   T contains only the following beyts : ١, ٢, ٣, ٧, ٨,

١٢, ١٥.

٣ کَی بفریبد (T).   ٦ سروَری (V).   ٧ جُملهٔ for جُمله

هرچه هست (V).   گُنج for کنز (V).   گُنج for کنز

VI.

O thou who art my soul's comfort in the season of
    sorrow,
O thou who art my spirit's treasure in the bitterness of
    dearth !
That which the imagination has not conceived, that
    which the understanding has not seen,
Visiteth my soul from thee ; hence in worship I turn
    toward thee.
By thy grace I keep fixed on eternity my amorous gaze,
Except, O king, the pomps that perish lead me astray.
The favour of that one, who brings glad tidings of thee,
Even without thy summons, is sweeter in mine ear than
    songs.
In the prostrations of prayer thought of thee, O lord,
Is necessary and binding on me as the seven verses.
To thee belongs mercy and intercession for the sin of
    infidels :
As regards me, thou art chief and principal of the stony-
    hearted.
If a never-ceasing bounty should offer kingdoms,
If a hidden treasure should set before me all that is,

٨   سِجده کُنَم من ز جان روی نِهَم من بخاك
      کُویَم ازینها همه عشقِ فُلانی مرا

٩   عُمرِ ابد پیشِ من هست زمانِ وِصال
      زآنکه نَگُنجد در او هیچ زمانی مرا

١٠   عُمر اوانیست وَصل شربتِ صافی در آن
      بی تو چه کار آیدم رنجِ اوانی مرا

١١   بیست هزار آرزو بود مرا پیش ازین
      در هَوَسش خَود نماند هیچ امانی مرا

١٢   از مددِ لُطفِ او ایمن گَشتَم از آنك
      کُوید سُلطانِ غیب جانِ جهانی مرا

١٣   گَوهرِ معنّی اوست پُر شُده جان و دلم
      او سِكِ کو گُفت و نیست ثالث و ثانی مرا

١٤   وَقتِ وِصالش بروح جِسمِ نکرد اِلتِفات
      گَرچه مُجَرَد ز تن گَشت عیانی مرا

١٥   پیر شُدم از غمش لیك چو تبریزرا
      نامِ بَری باز گَشت جُمله جوانی مرا

---

١٢ لستَ ترانی for جانِ جهانی (T).

I would bend down with my soul, I would lay my face
    in the dust,
I would say, 'Of all these the love of such an one for
    me !'
Eternal life, methinks, is the time of union,
Because time, for me, hath no place there.
Life is the vessels, union the clear draught in them ;
Without thee what does the pain of the vessels avail me?
I had twenty thousand desires ere this ;
In passion for him not even (care of) my safety remained.
By the help of his grace I am become safe, because
The unseen king saith to me, 'Thou art the soul of
    the world.'
The essence of the meaning of "He" has filled my heart
    and soul ;
"Au" cries the street-dog, and neither have I third or
    second.
The body, at the time of union with him, paid no regard
    to the spirit ;
Tho' incorporeal, he became visible unto me.
I aged with his affliction, but when Tabrīz
You name, all my youth comes back to me.

٧

Metre : مُضارِع مُثَمَّنِ اخرَبِ مكفوفِ مقصور

[– ∪ ᵜ | ∪ – – ∪ | ∪ – ∪ – | ∪ – –]

V.

١ باز آمد آن مَهی که ندیدش فَلَك بخواب

آوَرد آتشی که نمیرد بهیچ آب

٢ بنگَر بخانهٔ تن و بنگَر بجانِ من

از جامِ عشقِ او شُده این مست و آن حراب

٣ میرِ شرابخانه چو شُد با دلم حریف

خونِر شراب کُشت ز عشق و دلم کباب

٤ چون دیده پُر شَوَد ز خیالش ندا رسد

کاحَسنتَ ای پیاله و شاباش ای شراب

٥ چنگالِ عشق از بُن و از بیخ بر کَنَد

هر خانه کاندر او فُتَد از عشق آفتاب

٦ دریای عشقِرا چو دلم دید ناگهان

از من بجَست در وَی و گُفتا مرا بیاب

٧ خُرشیدِ رویِ مَفخَرِ تبریز شمسِ دین

اندر پَیش روان شُده دلهایِ چون سحاب

(V) contra metr. شمسُ آلدین ٧

VII.

That moon, which the sky ne'er saw even in dreams, has
    returned
And brought a fire no water can quench.
See the body's house, and see my soul,
This made drunken and that desolate by the cup of his
    love.
When the host of the tavern became my heart-mate,
My blood turned to wine and my heart to kabâb.
When the eye is filled with thought of him, a voice
    arrives :
'Well done, O flagon, and bravo, wine!'
Love's fingers tear up, root and stem,
Every house where sunbeams fall from love.
When my heart saw love's sea, of a sudden
It left me and leaped in, crying, 'Find me.'
The face of Shamsi Dîn, Tabrîz's glory, is the sun
In whose track the cloud-like hearts are moving.

٨

Metre : سَریع مطوِی مَوقوف [ـ∪ـ | ـ∪∪ـ | ـ∪∪ـ | ـ∪ـ]

L.	مردِ خُدا مست بُرَد بی شراب ۱
	مردِ خُدا سیر بُوَد بی کباب
	مردِ خُدا واله و حَیران بُوَد ۲
	مردِ خُدارا نبُوَد خَورد و خواب
	مردِ خُدا شاه بُوَد زیرِ دلق ۳
	مردِ خُدا کُنج بُوَد در خراب
	مردِ خُدا نیست ز باد و ز خاك ۴
	مردِ خُدا نیست ز نار و ز آب
	مردِ خُدا بحر بُوَد بی کِران ۵
	مردِ خُدا بارَد دُر بی سحاب
	مردِ خُدا دارد صد ماه و چرخ ۶
	مردِ خُدا دارد صد آفتاب
	مردِ خُدا عالِمِ از حق بُوَد ۷
	مردِ خُدا نیست فقیه از کِتاب

L Lakh. V

٤ ز خاك و ز آب (L). ۷ عالِمِ و از حق (L).
عالِمِ بر حق (V).

VIII.

The man of God is drunken without wine,

The man of God is full without meat.

The man of God is distraught and bewildered,

The man of God has no food or sleep.

The man of God is a king 'neath darvish-cloak,

The man of God is a treasure in a ruin.

The man of God is not of air and earth,

The man of God is not of fire and water.

The man of God is a boundless sea,

The man of God rains pearls without a cloud.

The man of God hath hundred moons and skies,

The man of God hath hundred suns.

The man of God is made wise by the Truth,

The man of God is not learned from book.

٨   مردِ خُدا زآن سویِ کُفرست و دین

مردِ خُدارا چه خطا و صواب

٩   مردِ خُدا کُشت سُوار از عَدَم

مردِ خُدا آمد عالی‌رِکاب

١٠   مردِ خُدا هست نِهان شمسِ دین

مردِ خُدارا تو بجوی و بیاب

---

۸ کُشتَ   (L). ٩ مردِ خُدارا بسویِ کُفر و دین

(L). The second miṣrā‘ in V reads بـسویِ عَدَم

١٠ نیست نِهان   (V). مردِ خُدا دارد عار از کِتاب

The man of God is beyond infidelity and religion,

To the man of God right and wrong are alike.

The man of God has ridden away from Not-being,

The man of God is gloriously attended.

The man of God is concealed, Shamsi Dīn ;

The man of God do thou seek and find !

٦

Metre: مُنْسَرِح مُثَمَّن مَطوِی [‒ᴗ×|‒ᴗᴗ‒|‒ᴗ‒‒ ‖ ‒ᴗᴗ‒|‒ᴗ‒‒]

V. ۱ هر نَفَس آوازِ عشق میرسد از چپ و راست

ما بفَلَك میرَویم عزمِ تماشا کِراست

۲ ما بفَلَك بوده ایم یارِ مَلَك بوده ایم

باز همآنجا رَویم خواجه که آن شهرِ ماست

۳ خَود ز فَلَك برتریم وَز مَلَك افزونتریم

زین دو چرا نگْذَریم منزلِ ما کِبریاست

۴ عالَمِ خاك از کُجا گَوهرِ پاك از کُجا

گَرچه فرود آمدیم باز دَویم این چه جاست

۵ بختِ جوان یارِ ما دادنِ جان کارِ ما

قافله‌سالارِ ما فخرِ جهان مُصطَفَی ست

٦ بویِ خَوشِ این نسیم از شِکَنِ زُلفِ اوست

شِعشِعهٔ این خیال از رُخِ چون وَالضُّحَی ست

_____

BCL Lakh. TV

۳ فَلَك and مَلَك transposed (V). هر دو جهان آنِ ماست

۴: منزلِ ما کِبریاست (L). بر چه فرود آمدند باز for

۴ این خیال for اختران (L). کُنید از کُجاست (L).

IX.

Every moment the voice of Love is coming from left and
    right.

We are bound for heaven: who has a mind to sight-seeing?

We have been in heaven, we have been friends of the
    angels ;

Thither, sire, let us return, for that is our country.

We are even higher than heaven and more than the angels;

Why pass we not beyond these twain? Our goal is majesty
    supreme.

How different a source have the world of dust and the
    pure substance !

Tho' we came down, let us haste back—what place is this?

Young fortune is our friend, yielding up soul our business;

The leader of our caravan is Muṣṭafā, glory of the world.

This gale's sweet scent is from the curl of his tresses,

This thought's radiance is from a cheek like "*by the
    morning bright.*"

٧   از رُخِ او مَه شِكافت دیدنِ او بر نتافت

ماه چنین بخت یافت او كه كمینه گُداست

٨   در دلِ ما در نِثرِ هر دم شقِّ قَمَر

كز نَظَرِ آن نَظَرِ چشمِ تو زآن سو چراست

٩   آمد مَوجِ اَلَست كِشتیِ قالب شِكست

باز چو كِشتی شِكست نَوبتِ وَصلِ لقاست

١٠   خلق چو مُرغابیان زاده ز دریایِ جان

كی كُند اینجا مقام مُرغ كزین بحر خاست

١١   بلكه بدریا دُریم جُمله در او حاضریم

وَرنه ز دریایِ جان مَوج پیاپی چراست

١٢   نَوبتِ وَصلِ لقاست نَوبتِ حُسنِ بقاست

نَوبتِ لُطف و عطاست بحرِ صفا در صفاست

١٣   مَوجِ عطا شُد پدید غُرِّشِ دریا رسید

صُبحِ سعادت دمید صُبح نه نورِ خُداست

---

٨ كز اثَرِ آن نَظَرِ چسمِ تو (C).   كز قَطَرِ آن قَطَر (V).

٩ كُشتیِ طاقت ببست (V).   ١١ بر او (V).

١٢ وَصل و لقاست (BL). حُسنِ بقاست for حشر و بقاست

١٣ درجِ عطا (B).   عرش ز دریا رسید (B).

ز نورِ خُداست (B).

By his cheek the moon was split: she endured not the
sight of him;

Such fortune the moon found—she that is an humble
beggar.

Behold a continual "cleaving of the moon" in our hearts,

For why should the vision of that vision transcend
thine eye?

Came the billow of "*Am I not?*" and wrecked the
body's ship;

When the ship wrecks once more is the time of union's
attainment.

Mankind, like waterfowl, are sprung from the sea—the
sea of soul;

Risen from that sea, why should the bird make here
his home?

Nay, we are pearls in that sea, therein we all abide;

Else, why does wave follow wave from the sea of soul?

'Tis the time of union's attainment, 'tis the time of
eternity's beauty,

'Tis the time of favour and largesse, 'tis the ocean of
perfect purity.

The billow of largesse hath appeared, the thunder of the
sea hath arrived,

The morn of blessedness hath dawned. Morn? No, 'tis
the light of God.

١۴ صورتِ تصویر کیست این شه و این میر کیست

این خِرَدِ پیر کیست این همه روپوشهاست

١٥ چارهٔ روپوشها هست چنین جوشها

چشمهٔ این نوشها در سر و چشمِ شُماست

١٦ در سرِ خَود هیچ لیك هست شُمارا دو سر

این سرِ خاك از زمین وآن سرِ پاك از سماست

١٧ ای بس سرهایِ پاك ریخته در زیرِ خاك

تا تو بدانی که سر زآن سرِ دیگر بپاست

١٨ آن سرِ اصلی نِهان وین سرِ فرعی عیان

زانکه پس از این جهان عالَمِ بی مُنتَهاست

١٩ مَشك ببند ای سقا مَی ببَر از خُمِّ ما

کوزهٔ اِدراکها تنگتر از تنگناست

٢٠ از سویِ تبریز تافت شمسِ حق و گُفتمش

نورِ تو هم مُتَّصِل با همه و هم جُداست

---

١٥ جوشها نوشها for (V).   ١٩ مبند (B). مَی نبَرَد خُمِّ ما

(L). مَی ببَرَد چشمِ ما (B).

Who is this pictured form, who is this monarch and
　　this prince ?
Who is this aged wisdom ?　They are all veils.
The remedy against veils is ecstasies like these,
The fountain of these draughts is in your own head
　　and eyes.
In the head itself is nought, but ye have two heads ;
This head of clay is from earth, and that pure head from
　　heaven.
O the many pure heads scattered beneath the clay,
That thou mayst know the head depends on that other
　　head !
That original head hidden, and this derived head manifest,
Forasmuch as behind this world lies the infinite universe.
Tie up the skin, O cup-bearer, fetch wine from our jar :
The vessel of perceptions is straiter than a strait pass.
From Tabrīz-ward shone the Sun of Truth, and I said
　　to him :
'Thy light is at once joined with all things and apart
　　from all.'

۱۰

Metre : مُجتَثٍّ مُثَمَّنِ مخبون [××ᴗ−|ᴗ−ᴗ−|ᴗᴗ−−|ᴗ−ᴗ−]

V. چه گَوهری که کَسیرا بکف بهایِ تو نیست ۱

جهان چه دارد در کف که آن عطایِ تو نیست

سزایِ آنکه زِیَد بی رُخ تو زآن بَتَراست ۲

سزایِ بنده مِده گرچه او سزایِ تو نیسب

میانِ مَوج حوادِث هرآنکه اُفتادست ۳

بآشنا نرَهَد چونکه آشنایِ تو نیست

بقا ندارد عالَم و گر بقا دارد ۴

فناش گیر چو او مَحرَمِ بقایِ تو نیست

چه فرُّخ است شهی کاو رُخ تُرا ماتست ۵

چه خَوشلقا بُودَ انکس که بی لقایِ تو نُیست

نِثارِ پایِ تو خواهم بَهر دمی دل و جان ۶

که خاک بر سرِ جانی که خاکپایِ تو نیست

مُبارَکست هوایِ تو بر همه مُرغان ۷ •

چه نامُبارَك مُرغی که در هوایِ تو نیست

CTV

───────────────

(V.) قیاس گیر ۴ (CV.) استادست ۳

X.

What pearl art thou that none possesseth the price of thee?
What does the world possess that is not thy gift?
Is there a worse punishment than his who lives away
    from thy face?
Punish not thy servant tho' he is unworthy of thee.
He that is fallen amid the surge of accidents
Escapes not by swimming, since he is no friend of thine.
The world has no permanence, and if it have,
Deem it perishable, because it is unfamiliar with thy
    permanence.
How happy the king that is mated by thy rook!
How fair company hath he who lacks not thine!
I desire continually to fling heart and soul at thy feet;
Dust on the head of the soul which is not the dust of
    thy feet!
Blessed to all birds is desire of thee;
How unblest the bird that desires thee not!

٨ ز زخمِ تو نگریزم که سخت خام بُوَد

دلی که سوختهٔ آتش بلایِ تو نیست

٩ کِرانه نیست ثنا و ثناگرانِ تُرا

کُدام ذرّه که سرگشتهٔ ثنایِ تو نیست

١٠ نظیرِ آنکه نِظامی بنظم میگوید

جفا مکُن که مرا طاقتِ جفایِ تو نیست

١١ جمال و مَفخَرِ آفاق شمسِ تبریزی

کُدام شاه که از جان و دل کُدایِ تو نیست

---

٨ سرد و خام (CT).   ١١ جمالِ مَفخَرِ آفاق (V).

I will not shun thy blow, for very crude

Is the heart ne'er burned in the fire of thy affliction.

To thy praise and praisers there is no end;

What atom but is reeling with thy praise?

Like that one of whom Nizāmī tells in verse,

Tyrannise not, for I cannot endure thy tyranny.

O Shamsi Tabrīz, beauty and glory of the horizons,

What king but is a beggar of thee with heart and soul?

١١

مُضارِع مُثَمَّنِ اخرَبِ مكفوف : Metre

$[\,-\,-\,\cup\,\mid\,-\,\cup\,-\,\cup\,\mid\,\cup\,-\,-\,\cup\,\mid\,-\,\cup\,\underset{\smile}{\cup}\,]$

L.

١ جانا جمالِ روح بسی خوب و بافَرست

لیکن جمال و حُسنِ تو خَود چیزِ دیگرست

٢ ای آنکه سالها صِفَتِ روح میکُنی

بنمای یك صِفَت كه بذاتش برابرست

٣ در دیده می فزاید نور از خیالِ او

با این همه به پیشِ وصالش مُكَدَّرست

٤ ماندم دهان‌باز ز تعظیمِ آن جمال

هر لحظه بر زبانِ دل اللهُ أُكبَرَست

٥ دل یافت دیدهٔ كه مُقیمِ هوایِ تُست

آوَخ كه آن هوا چه دل و دیده پرورَست

٦ چاكرنوازِیَست كه كردست عشقِ تو

وَرنه كُجا دلی كه بآن عشق درخَورست

٧ هر دل كه او بخُفت شبی در هوایِ تو

چون روزِ رَوشنست هوا زو مُنَوَّرست

١ جمالِ خوب (L). حور جمالِ (B²). ٣ خیالِ تو (L).
٥ در یافت دیدهٔ كه سقیمِ (L).

XI.

O Beloved, spiritual beauty is very fair and glorious,

But thine own beauty and loveliness is another thing.

O thou who art years describing spirit,

Show one quality that is equal to his essence.

Light waxes in the eye at the imagination of him,

But in presence of his union it is dimmed.

I stand open-mouthed in veneration of that beauty :

' God is most great ' is on my heart's lips every moment.

The heart hath gotten an eye constant in desire of thee.

Oh, how that desire feeds heart and eye !

'Tis slave-caressing thy love has practised ;

Else, where is the heart worthy of that love ?

Every heart that has slept one night in thy air

Is like radiant day : thereby the air is illumined.

٨ هر کس که بی مُراد شُد او چون مُریدِ تُست

بی صورتِ مُراد مُرادش مُیَسَّرست

٩ هر دوزخی که سوخت درین عشق و در فُتاد

در کَوثر او فُتاد که عشقِ تو کَوثرست

١٠ پایَم نمی رسد بزمین از اُمیدِ وَصل

هرچند در فِراقِ تو ام دست بر سرست

١١ غمگین مشَو دلا تو ازین ظُلمِ دُشمنان

و اندیشه کُن درین که دِلاوار داوَرست

١٢ از رویِ زعفرانِ من ار شاد شُد عدو

این رویِ زعفرانِ من از وَردِ احمرست

١٣ چون برترست خوبیِّ معشوقم از صِفَت

دردم چه فربه است و مدیحم چه لاغرست

١٤ آری که قاعدست که رنجورِ زاررا

هرچند رنج بیش بُوَد ناله کمترست

١٥ همچون قَمَر بتافت ز تبریز شمسِ دین

نی خَود قَمَر چه باشد کآن رویِ اقمرست

(L). سرسرست ١٠   (L). درین عشق اوفتاد ؟

(B²). نی روی   (B). بر روی   ١٢ In second miṣrā‘

(CL). از دَورِ احمرست   (L). وین روی

Every one that is without object is as thy disciple :

His object is gained without the semblance of object.

Each reprobate who has burned in this love and fallen in it,

Fell into Kauṣar : for thy love is Kauṣar.

From hope of union my foot comes not to earth :

While I am severed from thee, my hand is on my head.

Be not sorrowful, O heart, at this oppression of enemies,

And think on this, that the Sweetheart is judge.

If the foe is rejoiced at my sallow face,

This sallow face of mine is from the red rose.

Since the beauty of my Beloved is beyond description,

How fat is my grief and how lean my praise !

Yea, for it is a rule as regards the poor sick wretch,

That while his pain is more his plaint is less.

Shamsi Dīn shone, moon-like, from Tabrīz ;

No, what is the very moon ? for that is the moon's face
superlative.

۱۳

مُضارِع مُثَمَّنِ اخرَب [−−ᵕ|−ᵕ−|−−ᵕ‖−−ᵕ|−ᵕ−|ᵕ−] Metre:

L.

۱ هر نقشرا که دیدی جِنسش ز لامکانست
کُر نقش رفت غم نیست اصلش چو جاودانست

۲ هر صورتی که دیدی هر نُکته که شنیدی
بدِل مَشَو که رفت آن زیرا نه آن چنانست

۳ چون اصلِ چشمه باقیست فرعش همیشه ساقیست
چون هر دو بی زوالند از چه تُرا فُغانست

۴ جانرا چو چشمهٔ دان وین صُنعها چو جوها
تا چشمه هست باقی جوها ازو روانست

۵ غمرا بِرون کُن از سر وین آبِ جو همی خَور
از فَوتِ آب مندیش کین آب بی کِرانست

۲ زآن دم که آمدستی اندر جهانِ هستی
پیشت که تا برستی بنهاده نردُبانست

۷ اوّل جماد بودی آخِر نبات گَشتی
آنگَه شُدی تو حَیوان این بر تو چون نِهانست

_____

(L). بر دل مَشَو که رفتن ۲   (R). حُسنش ۱
(L). زآن غم که آمدستی ۶   (L). از قوتِ آب ۵

XII.

Every form you see has its archetype in the placeless world;
If the form perished, no matter, since its original is
  everlasting.
Every fair shape you have seen, every deep saying you
  have heard,
Be not cast down that it perished; for that is not so.
Whereas the spring-head is undying, its branch gives water
  continually;
Since neither can cease, why are you lamenting?
Conceive the Soul as a fountain, and these created things
  as rivers:
While the fountain flows, the rivers run from it.
Put grief out of your head and keep quaffing this river-
  water;
Do not think of the water failing; for this water is
  without end.
From the moment you came into the world of being,
A ladder was placed before you that you might escape.
First you were mineral, later you turned to plant,
Then you became animal: how should this be a secret
  to you?

٨ کُشتی از آن پس اِنسان با عِلمِ و عقل و ایمان

بنگر چه کُل شد آن تن کو جُزوِ خاکدانست

٩ ز اِنسان چو سَیر کردی بی شك فِرِشته گَردی

بی این زمین از آن پس جایَت بر آسمانست

١٠ باز از فِرِشتگی هم بگذر برَو در آن یَمِ

تا قطرهٔ تو بحری گَردد که صد عُمانست

١١ بگذر ازین وَلَد تو میگو ز جان اَحَد تو

گر پیر کُشت جِسمت چه غم چو جان جوانست

_____

(L). زین سان ٩

Afterwards you were made man, with knowledge, reason, faith ;

Behold the body, which is a portion of the dust-pit, how perfect it has grown !

When you have travelled on from man, you will doubtless become an angel ;

After that you are done with this earth : your station is in heaven.

Pass again even from angelhood : enter that ocean,

That your drop may become a sea which is a hundred seas of 'Omān.

Leave this 'Son,' say ever 'One' with all your soul ;

If your body has aged, what matter, when the soul is young ?

مُضارِعِ مُثَمَّنِ اخْرَبِ مكفوفِ مقصور :Metre

[ـ ˇ× | ـ ˇ ˇ | ـ ˇ ـ | ـ ـ ˇ ـ]

V.

۱	آن روحرا که عشقِ حقیقی شِعار نیست
	نابوده به که بودنِ او غَیرِ عار نیست
۲	در عشق مست باش که عشق است هرچه هست
	بی کار و بارِ عشق برِ یار بار نیست
۳	کُویند عشق چیست بُکو ترکِ اِختیار
	هر کاو ز اِختیار نَرَست اِختیار نیست
۴	عاشق شهِنشهیست دو عالَم برو نِثار
	هیچ اِلتفاتِ شاه بسوی نِثار نیست
۵	عشق است و عاشق است که باقیست تا ابد
	دل جُز برین منه که بجُز مُستعار نیست
۶	تا کی کِنار کِیری معشوقِ مُردهرا
	جانرا کِنار کِیر که اورا کِنار نیست
۷	آن کز بهار زاد بمیرد کَه خِزان
	کُلزارِ عشقرا مدد از نَوبهار نیست
۸	آن کُل که از بهار بُوَد خارِ یارِ اوست
	وآن مَی که از عصیر بُوَد بی خُمار نیست
۹	نظّارهکُر مباش درین راه مُنتظر
	والله که هیچ مرک بَتَر ز اِنتِظار نیست

(V). جُز این مُستعار ۵

XIII.

'Twere better that the spirit which wears not true love
    as a garment

Had not been : its being is but shame.

Be drunken in love, for love is all that exists;

Without the dealing of love there is no entrance to the
    Beloved.

They say, ' What is love ?' Say, ' Renunciation of will.'

Whoso has not escaped from will, no will hath he.

The lover is a monarch: two worlds lie at his feet;

The king pays no heed to what lies at his feet.

'Tis love and the lover that live to all eternity ;

Set not thy heart on aught else : 'tis only borrowed.

How long wilt thou embrace a dead beloved ?

Embrace the soul which is embraced by nothing.

What was born of spring dies in autumn,

Love's rose-plot hath no aiding from the early spring.

A thorn is the companion of the rose that comes of spring,

And the wine that comes of grape-juice is not free from
    headache.

Be not an expectant looker-on in this path ;

By God, there is no death worse than expectancy.

۱۰   بر نقد قلب زن تو اگر قلب نیستی

این نُکته گوش دار گَرَت گوشوار نیست

۱۱   بر اسپِ تن ملرز و سُبکتر پیاده شَو

پرَّش دِهد خُدای که بر تن سُوار نیست

۱۲   اندیشها رها کُن و دلساده شَو تمام

چون روی آینه که بنقش و نِگار نیست

۱۳   چون ساده شُد ز نقش همه نقشها دروست

زآن سادهروی روی کسی شرمسار نیست

۱۴   آئینه ساده خواهی خَودرا درو نِگر

کورا ز راستگوئی شرم و حذار نیست

۱۵   چون روی آهنی ز تمیز این صفا بیابت

تا روی دل چه باید کورا غُبار نیست

۱۶   لیکن میانِ آهن و دل این تفاوُتست

کین رازدار آمد و آن رازدار نیست

---

۱۰ بر نقد عشق (V). ۱۲ دلشاد شَو (V). ۱۳ آن سادهرو (V). ۱۴ ز روی کسی (B). ۱۴ از عیب ساده خواهی (B). جدار (CV). ۱۵ چون روی آینه (V). با روی دل (B). عیار نیست (B).

V has a seventeenth beyt, which I have omitted, as it not only seems to be corrupt but repeats the rhyme of the preceding couplet:

گویم چه باید او و بگوید خمُش کُنم

تا دلِستان نگوید کو رازدار نیست

Set thy heart on sterling coin, if thou be not false;

Give ear to this deep saying, if thou lack an earring.

Do not tremble on the steed of the body, but fare lighter on foot;

God lends him wings who is not mounted on the body.

Dismiss cares and be utterly clear of heart,

Like the face of a mirror without image and picture.

When it becomes clear of images, all images are contained in it;

No man's face is ashamed of that clear-faced one.

Wouldst thou have a clear mirror, behold thyself therein,

For it is not ashamed or afraid of telling the truth.

Since the steel face gained this purity by discrimination,

What needs the heart's face, which has no dust?

But betwixt the steel and the heart is this difference,

That the one is a keeper of secrets, while the other is not.

١۴

Metre: مُضارِع مُثَمَّنٍ اخرَب [--ᴗ|-ᴗ--||---ᴗ|-ᴗ--|-ᴗ-ᴢ]

L. ١ كُفتا كه كيست بر در كُفتم كمين غُلامت

كُفتا چه كار داری كُفتم مِها سلامت

٢ كُفتا كه چند رانی كُفتم كه تا بخوانی

كُفتا كه چند جوشی كُفتم كه تا قيامت

٣ دعَوَيِّ عشق كردم سَوگَندها بخَوردم

كز عشق ياوه كردم من مُلكت و شهامت

۴ كُفتا براِي دعوَی قاضی گُواه خواهد

كُفتم گُواه اشكم زردِيِّ رُخ علامت

٥ كُفتا گُواه جرحست ترداَمنست چشمت

كُفتم بفرِّ عدلت عدلند و بی غرامت

٦ كُفتا چه عزم داری كُفتم وَفا و ياری

كُفتا ز من چه خواهی كُفتم كه لُطفِ عامت

٧ كُفتا كه بود همره كُفتم خيالت ای شه

كُفتا كه خواندت اينجا كُفتم كه بوِي جامت

_____

BCL Lakh. V

(B). گُواه چرخست ٥ (L). اينجا مِها سلامت ١

XIV.

He said: 'Who is at the door?' Said I: 'Thy humble slave.'

He said: 'What business have you?' Said I: 'Lord, to greet thee.'

He said: 'How long will you push?' Said I: 'Till thou call.'

He said: 'How long will you glow?' Said I: 'Till resurrection.'

I laid claim to love, I took oaths
That for love I had lost sovereignty and power.

He said: 'A judge demands witness as regards a claim.'

Said I: 'Tears are my witness, paleness of face my evidence.'

He said: 'The witness is not valid; your eye is corrupt.'

Said I: 'By the majesty of thy justice they are just and clear of sin.'

He said: 'What do you intend?' Said I: 'Constancy and friendship.'

He said: 'What do you want of me?' Said I: 'Thy universal grace.'

He said: 'Who was your companion?' Said I: 'Thought of thee, O King.'

He said: 'Who called you here?' Said I: 'The odour of thy cup.'

٨   گُفتا کُجاست خَوشتر گُفتم که قصرِ قَیصر

     گُفتا چه دیدی آنجا گُفتم که صد کِرامت

٩   گُفتا چراست خالی گُفتم ز بیمِ رهزن

     گُفتا که کیست رهزن گُفتم که این ملامت

١٠   گُفتا کُجاست ایمن گُفتم بزُهد و تقوَی

     گُفتا که زُهد چه بوَد گُفتم رهِ سلامت

١١   گُفتا کُجاست آفت گُفتم بکویِ عشقت

     گُفتا که چونی آنجا گُفتم در اِستِقامت

١٢   بِسیارت آزمودم امّا نبود سودم

     مَن جَرَّبَ ٱلمُجَرَّب حَلَّت بِهِ ٱلنَّدَامَة

١٣   خاموش گر بگویم من نُکتهایِ اورا

     از خویشتن بر آئی نه در کشد نه بامت

---

٩ Begins in L: گُفتا کُجاست ایمن.   ١٠ Not in L, but evidently omitted by mistake.   ١٢ خَرَّبَ and حَلَّت (L).   ١٣ از خویشتن ندانی (L). کشد for بُوَد (L).

He said: 'Where is it pleasantest?' Said I: 'The Emperor's palace.'

He said: 'What saw you there?' Said I: 'A hundred miracles.'

He said: 'Why is it desolate?' Said I: 'From fear of the brigand.'

He said: 'Who is the brigand?' Said I: 'This blame.'

He said: 'Where is it safe?' Said I: 'In abstinence and piety.'

He said: 'What is abstinence?' Said I: 'The path of salvation.'

He said: 'Where is calamity?' Said I: 'In the neighbourhood of thy love.'

He said: 'How fare you there?' Said I: 'In steadfastness.'

I gave you a long trial, but it availed me nothing;

Repentance lights on him who tests one tested already.

Peace! if I should utter forth his mystic sayings,

You would go beside yourself, neither door nor roof would restrain you.

۱۵

Metre: هَزَجِ مُثَمَّنِ اخرَبِ مکفوفِ مقصور

$$[-\,-\,\cup\,|\,\cup\,-\,-\,\cup\,|\,\cup\,-\,-\,\cup\,|\,\cup\,-\,-\,]$$

L.	این خانه که پَیوَسته درو بِنگِ چُغانست	۱
	از خواجه بِپُرسید که این خانه چه خانست	
	این صورتِ بُت چیست گُر این خانهٔ کعبست	۲
	وین نورِ خُدا چیست گُر این دَیرِ مُغانست	
	گُنجیست درین خانه که در گَون نگُنجد	۳
	این خانه و این خواجه همه فِعل و بهانست	
	بر خانه منه دست که این خانه طِلِسمست	۴
	با خواجه مگُوئید که او مستِ شبانست	
	خاک و خِس این خانه همه مُشك و عبیرست	۵
	بامِ و دَرِ این خانه همه بَیت و تُرانست	
	فی آلجُمله هر آنکس که درین خانه رهی یافت	۶
	سُلطانِ زمینست و سُلَیمانِ زمانست	
	ای خواجه یکی سرِ تو ازین بامِ فرو کُن	۷
	کاندر رُخِ خوبِ تو ز اِقبالِ نِشانست	

۴ (L.) که این خانهٔ ظُلمست

XV.

This house wherein is continually the sound of the viol,
Ask of the master what house is this.

What means this idol-form, if this is the house of the Ka'ba?

And what means this light of God, if this is a Magian
    temple?

In this house is a treasure which the universe is too small
    to hold;

This house and this master is all acting and pretence.

Lay no hand on the house, for this house is a talisman;

Speak not with the master, for he is drunken overnight.

The dust and rubbish of this house is all musk and
    perfume;

The roof and door of this house is all verse and melody.

In fine, whoever has found the way into this house

Is sultan of the world and Solomon of the time.

O master, bend down thy head once from this roof,

For in thy fair face is a token of fortune.

٨ سَوگَند بجانِ تو که جُز دیدنِ رویَت

گر مُلکِ زمینست فسونست و فسانست

٩ حَیران شُده بُستان که چه برگ و چه شِکوفَست

واله شُده مُرغان که چه دامست و چه دانست

١٠ این خواجهٔ چرخست که چون زُهره و ماهَست

وین خانهٔ عشقَست که بی حدّ و کِرانست

١١ چون آینه جان نقشِ تو در دل بگرفتست

در دلِ سرِ زُلفِ تو فرو رفته چو شانست

١٢ در حضرتِ یوسُف که زنان دست بُریدند

ای جان تو بمن آی که جانان بمیانست

١٣ مستند همه خانه کسیرا خبری نیست

از هرکه در آید که فُلانست و فُلانست

١٤ سرمست بدر بر منشین خانه در آ زود

تاریک بُوَد آنکه ورا جایِ ستانست

١٥ مستانِ خُدا گرچه هزارند یکی اند

مستانِ هوا گرچه یکانست دوگانست

١٦ در بیشهٔ شیران رَو و از زخم مَیَندیش

کاندیشه و ترس این همه اشکالِ زنانست

---

(٧). کاندیشه و ترسیدن از اشکالِ زبانه است ١٦

I swear by thy soul that save the sight of thy countenance,

All, tho' 'twere the kingdom of the earth, is fantasy
and fable.

The garden is bewildered to know which is the leaf, and
which the blossom;

The birds are distracted to know which is the snare and
which the bait.

This is the Lord of heaven, who resembles Venus and
the moon,

This is the house of Love, which has no bound or end.

Like a mirror, the soul has received thy image in its heart;

The tip of thy curl has sunk into the heart like a comb.

Forasmuch as the women cut their hands in Joseph's
presence,

Come to me, O soul, for the Beloved is in the midst.

All the house are drunken—none has knowledge

Of each who enters that he is so-and-so or so-and-so.

Do not sit intoxicated at the door: come into the
house quickly;

He is in the dark whose place is the threshold.

Those drunk with God, tho' they be thousands, are yet one;

Those drunk with lust—tho' it be a single one, he is a
double.

Go into the wood of lions and reck not of the wound,

For thought and fear—all these are figments of women.

۱۷   کآنجا نبُوَد زخم همه رحمت و مهرست

لیکن پس در وَهمِ تو ماننده‌ٔ فانست

۱۸   در بیشه بزن آتش و خاموش کُن ای دل

در کِش تو زبان زاآنکه زبانِ تو زبانست

_____

۱۸ مزن آتش (۷).   است زبانه تو زبانِ (۷).

For *there* is no wound: all is mercy and love,

But thy imagination is like a bar behind the door.

Set fire to the wood, and keep silence, O heart;

Draw back thy tongue, for thy tongue is harmful.

۱٦

مُضارِع مُثَمَّنِ اخرَبِ مكفوفِ مقصور :Metre

[ـ ـ ᴗ | ـ ᴗ ـ ᴗ | ᴗ ـ ـ ᴗ | ـ ᴗ ˣ]

V.

١ بنمای رُخ که باغ و گُلِستانم آرزوست
بکشای لب که قندِ فراوانم آرزوست

٢ ای آفتاب رُخ بنُمای از نِقابِ ابر
كآن چِهرهٔ مُشَعشَعِ تابانم آرزوست

٣ بشنیدم از هوایِ تو آوازِ طبلِ باز
باز آمدم که ساعِدِ سُلطانم آرزوست

۴ گُفتی ز ناز بیش مرنجان مرا بَرو
آن گُفتنت که بیش مرنجانم آرزوست

٥ وآن دفع گُفتنت که بِرون شَو بخانه نیست
وآن ناز و کِبر و تُندیِ دربانم آرزوست

٦ ای بادِ خَوش که از چَمَنِ دوست می وَزی
بر من بَوز که مُژدهٔ رَیحانم آرزوست

٧ آن نان و آبِ چرخ چو سَیلیست بی وَفا
من ماهیِ نِهنگُم و عُمّانم آرزوست

(V). ماهی و نِهنگم ٧

XVI.

Show thy face, for I desire the orchard and the rose-garden;

Ope thy lips, for I desire sugar in plenty.

O sun, show forth thy face from the veil of cloud,

For I desire that radiant glowing countenance.

From love for thee I hearkened to the sound of the falcon-drum;

I have returned, for the sultan's arm is my desire.

'Vex me no more,' thou saidst capriciously, 'begone!'

I desire that saying of thine, 'Vex me no more.'

And thy bidding off with 'Depart, he is not at home,'

And the airs and pride and harshness of the door-keeper I desire.

O sweet zephyr, that blowest from the flower-plot of the Friend,

Blow on me, for I desire news of the basil.

The bread and water of destiny is like a treacherous flood;

I am a great fish and desire the sea of 'Omān.

٨ یعقوب‌وار وا اَسَفاها همی زنم
 دیدارِ خوبِ یوسُفِ کنعانم آرزوست

٩ بِلله که شهر بی تو مرا حبس میشَوَد
آوارگیِّ کوه و بیابانم آرزوست

١٠ یک دست جامِ باده و یک دست زُلفِ یار
رقصی چنین میانهٔ میدانم آرزوست

١١ زین همرهانِ سُست‌عناصر دلم گِرِفت
شیرِ خُدا و رُستمِ دستانم آرزوست

١٢ در دستِ هر که هست ز خوبی قُراضه‌هاست
آن معدنِ ملاحت و آن کانم آرزوست

١٣ هرچند مُفلِسم نَپذیرم عقیقِ خُرد
کانِ عقیقِ نادرِ لرزانم آرزوست

١۴ زین خلق پُر شِکایَت گِریانم و ملول
آن های و هوی و زاریِ مستانم آرزوست

١۵ جانم ملول گشت ز فِرعَون و ظُلمِ او
آن نورِ رویِ موسَیِ عِمرانم آرزوست

عزیزئی ١٢ (L.) یعقوب‌وار زآن نَفَس آتشین زنم ٨
آن معدنِ لطافت و ارکانم آرزوست (V.) قُراضه‌هاست for
چو بدیدم عقیقِ تو ١٣ (V.) (V.)

Like Jacob I am uttering cries of grief,

I desire the fair face of Joseph of Canaan.

By God, without thee the city is a prison to me,

O'er mountain and desert I desire to wander.

In one hand a wine-cup and in one hand a curl of the
　　Beloved :

Such a dance in the midst of the market-place is my desire.

My heart is weary of these weak-spirited companions;

I desire the Lion of God and Rustam, son of Zāl.

Filings of beauty are in the possession of every one that
　　exists;

I desire that quarry and that mine of exquisite loveliness.

Bankrupt tho' I be, I will not accept a small carnelian;
The mine of rare tremulous carnelian is my desire.

Of this folk I am full of complaint, weeping and weary;

I desire the drunkards' wailing and lamentation.

My soul is grown weary of Pharaoh and his tyranny ;

I desire the light of the countenance of Moses, son of
　　'Imrān.

۱٦ کُفتند یافت نیست بسی جُسته ایم ما
چیزی که یافت می نشَود آنم آرزوست

۱۷ گویاترم ز بُلبُل و امّا ز رشك عام
مُهریست بر زبانم و افغانم آرزوست

۱۸ دی شَیخ با چِراغ همی گُشت گِردِ شهر
کز دیو و دد ملولم و انسانم آرزوست

۱۹ خَود کارِ من گُذشت ز هر آز و آرزو
از گَون و از مکان سوِي ارکانم آرزوست

۲۰ پنهان ز دیدها و همه دیدها ازو
آن آشکارصُنعت پنهانم آرزوست

۲۱ گوشم شنید قِصّهٔ ایمان و مست شُد
کو قِسمِ و جِسم و صورتِ ایمانم آرزوست

۲۲ من خَود رباب عشقم و عشقم ربابی است
دست و کِنار و نغمهٔ عُثمانم آرزوست

۲۳ میگویَد آن رباب که هر دم ز اِشتیاق
آن لُطفهای رحمتِ رحمانم آرزوست

۲٤ ای مُطرِب ظریف تو باقّي این غَزَل
زین سان همی شُمار که زین سانم آرزوست

۲۵ بنمای شمس مفخرِ تبریز شرقِ عشق
من هُدهُدم حُضورِ سُلَیمانم آرزوست

They said, 'He is not to be found, we have sought Him
    long.'

A thing which is not to be found—*that* is my desire.

I am more eloquent than the nightingale, but because
    of vulgar envy

A seal is on my tongue, tho' I desire to moan.

Yesterday the Master with a lantern was roaming about
    the city,

Crying, 'I am tired of devil and beast, I desire a man.'

My state has passed even beyond all yearning and
    desire ;

I desire to go from Being and Place toward the Essentials.

He is hidden from our eyes, and all objects are from Him ;

I desire that hidden One whose works are manifest.

Mine ear listened to the tale of faith and was intoxicated ;

Say, 'The limbs and the body and the form of faith are
    my desire.'

I myself am Love's rebeck, and Love is a rebeck to me ;

I desire the hand and bosom and modulation of 'Othmān.

That rebeck is saying, 'Every moment passionately

I desire the favours of the mercy of the Merciful.'

O cunning minstrel, con the rest of this ode

After this fashion, for after this fashion I desire.

Display, O Sun who art Tabrīz's glory, the dawning of
    Love ;

I am the hoopoe: the presence of Solomon is my desire.

Metre : مُتَقارِب مُثَمَّن مقصور [∪ـ | ـ∪ـ | ∪ـ | ـ∪ـ | ∪ـ | ـ∪ـ | ∪ـ | ـ∪ـ]

V.　　١　من آن روز بودم که اسما نبود

　　　　نِشان از وُجودِ مُسمّا نبود

　　٢　ز ما شُد مُسمّا و اسما پدید

　　　　در آن روز کانجا من و ما نبود

　　٣　نِشان گَشت مَظهَر سرِ زُلفِ یار

　　　　هنوز آن سرِ زُلفِ زیبا نبود

　　٤　چلیپا و نصرانیان سر بسر

　　　　بپیمودم اندر چلیپا نبود

　　٥　به بُتخانه رفتم بدَیرِ کُهَن

　　　　درو هیچ رنگی هُوَیدا نبود

　　٦　بکوهِ هرا رفتم و قندهار

　　　　بدیدم در آن زیر و بالا نبود

RV

٣ نِشانِ مُطَهَّر سرِ زُلفِ یار (V).　٤ بپیوَندم (V).
٥ در بُتخانه به for بدَیرِ کُهَن (V).　٦ حری for هرا (V).
بکوی هرا (R).　This couplet is followed in V by another
which I have omitted as it repeats the rhyme :

ز زیر و ز بالا فرو دیدمش
که نزدیکِ وَی زیر و بالا نبود

XVII.

I was on that day when the Names were not,

Nor any sign of existence endowed with name.

By me Names and Named were brought to view

On the day when there were not 'I' and 'We.'

For a sign, the tip of the Beloved's curl became a
centre of revelation;

As yet the tip of that fair curl was not.

Cross and Christians, from end to end,

I surveyed; He was not on the Cross.

I went to the idol-temple, to the ancient pagoda;

No trace was visible there.

I went to the mountains of Herát and Candahár;

I looked; He was not in that hill-and-dale.

٧   بِعَمداً شُدم بر سرِ کوهِ قاف

در آن جای جُز جاي عنقا نبود

٨   بکعبه کشیدم عِنانِ طَلَب

در آن مقصدِ پیر و برنا نبود

٩   بپُرسیدم از اِبن سیناش حال

بر اندازهٔ اِبن سینا نبود

۱۰   سوِي منظرِ قابَ قَوْسَیْن شُدم

در آن بارگاهِ مُعلّا نبود

۱۱   نِگه کردم اندر دلِ خویشتن

در آن جاش دیدم دِگر جا نبود

۱۲   بجُز شمسِ تبریزِ پاکیزهجان

کسی مست و مخمور و شَیدا نبود

(R). در آنجا نِشانی ز عنقا نبود ٧

With set purpose I fared to the summit of Mount Qáf;

In that place was only the 'Anqá's habitation.

I bent the reins of search to the Ka'ba;

He was not in that resort of old and young.

I questioned Ibn Sīnā of his state;

He was not in Ibn Sīnā's range.

I fared towards the scene of *"two bow-lengths' distance"*;

He was not in that exalted court.

I gazed into my own heart;

There I saw Him; He was nowhere else.

Save pure-souled Shamsi Tabrīz

None ever was drunken and intoxicated and distraught.

١٨

Metre: هَزَج مُثَمَّنِ اخرَب [ـ‌ـ‌ـ‌خ| ـ‌ـ‌ـ‌ʊ| ـ‌ـ‌ـ‌ʊ| ʊ‌ـ‌ـ]

C.	جان پیشِ تو هر ساعت میریزد و میرویَد ۱
	وَز بهرِ یکی جان کس چون با تو سُخُن گُویَد
	هر جای نِهی پائی از خاك برویَد سر ۲
	از بهرِ یکی سر کس دست از تو کُجا شویَد
	روزی که بپرّد جان از لذّتِ بوي تو ۳
	جان داند و جان داند کز دوست چه میبویَد
	یکدم که خُمارِ تو از مغز شَوَد کمتر ۴
	صد نَوحه بر آرد سر هر موی همی مویَد
	من خانه تِهی کردم کز رخت بپردازم ۵
	میکاهم تا عشقت افزایَد و افزویَد
	از بهرِ چنین سودی جان باختن اولَی‌تر ۶
	خامُش که همآن ارزد ای خواجه که میجویَد
	جانم ز پَی عشقت شمَسِ آلحقِ تبریزی ۷
	بی پای چو کِشتیها در بحر همی پویَد

CT

(T). کز رختِ تو پردازم ۵

XVIII.

Before thee the soul is hourly decaying and growing,

And for one soul's sake how should any plead with thee?

Wherever thou settest foot a head springs up from the
earth ;

For one head's sake why should any wash his hands of
thee ?

That day when the soul takes flight enraptured by thy
fragrance,

The soul knows, the soul knows what fragrance is the
Beloved's.

As soon as thy fumes vanish out of the brain,

The head heaves a hundred sighs, every hair is lamenting.

I have emptied house, to be quit of the furniture ;

I am waning, that thy love may increase and wax.

'Tis best to gamble the soul away for so great a gain.

Peace ! for it is worth, O master, just that which it seeks.

My soul in pursuit of thy love, Shamsu 'l Ḥaqq of Tabrīz,

Is scudding without feet, ship-like, over the sea.

١٩

هَزَجِ مُثَمَّنِ اخرَبِ مكفوفِ مقصور :Metre
[ـ ـ ـ ٴ | ٴ ـ ـ ٴ | ٴ ـ ـ ٴ | ٴ ـ ـ]

١	بر چرخِ سَحرگَاه یکی ماه عیان شُد	L.
	وَز چرخ بزیر آمد و بر ما نِگران شُد	
٢	چون باز که بِرباید مُرغی بَّهِ صَید	
	بِربود مرا آن مَه و بر چرخ روان شُد	
٣	در خَود چو نظَر کردم خَودرا بِنَدیدم	
	زیراکه در آن مَه تنم از لُطف چو جان شُد	
٤	در جان چو سَفَر کردم جُز ماه ندیدم	
	تا سِرِّ تجلیّ ازل جُمله بیان شُد	
٥	نه چرخِ فلك جُمله در آن ماه فرو شُد	
	کِشتیّ وُجودم همه در بَحر نِهان شُد	
٦	آن بَحر بزد مَوج و خِرَد باز بر آمد	
	و آوازه در افکند چنین گُشت و چنان شُد	
٧	آن بَحر کَفی کرد بَهَر پاره از آن کَف	
	نقشی ز فُلان آمد و جِسمی ز فُلان شُد	

BCL Lakh. TV

XIX.

At morning-tide a moon appeared in the sky,

And descended from the sky and gazed on me.

Like a falcon which snatches a bird at the time of hunting,

That moon snatched me up and coursed over the sky.

When I looked at myself, I saw myself no more,

Because in that moon my body became by grace even
as soul.

When I travelled in soul, I saw nought save the moon,

Till the secret of the eternal Theophany was all revealed.

The nine spheres of heaven were all merged in that moon,

The vessel of my being was completely hidden in the sea.

The sea broke into waves, and again Wisdom rose

And cast abroad a voice; so it happened and thus it befell.

Foamed the sea, and at every foam-fleck

Something took figure and something was bodied forth.

٨   هر پاره كفِ جسم كز آن بحر نشان يافت

در حال كُدازيد و درين بحر روان شُد

٩   بی دَولتِ مخدومیِ شمسِ آلحقِ تبريز

نی ماه توان ديدن و نی بحر توان شُد

(L). نی ماه توان بودن ٩

Every foam-fleck of body, which received a sign from
    that sea,

Melted straightway and turned to spirit in this ocean.

Without the power imperial of Shamsu 'l Ḥaqq of Tabrīz

One could neither behold the moon nor become the sea.

٢.

Metre: مُجتثتِ مُثَمَّنِ مخبون [ᴗ−−|ᴗ−ᴗ−|ᴗᴗ−−|ᴗ−ᴗ−|−−ᴗᴗ]

B.

١ بگیر دامنِ لُطفش که ناگهان بگُریزد

ولی مکش تو چو تیرش که از کمان بگُریزد

٢ چه نقشها که ببازد چه حیلها که بسازد

بِنقش حاضر باشد ز راهِ جان بگُریزد

٣ در آسمانش بجوئی چو مَه در آب بتابد

در آب چونکه در آئی بآسمان بگُریزد

۴ ز لامکانش بجوئی نِشان دِهد بمکانت

چو در مکانش بجوئی بلامکان بگُریزد

۵ چو تیر می بَرَوَد از کمان چو مُرغ گُمانت

یقین بِدان که یقین‌وار از گُمان بگُریزد

٦ از این و آن بگُریزم ز ترس نی ز ملولی

که آن نِثارِ لطیفم از این و آن بگُریزد

BCTV

(B²). چو تیر می بَرَوَد از وُجود مُرغ کمان او ۵
(V). وار for تیر. (V). چو مُرغ for همچو

XX.

Grasp the skirt of his favour, for on a sudden he will flee ;

But draw him not, as an arrow, for he will flee from
the bow.

What delusive forms does he take, what tricks does he
invent !

If he is present in form, he will flee by the way of spirit.

Seek him in the sky, he shines in water, like the moon ;

When you come into the water, he will flee to the sky.

Seek him in the placeless, he will sign you to place ;

When you seek him in place, he will flee to the placeless.

As the arrow speeds from the bow, like the bird of your
imagination,

Know that the Absolute will certainly flee from the
Imaginary.

I will flee from this and that, not for weariness, but
for fear

That my gracious Beauty will flee from this and that.

۷ گُریزپای چو بادم ز عشقِ گُل چو صبا ام

گُلی ز بیمِ خزانی ز بوستان بگُریزد

۸ چنان گُریزد نامش چو قصدِ گُفتن بیند

که گُفت نیز نتابی که آن فلان بگُریزد

۹ چنان گُریزد از تو که گر نَویسی نقشش

ز لَوح نقش بپَّرد ز دل نِشان بگُریزد ۰

---

۷ ز بیمِ بادِ خزانی (T.) چو صبا ام for نه گُلی کو

(B.) چو قصدِ گُفتم شُد (T.) ۸ گُلی ز بیمِ خزانی for

(V.) که گُفته اند ندانی (B.) نیز نتابی for بند ندانی

As the wind I am fleet of foot, from love of the rose I
am like the zephyr ;

The rose in dread of autumn will flee from the garden.

His name will flee, when it sees an attempt at speech,

So that you cannot even say, 'Such an one will flee.'

He will flee from you, so that if you limn his picture,

The picture will fly from the tablet, the impression will
flee from the soul.

٢١

Metre: هَزَجِ مُثَمَّنِ سالِم [×--ᵕ|---ᵕ|---ᵕ|---ᵕ]

١   بُتى كو زُهره و مَهرا همه شب شيوَه آموزد   L.

دو چشمِ او بجادوئى دو چشمِ چرخ بر دوزد

٢   شُما دلها نِگه داريد من بارى مُسلمانان

چنان آميختمِ با او كه دل با من نياميزد

٣   نُخُست از عشقِ او زادم بآخِر دل بِدو دادم

چو ميوَه زايَد از شاخى بدآن شاخ اندر آويزد

٤   سرِ زُلفش همى كُويد هلا رَو بر رسن‌بازى

رُخِ شمعش همى كُويد كُجا پروانه تا سوزد

٥   براىِ آن رسن‌بازى دلا زو باش چَنبَر شَو

در افگن خويش بر آتش چو شمعِ او بر افروزد

٦   چو ذَوقِ سوختن ديدى دِگُر نشكيبى از آتش

اگُر آبِ حيات آيد تُرا ز آتش نَينگيزد

CL Lakh.

(L) contra metr. كه من بارى ٢

XXI.

A beauty that all night long teaches love-tricks to Venus
    and the moon,
Whose two eyes by their witchery seal up the two eyes
    of heaven.
Look to your hearts! I, whate'er betide, O Moslems,
Am so mingled with him that no heart is mingled with me.
I was born of his love at the first, I gave him my heart
    at the last;
When the fruit springs from the bough, on that bough
    it hangs.
The tip of his curl is saying, 'Ho! betake thee to rope-
    dancing.'
The cheek of his candle is saying, 'Where is a moth
    that it may burn?'
For the sake of dancing on that rope, O heart, make
    haste, become a hoop;
Cast thyself on the flame, when his candle is lit.
Thou wilt never more endure without the flame, when
    thou hast known the rapture of burning;
If the water of life should come to thee, it would not
    stir thee from the flame.

٢٢

Metre : سريعِ مَطوِيِ مَوقوف [–∪∪– | –∪∪– | –∪∪– | –∪x]

B.

١   كُفت كسى خواجه سنائى بمُرد

مرگِ چنين خواجه نه كاريست خُرد

٢   كاه نبود او كه ببادى پريد

آب نبود او كه بسرما فُسُرد

٣   شانه نبود او كه بموئى شِكست

دانه نبود او كه زمينش فُشُرد

٤   كُنجِ زرى بود درين خاكدان

كو دو جهانرا بجَوى مى شُمُرد

٥   قالِبِ خاكى سوىِ خاكى فِگَند

جان و خِرَد سوىِ سَموات بُرد

٦   صاف بر آميخته با دُردِ مَى

بر سرِ خُمِ رفت و جُدا گَشت دُرد

٧   جانِ دُومرا كه ندانند خلق

والله گُويمر كه بجانان سُپُرد

BLT

٧ جامِ دُومرا (L).   مغلطه گُويمر و بجانان سُپُرد (B).

XXII.

Quoth some one, 'Master Sanā'ī is dead.'

The death of such a master is no little thing.

He was not chaff which flew on the wind,

He was not water which froze in winter.

He was not a comb which was broken with an hair,

He was not a seed which the earth crushed.

He was a treasure of gold in this dust-pit,

For he valued the two worlds at a barley-corn.

The earthly frame he flung to the earth,

Soul and intellect he bore to heaven.

The pure elixir mingled with the wine-dregs

Came to the jar's surface, and the lees settled apart.

The second soul which the vulgar know not

I protest by God that he surrendered to the Beloved.

٨   در سَفَر اُفتند بِهَم ای عزیز

مروَزی و رازی و رومی و کُرد

٩   خانهٔ خَود باز رَوَد هر یکی

اطلس کی باشد همتای مُرد

١٠   خامُش کُن چون نُقَط ایرا مَلِك

نامِ تو از دفترِ گُفتـن سُتُرد

---

٨ مـرغزی و تـازی (B).   ٩ همتای بُرد (B°).

گُفت حمُش (L).   ١٠ خامُش و شو کین سُخُنت‌را مَلِك

چون مَلِك نُطق عشق (B°).

In travel, dear friend, there meet together

The native of Marv and of Rai, the Roman and the Kurd.

Each one returns to his home ;

How should an old man be the companion of youths ?

Keep silence, like the points (of a compass), because the
King

Has erased thy name from the book of speech.

Metre : مُضارِع مُثَمَّنِ اخرَبِ مكفوفِ مقصور

$[--\cup | -\cup-\cup | \cup--\cup | -\cup \overset{\times}{-}]$

		L.
۱	لُطفی نماند کآن صنمِ خَوشلِقا نکرد	
	مارا چه جُرمِ گر کَرَمش با شُما نکرد	
٢	تشنیع می زنی که جفا کرد آن نِگار	
	خوبی که دید در دو جهان که جفا نکرد	
٣	عشقش شَکَرنَیَست اگر او شَکَر نداد	
	حُسنش همه وَفاست اگر او وَفا نکرد	
۴	بنمای خانهٔ که ازو نیست پُر چِراغ	
	بنمای صُفّهٔ که رُخش پُر صفا نکرد	
۵	چون روح در نظاره فنا کُشت این بگُفت	
	نظّارهٔ جمالِ خُدا جُز خُدا نکرد	
٦	این چشم و آن چِراغ دو نورند هر یکی	
	چون این بهمِ رسید کسی‌شان جُدا نکرد	

BCL Lakh. T

There are two versions of this ghazal in L. The former (Lᵃ) contains only five couplets (۱ ۲ ۳ ۴ ٦ above). I give here the text of the second (Lᵇ).

حُسنِ (Lᵇ). عشقِ تو شگّرست (Lᵃ). عشقش شکریست ٣
کس از ایشان جُدا (Lᵃ). کس آسان جُدا ٦ ۰. (Lᵇ). شُما
(Lᵇ).

XXIII.

No favour was left which that winsome beauty did not
    bestow.

What fault of ours, if he failed in bounty towards you?

Thou art reviling, because that charmer wrought tyranny;

Who ever saw in the two worlds a fair one that played
    not the tyrant?

His love is a sugar-cane, tho' he gave not sugar;

His beauty is perfect faith, tho' he kept not faith.

Show a house that is not filled by him with lamps,

Show a portico that his face filled not with loveliness.

When the spirit became lost in contemplation, it said this:

'None but God has contemplated the beauty of God.'

This eye and that lamp are two lights, each individual;

When they came together, no one distinguished them.

٧ هر يك ازين مِثال بيانست و مغلطه

حق جُز برشكِ نورِ رُخش وَٱلضّحَى نكرد

٨ خَيّاطِ روزگار بباَلاي هيچكس

پيراهنى ندوخت كه اورا قبا نكرد

٩ خُرشيدِ رويِ مفخرِ آفاق شمسِ دين

بر فانئى نتافت كه اورا بقا نكرد

---

٧ و (L[b]). نور و رُخش om. (CL[b]).

Each of these metaphors is at once an explanation and
    a misconception ;
God revealed "*By the morning splendour*" in envy of
    the light of his countenance.
Never did the tailor, Destiny, to any one's measure
Stitch a shirt but he tore it in pieces.
The sun of the face of Shamsi Dín, glory of the horizons,
Never shone upon aught perishable but he made it
    eternal.

Metre: مُجتَّتِ مُثَمَّنِ مخبون [−∪−∪−|∪∪−−|∪−∪−|∞−]

B.	بروزِ مرگ چو تابوتِ من روان باشد	۱
	گُمان مَبَر که مرا دل درین جهان باشد	
	براي من مثٓري و مگو دريغ دريغ	۲
	بدامِ ديو در اُفتى دريغ آن باشد	
	جنازهام چو ببينى مگو فِراق فِراق	۳
	مرا وصال و مُلاقات آن زمان باشد	
	مرا بگٓور سپارى مگو وِداع وِداع	۴
	که گٓور پردهٔ جمعيّتِ جِنان باشد	
	فرو شُدن چو بديدى بر آمدن بنِگٓر	۵
	غُروب شمس و قمررا چرا زِيان باشد	
	تُرا غُروب نمايد ولى شُروق بُوَد	۶
	لَحَد چو حبس نمايد خلاصِ جان باشد	

BCL Lakh. TV
───────────

(B). بدوغِ ديو ۲   (L). دردِ اين جهان باشد ۱

۳ For the second miṣrā' of this beyt B and V substitute the second miṣrā' of ۴.   ۴ For the second miṣrā' of this beyt B and V substitute the second miṣrā' of ۳.

(L). جمعيّتِ جِنان for ارواحِ ساكِنان

XXIV.

When my bier moveth on the day of death,

Think not my heart is in this world.

Do not weep for me and cry ' Woe, woe !'

Thou wilt fall in the devil's snare : that is woe.

When thou seest my hearse, cry not ' Parted, parted !'

Union and meeting are mine in that hour.

If thou commit me to the grave, say not ' Farewell,
   farewell !'

For the grave is a curtain hiding the communion of
   Paradise.

After beholding descent, consider resurrection ;

Why should setting be injurious to the sun and moon ?

To thee it seems a setting, but 'tis a rising ;

Tho' the vault seems a prison, 'tis the release of the soul.

و	كدام دانه فرو رفت در زمین که نرُست

چرا بدانهٔ انسانت این گُمان باشد

٨	كدام دَلو فرو شُد که پُر برون نآمد

ز چاه یوسُفِ جانرا چرا فُغان باشد

٩	دهان ببند ازین سو و زآن طَرَف بگُشای

که های و هویِ تو در جَوِّ لامکان باشد

_____

٩ دهانِ خَود به نبستی (L.) جَوفِ لامکان (V.)

What seed went down into the earth but it grew?

Why this doubt of thine as regards the seed of man?

What bucket was lowered but it came out brimful?

Why should the Joseph of the spirit complain of the well?

Shut thy mouth on this side and open it beyond,

For in placeless air will be thy triumphal song.

٢٥

Metre: مُجْتَثّ مُثَمَّنِ مخبونِ مقصور

$$[\cup - \cup - | \cup \cup - - | \cup - \cup - | \simeq -]$$

V. ‏۱ بِمن نِگر که توئی مؤنِسِ من اندر گُور

در آن شبی که کُنی از دُکان و خانه عُبور

‏۲ سلامِ من شِنَوی در لَحَد خَبَر شَوَدت

که هیچ وَقت نبودی ز چشمِ من مستور

‏۳ منم چو عقل و خِرَد در درونِ سینهٔ تو

بِوَقتِ لذّت و شادی بِوَقتِ رنج و ضرور

‏۴ شبِ غریب چو آوازِ آشنا شِنَوی

رَهی ز ضربتِ مار و جِهی ز وَحشتِ مور

‏۵ خُمارِ عشق در آرد بِگُورِ تو تُحفه

شراب و شاهِد و شمع و کَباب و نُقل و بخور

‏۶ در آن زمان که چِراغِ خِرَد بِگِیرانند

چه های هو که بر آید ز مُردِگانِ قُبور

BC Lakh. TV

(BV). رنجِ ضرور ۳   (CT). منم مؤنِس تو ۱
(BCT). بگِیرانم ۶

XXV.

Look on me, for thou art my companion in the grave

On the night when thou shalt pass from shop and dwelling.

Thou shalt hear my hail in the hollow of the tomb : it
shall become known to thee

That thou wast never concealed from mine eye.

I am as reason and intellect within thy bosom

At the time of joy and gladness, at the time of sorrow
and distress.

O strange night when thou hear'st the well-known voice,

Scap'st from the stroke of asp, and leap'st from the
horror of ant !

Love's intoxication will bring to thy grave, as a gift,

Wine and mistress and candle and meats and sweets and
incense.

In the hour when the intellectual lamp is lighted,

What a paean goes up from the dead men in the tombs !

٧ ز های و هوی شَوَد خیره خاكِ گورستان

ز بانكِ طبلِ قیامت ز طُمطُراقِ نُشور

٨ كَفَن دریده گِرِفته دو گوشِ خَود از بیم

دِماغ و گوش چه باشد به پیشِ نفخهٔ صور

٩ تو چشمِ خویش نِگه دار تا غَلَط نكُنی

كه تا یكی بُوَدت عَینِ ناظِر و منظور

۱۰ بَهَر طَرَف نِثَری صورتِ مرا بینی

اِگَر بخَود نِثَری یا بسویِ آن شر و شور

۱۱ ز احوَالِ بتُریز و دو چشمِ نیكو كُن

كه چشمِ بد بُوَد آن لحظه از جمالِم دور

۱۲ بصورتِ بَشَرَم هان و هان غَلَط نكُنی

كه روح سخت لطیفست و عشق سخت غیور

۱۳ چه جایِ صورت اگَر خَود نَمَد شَوَد صدتو

شُعاعِ آینه جان عالَم آوَرَد بظُهور

۱۴ بجایِ لُقمه و پول ار خُدای جُستندی

نِشسته بر لبِ خَندق ندیدئی یك كور

The earth of the grave-yard is confounded by their cries,

By the din of the drums of resurrection, by the pomp
of rising from the dead.

They have rent their shrouds, they have pressed tight
their two ears in terror;

What is brain and ear before the blast of the trumpet?

Look to thine eye, that thou mistake not,

That unto thee the essence of seer and seen may be one.

To whatever side thou gaze, my form thou shalt espy,

Whether thou gaze on self or towards that moil and mell.

Shun distorted vision and heal thine eyes,

For in that moment the evil eye shall be far from my
beauty.

O take heed, lest thou misconceive me in human shape,

For spirit is very subtle, and love is very jealous.

What room for form, if the felt is hundredfold?

'Tis the rays of the soul's mirror that bring the world
to view.

Had they sought God instead of morsel and pittance,

Thou hadst not seen a single blind man seated on the
moat-edge.

١٥   بشهرِ ما تو چو غمّاز خانه بكشادى

دهان ببسته و غمّاز باش همچون نور

١٦   خموش كردم و از غَيرِ اهل بنهُفتم

خُود اهلِ جُمله توئى راز شُد ز من مستور

١٧   بيا بجانِبِ مشرِق چو شمسِ تبريزى

ببين تو كَوكبهٔ فتح و رايتِ منصور

(C). اهلِ غَير ١٦   (CV). چو تو ١٥

Since Thou hast opened house in our city as dealer in
    amorous glances,

Deal out glances, like light, with closed lips.

I hold my peace and keep the unworthy in the dark ;

Thou art all that is worthy : the mystery is veiled from me.

Come, like the Sun of Tabrīz, towards the east ;

See the star of victory and the conqueror's banner !

۲٦

Metre: رَمَلِ مُثَمَّنِ مقصور [‏ـ ᴗ – –|– ᴗ – –|– ᴗ – –|– ᴗ –]

B.

١ از كِنارِ خویش یابمر هر دمی من بویِ یار
چون نكیرمر خویشتن‌را هر شبی اندر كِنار

٢ دوش باغِ عشق بودمر این هَوَس بر سر دوید
مِهرِ او از دیده سر بر زد روان شُد جویبار

٣ هر كُلِ خندان كه رویَد از لبِ خندانِ او
رَسته بود از خارِ هستی جَسته بود از ذو آلفِقار

٤ هر درختی و گیاهی در چَمَن رقصان شُده
لیك اندر چشمِ عامه بسته بود و بر قرار

٥ ناگهان اندر رسید از یك طَرَف آن سروِ ما
تا كه بیخَود گَشت باغ و دست برهمر زد چُنار

٦ رو چو آتش مَی چو آتش عشق آتش هر سِه خَوش
جان ز آتشهایِ برهمر در فُغان أیْنَ آلِفِرار

٧ در جهانِ وحدتِ شَه این عددرا كُنج نیست
وین عدد هست از ضرورت در جهانِ پنج و چار

(C). او چو آتش ٦   · (B). ناگه بیخَود ٥

XXVI.

From the bosom of Self I catch continually a scent of
　　the Beloved :

How should I not, every night, take Self to my bosom ?

Yestereve I was in Love's garden : this desire came into
　　my head :

His sun peeped forth from mine eye : the river (of tears)
　　began to flow.

Each laughing rose that springs from his laughing lip

Had escaped the thorn of being, had avoided <u>Dh</u>ū 'lfiqār.

Every tree and blade of grass was dancing in the meadow,

But in the view of the vulgar they were bound and at
　　rest.

Suddenly on one side our Cypress appeared,

So that the garden became senseless and the plane clapped
　　its hands.

A face like fire, wine like fire, Love afire—all three
　　delectable ;

The soul, by reason of the mingled fires, was wailing
　　'Where shall I flee ?'

In the world of Divine Unity is no room for Number,

But Number necessarily exists in the world of Five and
　　Four.

۸   صد هزاران سیبِ شیرین بِشمَری در دستِ خویش

گر یکی خواهی که گردد جُمله‌را درهمِ فِشار

۹   بی شُمارِ حرفها این نُطق در دل بین که چیست

ساده‌رنگی هست شکلی آمده از اصلِ کار

۱۰ شمسِ تبریزی نِشسته شاهوار و پیشِ او

شِعرِ من صفها زده چون بندگانِ اِختیار

You may count a hundred thousand sweet apples in
    your hand :

If you wish to make One, crush them all together.

Behold, without regarding the letters, what is this lan-
    guage in the heart ;

Pureness of colour is a quality derived from the Source
    of Action.

Shamsi Tabriz is seated in royal state, and before him

My rhymes are ranked like willing servants.

Metre: مُجتَثِ مُثَمَّنِ مخبونِ مقصور

$$[- - \cup - | \cup \cup - - | \cup - \cup - | \overline{\cup} -]$$

V.

١ درخت اگر مُتحرِّک بُدی بپا و بپر
نه رنجِ اَرّه کشیدی نه زخمهایِ تَبَر

۲ وَر آفتاب نرفتی بپر و پا هر شب
جهان چگُونه مُنَوَّر شُدی بگاهِ سَحَر

۳ وَر آبِ تلخ نرفتی ز بحرِ سویِ اُفُق
کُجا حیاتِ گُلستان شُدی بسَیل و مَطَر

۴ چو قطره از وَطَنِ خویش رفت و باز آمد
مُصادِفِ صَدَفی گَشت و شُد یکی گَوهر

۵ نه یوسُفی بسَفَر رفت از پِدَر گِریان
نه در سَفَر بسعادت رسید و مُلک و ظَفَر

۶ نه مُصطفَی بسَفَر رفت جانِبِ یَثرِب
بیافت سلطنت و گَشت شاهِ صد کِشَوَر

BCTV

۵ نه یوسُفی .(V) ۴ مُصادِق .(V) بپا و بپر ا
پِسَری .(V)

XXVII.

If a tree might move by foot and wing,

It would not suffer the pain of the saw or the blows of the axe.

And if the sun did not fare by wing and foot every night,

How would the world be illuminated at morning-tide?

And if the salt water did not go up from the sea to the sky,

Whence would the garden be quickened by river and rain?

When the drop departed from its native home and returned,

It found a shell and became a pearl.

Did not Joseph go on a journey from his father, weeping?

Did he not, in the journey, come to fortune and kingdom and victory?

Did not Muṣṭafā go a-journeying toward Medīna,

Gain sovereignty and become lord of an hundred lands?

و گُر تو پای نداری سَفَر گُزین در خویش ۷

چو كانِ لعل پذيرا شَو از شُعاعِ اثر

ز خویشتن سَفَری كُن بخویش ای خواجه ۸

كه از چُنین سَفَری گُشت خاك معدنِ زر

ز تلخی و تُرُشی رَو بسويِ شیرینی ۹

چنانك رُست ز تلخی هزار گُونه ثَمَر

ز شُمس مفخرِ تبریز این عجائب بین ۱۰

از آنكه هر شَجَر از نورِ شمس یابد فر

---

۹ V substitutes for the second miṣrā' of this beyt the second miṣrā' of ۱۰, and vice versa; the sense, however, seems to require the order given above, which is also found in T. (CT). ۱۰ جوی شیرینی for این عجائب بین

Tho' you have no feet choose to journey in yourself,

Like the ruby-mine receive a print from the sunbeams.

Make a journey out of self into self, O master,

For by such a journey earth becomes a quarry of gold.

From sourness and bitterness advance to sweetness,

Even as from briny soil a thousand sorts of fruit spring up.

From the Sun, the pride of Tabrīz, behold these miracles,

For every tree gains beauty by the light of the sun.

۲۸

Metre : رَجَزِ مُثَمَّنِ مَطوی [‒∪∪‒|‒∪∪‒|‒∪∪‒|‒∪∪×]

L. بانگ زدم نیمِ شبان کیست درین خانۀ دل   ۱

کُفت منم کز رُخِ من شُد مَه و خُرشید خجل

کُفت که این خانۀ دل پُر همه نقشست چرا   ۲

کُفتم کین عکسِ تو است ای رُخِ تو شمعِ چِگِل

کُفت که این نقشِ دِگَر چیست پُر از خونِ جِگَر   ۳

کُفتم کین نقشِ منِ خسته دل و پای بگِل

بستم من گُردنِ جان بُردم پیشش بنشان   ۴

محرمِ عشقست مکُن محرمِ خُودرا تو بجِل

داد سرِ رِشته بمن رِشتۀ پُر فِتنه و فن   ۵

کُفت بکَش تا بکَشم هم بکَش و هم مگُسِل

_____

۲ کین نقشِ تو است (B).   ۳ تَر از خون (B).
۴ مُجرمِ عشقست (BL).   محرمِ مارا تو بجِل (L).   بکش
مکُن (B) for

XXVIII.

I cried out at midnight, 'Who is in this house of the heart?'

He said, ''Tis I, by whose countenance moon and sun are shamed.'

He said, 'Why is this house of the heart filled with diverse images?'

Said I, 'They are the reflexion of thee, O thou whose face is a candle of Chigil.'

He said, 'What is this other image, bedabbled with heart's blood?'

Said I, 'This is the image of me, heart-sore and with feet in the mire.'

I bound the neck of my soul and brought it to him as a token:

'It is the confidant of Love; do not sacrifice thine own confidant.'

He gave me the end of a thread—a thread full of mischief and guile—

'Pull,' he said, 'that I may pull, and break it not in the pulling.'

٦ تافت از آن خَرگَهِ جان صورتِ تُرکم بِه از آن
دست بِبُردمِ سوِي او دستِ مرا زد که بِهِل

٧ گُفتمِ تو همچو فُلان تُرش شُدی گُفت بدان
من تُرُش مصلحتم نه تُرُش کینه و غِل

٨ هرکه در آید که منهِ بر سرِ شاخش بزنهِ
کین حَرَمِ عشق بُوَد ای حَیَوان نیست اغل

٩ هست صلاحِ دل و دین صورتِ آن تُرک یقین
چشمِ فرو مال و ببین صورتِ دِل صورتِ دِل

---

٦ بافت از آن خَرگَهِ دل (L). یافت (B³).

From the tent of the soul flashed out the form of my
  Beloved, fairer than before ;

I stretched my hands to him ; he struck my hand, saying,
  'Let go.'

I said, 'Thou art harsh, like such an one.' 'Know,' he
  replied,

'That I am harsh for good, not from rancour and spite.

Whoever enters saying, "'Tis I," I smite him on the brow ;

For this is the shrine of Love, O fool ! It is not a
  sheep-cote.'

Assuredly Ṣalāḥi dil u dīn is the image of that Fair
  One ;

Rub thine eyes, and behold the image of the heart, the
  image of the heart.

مُجتَثِ مُثَمَّنِ مخبونِ مقصور : Metre

$$[- \overline{\smile\smile} - | \smile - \smile - | \smile\smile - - | \smile - \smile -]$$

		L.
۱	چگونه بر نَپَرَد جان چو از جنابِ جلال	
	خطابِ لُطفِ چو شکّر بجان رسد که تعال	
۲	در آب چون نجِهَد زود ماهی از خُشکی	
	چو بانگِ مَوج بگوشش رسد ز بحرِ زُلال	
۳	چرا ز صَید نپَرَّد بسویِ سُلطان باز	
	چو بشنَوَد خبرِ ارْجِعی ز طبل و دُوال	
۴	چرا چو ذرّه نیاید برقص هر صوفی	
	در آفتابِ بقا تا رهاندش ز زوال	
۵	چنان لطافت و خوبی و حُسن و جان‌بخشی	
	کسی ازو بشکیبد زهی شقا و ضلال	
۶	بپر بپر هله ای مُرغ سویِ معدنِ خویش	
	که از قفس برهیدی و باز شُد پر و بال	
۷	از آبِ شور سفر کُن بسویِ آبِ حیات	
	رُجوع کن بسویِ صدرِ جان ز صفِّ نِعال	

BCL Lakh. TV

۱ رسد همی بجانها (BCV). ۳ خبری (L).

۵ حُسنِ جان‌بخشی (BCT). کسی کزو (CT). شفا (L).

XXIX.

Why does not the soul take wing, when from the glorious
    Presence
A speech of sweet favour comes to it, saying, 'Aloft'?
How should a fish not leap nimbly from the dry land
    into the water,
When the sound of waves reaches its ear from the cold
    ocean ?
Why should a falcon not fly from the quarry towards
    the King,
When it hears by drum and drum-stick the notice of
    " *Return* " ?
Why should not every Sūfī begin to dance, like a mote,
In the sun of eternity, that it may deliver him from
    decay ?
Such grace and beauty and loveliness and bestowal of life!
O misery and error, if any one dispense with Him !
Fly, fly, O bird, to thy native home,
For thou hast escaped from the cage, and thy pinions
    are outspread.
Travel away from the bitter stream towards the water
    of life,
Return from the vestibule to the high seat of the soul.

٨ بَرو بَرو تو كه ما نيز ميرسيم اى جان

ازين جهانِ جُدائى بدآن جهانِ وِصال

٩ چو كودكان هله تا چند ما بعالَمِ خاك

كُنيم دامنِ خَود پُر ز خاك و سنگ و سِفال

١٠ ز خاك دست بداريم و بر سما پَريم

ز كودكى بگُريزيم سوىِ بزمِ رِجال

١١ ببين كه قالِبِ خاكى چه در جُوالت كرد

جُوالرا بشِكاف و بر آر سر ز جُوال

١٢ بدستِ راست بگِير از هوا تو اين نامه

نه كودكى كه ندانى يمينِ خَود ز شِمال

١٣ بگُفت پَيكِ خِردرا خُدا كه پا بر كِير

بگُفت دستِ اجَلرا كه گُوشِ حِرص بمال

١٤ ندا رسيد روانرا روان شَو اندر غَيب

منال و كُنج بگِير و دِگُر ز رنج منال

١٥ تو كُن نِدا و تو آوازه دِه كه سُلطانى

تُراست لُطفِ جواب و تُراست عِلمِ سؤال

Haste, haste! for we too, O soul, are coming

From this world of severance to that world of union.

O how long shall we, like children, in the earthly sphere

Fill our lap with dust and stones and sherds?

Let us give up the earth and fly heavenwards,

Let us flee from childhood to the banquet of men.

Behold how the earthly frame has entrapped thee!

Rend the sack and raise thy head clear.

Take from Love this scroll with thy right hand;

Thou art no child, not to know thy right from thy left.

God said to Reason's messenger, 'Begone,'

To the hand of Death he said, 'Chastise worldly desire.'

A voice came to the spirit, 'Spirit thee away to the Unseen,

Take the gain and the treasure and lament the pain no more.'

Cry out and proclaim that thou art King;

Thine is the grace of answer, and thine is the knowledge of question.

۳۰.

Metre: هَزَج مُسَدَّس مقصور [∪−−−|∪−−−|∪−−×]

L.

۱   من از عالَمْ تُرا تنها گُزینمْ

روا داری که من غمگین نِشینمْ

۲   دلِ من چون قَلَمْ اندر کفِ تُست

ز تُست ار شادمانمْ وَر حزینمْ

۳   بِجُز آنچه تو خواهی من چه خواهمْ

بِجُز آنچه نُمائی من چه بینمْ

۴   کَه از من خار رویانی کَهی گُل

کَهی گُل بویمْ و کَه خار چینمْ

۵   مرا گر تو چنان داری چنانمْ

مرا گر تو چنین خواهی چنینمْ

۶   در آن حُمّی که دلرا رنگ بخشی

که باشمْ من چه باشد مِهر و کینمْ

BCL Lakh.

There are two versions of this ghazal in L. I give the
text of the second (L^b) with a few changes. ۳ باشی for
خواهی (L^b). ۴ کَهی از من (L^b) contra metr.
۵ In first کَه از من گُل بروید گَاه خاری (L^a).
misrā', مرا چون (L^b). ۶ در آن زخمی که دلرا رشك
بخشی (B). چه باشد for چنین با (L^a).

XXX.

Thee I choose, of all the world, alone ;

Wilt thou suffer me to sit in grief ?

My heart is as a pen in thy hand,

Thou art the cause if I am glad or melancholy.

Save what thou williest, what will have I ?

Save what thou showest, what do I see ?

Thou mak'st grow out of me now a thorn and now a rose ;

Now I smell roses and now pull thorns.

If thou keep'st me that, that I am ;

If thou would'st have me this, I am this.

In the vessel where thou givest colour to the soul

Who am I, what is my love and hate ?

٧   تو بودی اوّل و آخِر تو باشی

تو بِه کُن آخِرم از اوّلینم

٨   چو تو پنهان شَوی از اهلِ کُفرم

چو تو پَیدا شَوی از اهلِ دینم

٩   بِجُز چیزی که دادی من چه دارم

چه می جوئی ز جَیب و آستینم

---

٧ اوّلین و آخِرینم (L^a).   ٨ چو پنهان گُشتی از

٨ من اهلِ کُفرم (L^b).   هُوَیدا آمدی من اهلِ دینم (L^b)

٩ من چه باشم (L^b).

Thou wert first, and last thou shalt be;

Make my last better than my first.

When thou art hidden, I am of the infidels;

When thou art manifest, I am of the faithful.

I have nothing, except thou hast bestowed it;

What dost thou seek from my bosom and sleeve?

۳۱

Metre: هَزَج مُثَمَّنِ سالِم [ؚؖؖؖؖ]

V.   چه تدبير اى مُسلمانان كه من خَودر نميدانم   ۱
نه ترسا نه يهودر من نه گُبرم نه مُسَلمانم

نه شرقيّم نه غربيّم نه بَرّيّم نه بحريّم   ۲
نه از كانِ طبيعيّم نه از افلاكِ گُردانم

نه از خاكم نه از آبم نه از بادم نه از آتش   ۳
نه از عرشم نه از فرشم نه از كَونم نه از كانم

نه از هندم نه از چينم نه از بُلغار و سقسينم   ۴
نه از مُلكِ عِراقَينم نه از خاكِ خُراسانم

نه از دُنَيى نه از عُقبَى نه از جنّت نه از دوزخ   ۵
نه از آدم نه از حوّا نه از فِردَوس و رِضوانم

مكانم لامكان باشد نِشانم بى نِشان باشد   ۶
نه تن باشد نه جان باشد كه من از جانِ جانانم

TV

T contains only the following beyts: ۲۰ . ۱۰ ۷ ۶ ۳ ۲ ۱.

۱ نه ترسا و يهودم (V). ۶ كه من خَود جانِ جانانم (T).

XXXI.

What is to be done, O Moslems? for I do not recognise
  myself.

I am neither Christian, nor Jew, nor Gabr, nor Moslem.

I am not of the East, nor of the West, nor of the land,
  nor of the sea;

I am not of Nature's mint, nor of the circling heavens.

I am not of earth, nor of water, nor of air, nor of fire;

I am not of the empyrean, nor of the dust, nor of existence, nor of entity.

I am not of India, nor of China, nor of Bulgaria, nor
  of Saqsīn;

I am not of the kingdom of 'Irāqain, nor of the country
  of Khorāsān.

I am not of this world, nor of the next, nor of Paradise,
  nor of Hell;

I am not of Adam, nor of Eve, nor of Eden and Riẓwān.

My place is the Placeless, my trace is the Traceless;

'Tis neither body nor soul, for I belong to the soul of the
  Beloved.

٧ دوئی از خَود بَدَر کردم یکی دیدم دو عالَمرا

یکی جویم یکی دانم یکی بینم یکی خوانم

٨ هُوَ ٱلأَوَّل هُوَ ٱلآخِر هُوَ ٱلظاهِر هُوَ ٱلباطِن

بِجُز یا هو و یا من هو کسی دیگر نمیدانم

٩ ز جامِ عشق سرمستم دو عالَم رفته از دستم

بِجُز رِندی و قلّاشی نباشد هیچ سامانم

١٠ اگر در عُمرِ خَود روزی دمی بی تو بر آوَردم

از آن وقت و از آن ساعت ز عُمرِ خَود پشیمانم

١١ اگر دستم دِهد روزی دمی با تو درین خلوَت

دو عالَم زیرِ پایِ آرم همی دستی بر افشانم

١٢ الا ای شمسِ تبریزی چنین مستم درین عالَم

که جُز مستی و قلّاشی نباشد هیچ دستانم

---

١١ دمی for همی (V).   ١٢ دِگر چیزی نمیدانم for دیگر چیزی نمیدانم

نباشد الخ (T).

I have put duality away, I have seen that the two worlds
    are one ;

One I seek, One I know, One I see, One I call.

*He is the first, He is the last, He is the outward, He is
    the inward ;*

I know none other except 'Yā Hū' and 'Yā man Hū.'

I am intoxicated with Love's cup, the two worlds have
    passed out of my ken ;

I have no business save carouse and revelry.

If once in my life I spent a moment without thee,

From that time and from that hour I repent of my life.

If once in this world I win a moment with thee,

I will trample on both worlds, I will dance in triumph
    for ever.

O Shamsi Tabrīz, I am so drunken in this world,

That except of drunkenness and revelry I have no tale
    to tell.

۳۲

مُضارِع مُثَمَّن اخرَب :Metre [ـ ـ ٮ | ـ ٮ ٮ | ـ ـ ٮ | ـ ٮ ـ]

L.	۱ اندر دو کَون جانا بی تو طَرَب ندیدم
	دیدم بسی عجائِب چون تو عَجَب ندیدم
	۲ گُویند سوزِ آتش باشد نصیبِ کافِر
	محرومم از آتشِ تو جُز بو لَهَب ندیدم
	۳ من بر دریچهٔ دل بس کُوشِ جان نِهادم
	چندان سُخُن شنیدم امّا دو لب ندیدم
	۴ بر بنده ناگهانی کردی نِثارِ رحمت
	جُز لُطفِ بی حدِ تو آنرا سَبَب ندیدم
	۵ ای ساقِی گُزیده مانندت ای دو دیده
	اندر عَجَم نیامد اندر عَرَب ندیدم
	۶ چندان بریز باده کز خَود شَوَم پیاده
	کاندر خَودی و هستی غَیرِ تَعَب ندیدم

CL Lakh. T
_____

۴ کردی بناز رحمت (L).

XXXII.

No joy have I found in the two worlds apart from thee, Beloved.

Many wonders I have seen: I have not seen a wonder like thee.

They say that blazing fire is the infidel's portion:

I have seen none, save Abū Lahab, excluded from thy fire.

Often have I laid the spiritual ear at the window of the heart:

I heard much discourse, but the lips I did not see.

Of a sudden thou didst lavish grace upon thy servant:

I saw no cause for it but thy infinite kindness.

O chosen Cup-bearer, O apple of mine eyes, the like of thee

Ne'er appeared in Persia, nor in Arabia have I found it.

Pour out wine till I become a wanderer from myself;

For in selfhood and existence I have felt only fatigue.

٧ ای شیر و ای شَکَر تو ای شمس و ای قَمَر تو

ای مادر و پِدَر تو جُز تو نَسَب ندیدم

٨ ای عشقِ بی تباهی ای مُطرِبِ اِلاهی

هم پُشت و هم پناهی کفوَت لَقَب ندیدم

٩ پولادپارهائیم آهن‌رُباست عشقت

اصلِ همه طَلَب تو در خود طَلَب ندیدم

١٠ خاموش ای بِرادر فضل و ادَب رها کُن

· تا تو ادَب نخواندی جُز تو ادَب ندیدم

خَود for تو ٩ (CT). ٨ وَی for ای bis (L). ٨

بخواندی (T). جُز for در (CT). ١٠

O thou who art milk and sugar, O thou who art sun
and moon,

O thou who art mother and father, I have known no
kin but thee.

O indestructible Love, O divine Minstrel,

Thou art both stay and refuge : a name equal to thee
I have not found.

We are pieces of steel, and thy love is the magnet :

Thou art the source of all aspiration, in myself I have
seen none.

Silence, O brother! put learning and culture away :

Till Thou namedst culture, I knew no culture but Thee.

٣٣

Metre: **رَمَل مُثَمَّنِ مشكول** [ﮞ– – | ﮞﮞ– ﮞ | – ﮞ– – | ﮞﮞ– ﮞ]

L.

١ منم آن نِیازمندی که بتو نِیاز دارم

غمِ چون تو نازنینی بهزار ناز دارم

٢ توئی آفتابِ چشمم بجمالِ تُست رَوشن

اگر از تو باز گیرم بکه چشم باز دارم

٣ بجفا نمودنِ تو ز وَفات بر نگردم

بوَفا نمودنِ خُود ز جفات باز دارم

۴ گِله کردم از تو گُفتی که بساز چارهٔ خَود

منم آن که در غمِ آلحق دلِ چارهساز دارم

۵ غمِ دل بتو نگویم که تُرا ملال گیرد

کنم این حدیث کوته که غمِ دراز دارم

LT

❘ T inverts the order of the second miṣrā's of the first
two beyts, reading باز گیرم for باز دارم.

XXXIII.

I am that supplicant who make supplication to thee ;
The anguish inspired by a charmer like thee hath for
    me a thousand charms.
Thou art the sun of mine eyes—they are radiant with
    thy beauty ;
If I draw them away from thee, to whom shall I look
    again ?
I will not become inconstant to thee on account of thy
    cruel treatment ;
By remaining constant myself I will restrain thee from
    cruelty.
I complained of thee, thou saidst : 'Provide thine own
    remedy.'
I am one whose heart provides a remedy for Divine
    affliction.
I will not tell thee my heart's grief, for it would weary
    thee ;
I will shorten this tale, for mine is a long grief.

۳۴

B³.	صورتگرِ نقّاشم هر لحظه بُتی سازم	۱
	و آنکه همه بُتهارا در پیشِ تو بگُدازم	
	صد نقش بر انگیزم با روح در آمیزم	۲
	چون نقش تُرا بینم در آتشش اندازم	
	تو ساقیِ خمّاری یا دُشمنِ هُشیاری	۳
	یا آنکه کُنی ویران هر خانه که بر سازم	
	جان ریخته شُد با تو آمیخته شُد با تو	۴
	چون بویِ تو دارد جان جانرا هله بنوازم	
	هر خون که ز من روید با خاكِ تو میگوید	۵
	با مِهرِ تو همرنگم با عشقِ تو انبازم	
	در خانهٔ آب و گِل بی تُست خراب این دل	۶
	یا خانه در آ ای جان یا خانه بپردازم	

B³CT

۲ پُر آمیزم (T). ۳ با آنکه (B³). ۴ خون ریخته (C).
۵ همرازم ننوازم (T). ۶ انبازم for انبازم (C). تا خانه بپردازم
(C).

XXXIV.

I am a painter, a maker of pictures; every moment I
    shape a beauteous form,
And then in thy presence I melt them all away.
I call up a hundred phantoms and indue them with a
    spirit;
When I behold thy phantom, I cast them in the fire.
Art thou the Vintner's cup-bearer or the enemy of him
    who is sober,
Or is it thou who mak'st a ruin of every house I build?
In thee the soul is dissolved, with thee it is mingled;
Lo! I will cherish the soul, because it has a perfume
    of thee.
Every drop of blood which proceeds from me is saying
    to thy dust:
'I am one colour with thy love, I am the partner of
    thy affection.'
In the house of water and clay this heart is desolate
    without thee;
O Beloved, enter the house, or I will leave it.

۳۵

Metre : هَزَجِ مُسَدَّسِ اخرَبِ مقبوضِ مقصور

[ـ ـ ◡ | ◡ ـ ◡ ـ | ◡ ـ ⊻]

		T.
۱	عشق است در آسمان پریدن	
	صد پرده بَهَر نَفَس دریدن	
۲	اوّل نَفَس از نَفَس گُسِستن	
	آخِر قَدَم از قَدَم بُریدن	
۳	نادیده گِرِفتن این جهانرا	
	مر دیدهٔ خویشرا ندیدن	
۴	گُفتم که دلا مُبارکت باد	
	در حلقهٔ عاشِقان رسیدن	
۵	زآن سویِ نَظَر نظاره کردن	
	در کوچهٔ سینها دویدن	
۶	ای جان ز کُجا رسیدت این دم	
	ای دل ز کُجاست این طپیدن	

B⁹CT

.(B⁹) اوّل قَدَم ۲

XXXV.

This is Love: to fly heavenward,

To rend, every instant, a hundred veils.

The first moment, to renounce life;

The last step, to fare without feet.

To regard this world as invisible,

Not to see what appears to one's self.

'O heart,' I said, 'may it bless thee

To have entered the circle of lovers,

To look beyond the range of the eye,

To penetrate the windings of the bosom!

Whence did this breath come to thee, O my soul,

Whence this throbbing, O my heart?

٧   ای مُرغ بگو زبانِ مُرغان

من دانمِ رمزِ تو شنیدن

٨   دل گُفت بکارخانه بودمِ

تا خانهٔ آب و گِل پزیدن

٩   از خانهٔ صُنع می پریدمِ

تا خانهٔ صُنع آفریدن

١٠   چون پای نماند می کشیدند

چون گُویمِ صورتی کشیدن

---

٩ در خانهٔ صُنع می پزیدمِ (CT).

O bird, speak the language of birds :

I can understand thy hidden meaning.'

The soul answered : ' I was in the (divine) Factory

While the house of water and clay was a-baking.

I was flying away from the (material) workshop

While the workshop was being created.

When I could resist no more, they dragged me

To mould me into shape like a ball.'

٣٦

Metre : رَجَزِ مُثَمَّنِ سالِم [ـحٮٮ|ـ--|--ں-|--ں-|--ں-|--ں-|--ں-|--ں-]

١ ای عاشِقان ای عاشِقان هنگامِ کوچست از جهان C.

در گُوشِ جانم میرسد طبلِ رحیل از آسمان

٢ نك ساربان بر خاسته قطارها آراسته

از ما حلالی خواسته چه خُفته اید ای کاروان

٣ این بانگها از پیش و پس بانگِ رحیلست و جَرَس

هر لحظهٔ نفس و نَفَس سر میکُنند در لامکان

٤ زین شمعهایِ سرنگُون زین پردهایِ نیلگُون

خلقی عجب بِرون آمد تا غَیبها گُردد عیان

٥ زین چرخِ دولابی تُرا آمد گِران خوابی تُرا

فریاد ازین عُمرِ سبُك زِنهار ازین خوابِ گِران

٦ ای دل سویِ دلدار شَو ای سویِ یار شَو

ای پاسبان بیدار شَو خُفته نشاید پاسبان

B²B³CT

خواسته ٢ جُدائی (B²). جلالی (B³). ٣ هرلحظه این

(B²T). آمد for آید ٤ (B³T). سر میکشد (C).

XXXVI.

O lovers, O lovers, it is time to abandon the world;
The drum of departure reaches my spiritual ear from heaven.
Behold, the driver has risen and made ready the files of camels,
And begged us to acquit him of blame: why, O travellers, are you asleep?
These sounds before and behind are the din of departure and of the camel-bells;
With each moment a soul and a spirit is setting off into the Void.
From these (stars like) inverted candles, from these blue awnings (of the sky)
There has come forth a wondrous people, that the mysteries may be revealed.
A heavy slumber fell upon thee from the circling spheres:
Alas for this life so light, beware of this slumber so heavy!
O soul, seek the Beloved, O friend, seek the Friend,
O watchman, be wakeful: it behoves not a watchman to sleep.

٧ هر سوی بانگ و مشغله هر کوی شمع و مشعله
كامشب جهانِ حاملَه زايد جهانِ جاودان

٨ تو كُل بُدی و دل شُدی جاهل بُدی عاقل شُدی
آن کو کشيدت اين چنين آن سو کشاند آن چنان

٩ اندر کشاکشهایِ او نوشست ناخوشهایِ او
آبست آتشهایِ او بر وَی مکُن رورا کُران

١٠ در جان نِشستن کارِ او توبه شِکستن کارِ او
از حيلهٔ بِسيارِ او اين ذرّها لرزان دِلان

١١ ای ریش خندِ رخنه جه یعنی منم سالار ده
تا کی جِهی کُردن بِنه وَر نی کشندت چون کمان

١٢ تُخمِ دَغَل میکاشتی افسوسها میداشتی
حق را عَدَم پِنداشتی اکنون ببین ای قلتبان

١٣ ای خر بکاه اولَی تری ديگی سِياه اولَی تری
در قعرِ چاه اولَی تری ای ننگِ خان و خاندان

---

٧ شمع و مشعله and مشغله و بانگ transposed (B²B³T).
٨ هر کوی for هر کوی (B²B³). هر سو (T). ز آن سو
for آن کو (B³). آن کو (B³B³T). کشکشان for آن چنان
٩ کُران رو بِکُردان بر وَی (C). ١٠ در جا (B³T).
لرزان لزان (B²). وَر بر ١١ (T). افسوسها پِنداشتی ١٢ (C).
عَدَم میداشتی (C). ١٣ دیگِ سِياه (B³T). خانه خاندان (C).

On every side is clamour and tumult, in every street
 are candles and torches,

For to-night the teeming world gives birth to the world
 everlasting.

Thou wert dust and art spirit, thou wert ignorant and
 art wise ;

He who has led thee thus far will lead thee further also.

How pleasant are the pains he makes thee suffer while
 he gently draws thee to himself!

His flames are as water : do not frown upon him.

To dwell in the soul is his task, to break vows of penitence is his task ;

By his manifold artifice these atoms are trembling at
 their core.

O ridiculous puppet that leapest out of thy hole, as if
 to say, 'I am the lord of the land,'

How long wilt thou leap? Abase thyself, or they will
 bend thee, like a bow.

Thou didst sow the seed of deceit, thou didst indulge
 in derision,

Thou didst regard God as nothing: see now, O miscreant !

O ass, thou wert best with straw; thou art a caldron :
 thou wert best black ;

Thou wert best at the bottom of a well, O disgrace of
 thy house and family !

۱۴ در من کسی دیگر بُوَد کین چشمها از وَی جِهد

کر آب سوزانی کُند ز آتش بُوَد این‌را بدان

۱۵ در کف ندارم سنك من با کس ندارم جنك من

بر کس نكیرم تنك من زیرا خَوشم چون كُلستان

۱۶ پس چشمِ من ز آن سر بُوَد وز عالمِ دیگر بُوَد

این سو جهان آن سو جهان بنشسته من بر آستان

۱۷ بر آستان آنکس بُوَد کو ناطقِ اخرَس بُوَد

این رمز كُفتن بس بُوَد دیگر مكو در كش زبان

---

۱۴ سوزائی (B⁹). ۱۵ ندانم سنك (C). نكیرم ننك (C).

۱۶ این سو for آن سو (C). بر آسمـان (B²B³C).

۱۷ بر آسمان (B²B³C). اخرسِ ناطق (C). رمز for امر (C).

كُفتی (T).

In me there is Another by whom these eyes sparkle;
If water scalds, 'tis by fire; understand this.
I have no stone in my hand, I have no quarrel with
    any one,
I deal harshly with none, because I am sweet as a
    garden of roses.
Mine eye, then, is from that source and from another
    universe;
Here a world and there a world: I am seated on the
    threshold.
On the threshold are they alone whose eloquence is mute;
'Tis enough to utter this intimation: say no more, draw
    back thy tongue.

۳۷

مُضارِعِ مُثَمَّنِ اخَرَبِ مكفوفِ مقصور :Metre

[‒ ‒ ∪ | ∪ ‒ ∪ ‒ | ∪ ‒ ‒ ∪ | ‒ ∪ ‒]

V.

۱ بِشنیده ام که عزمِ سَفَر میکُنی مکُن
مِهرِ حریف و یارِ دِگَر میکُنی مکُن

۲ تو در جهان غریبی و غُربت ندیدهٔ
قصدِ کُدام خستهجِگَر میکُنی مکُن

۳ از ما مُدزد خویش و به بیگانگان مَرو
دُزدیده سویِ غَیر نَظَر میکُنی مکُن

۴ ای مَه که چرخ زیر و زَبَر از برایِ تُست
مارا خراب و زیر و زَبَر میکُنی مکُن

۵ کو عهد و کو وَثیقه که با ما تو کردهٔ
از قَول و عهدِ خویش عَبَر میکُنی مکُن

۶ چه وعده میدِهی و چه سَوگُند میخَوری
سَوگُند و عِشوَهرا چه سِپَر میکُنی مکُن

BCL Lakh. V

۱ حریف یار (V).   ۲ عزیزی for غریبی (L).   چه میکُنی
۴ ندیدهٔ for (BCL).   این ماهِ چرخ (L).   for

XXXVII.

I have heard that thou dost intend to travel: do not so.

That thou bestowest thy love on a new friend and companion: do not so.

Tho' in the world thou art strange, thou hast never known estrangement;

What heart-stricken wretch art thou attempting? do not so.

Steal not thyself away from me, go not to aliens;

Thou art stealthily glancing at another: do not so.

O moon for whose sake the heavens are bewildered,

Thou makest me distraught and bewildered: do not so.

Where is the pledge and where the compact thou didst make with me?

Thou departest from thy word and pledge: do not so.

Why give promises and why utter protestations,

Why make a shield of vows and blandishments? do not so.

٧   ای برتر از وُجود و عَدَم پایگاهِ تو

این لحظه از وُجود گُذَر میکُنی مکُن

٨   ای دوزخ و بهِشت غُلامانِ امرِ تو

بر ما بهِشت همچو سَفَر میکُنی مکُن

٩   اندر شَکَرِستانِ تو از زهر اینمر

آن زهررا حریفِ شَکَر میکُنی مکُن

١٠   جانم چو کورهٔ پُر آتش بَسَت نکرد

روی من از فِراق چو زَر میکُنی مکُن

١١   چون روی در کشی تو شَوَد مَه ز غمِ سیَه

قصدِ کُسوفِ قُرصِ قَمَر میکُنی مکُن

١٢   ما خُشکلب شُویم چو تو خُشک آوری

چشمِ مرا بِاشک چه تَر میکُنی مکُن

١٣   چون طاقتِ عقیلهٔ عُشّاق نیست

پس عقلرا چه خیرهنِگر میکُنی مکُن

---

٧ پایگاه for بارگاه (L).   از خِطّهٔ وُجود (BCL).

١٠ کوزهٔ (BCLV).   جانِ مرا چو کوزهٔ آتش چه میکُنی (L).

١١ خُسوف (BC).   ١٢ خُشکی آوری (BL).   چو تر (V).

O thou whose vestibule is above existence and non-existence,

At this moment thou art passing from existence : do not so.

O thou whose command Hell and Paradise obey,

Thou art making Paradise like Hell-fire to me : do not so.

In thy plot of sugar-canes I am secure from poison ;

Thou minglest the poison with the sugar : do not so,

My soul is like a fiery furnace, yet it sufficed thee not;

By absence thou art making my face pale as gold : do not so.

When thou withdrawest thy countenance, the moon is darkened with grief ;

Thou art intending the eclipse of the moon's orb : do not so.

Our lips become dry when thou bringest a drought ;

Why art thou moistening mine eye with tears ? do not so.

Since thou canst not endure the reasoning faculty of lovers,

Then why dost thou dazzle the eye of reason ? do not so.

۱۴   حلوا نمی دِهی تو برنجور از اِحتِما

رنجورِ خویشرا تو بَتَر میکُنی مکُن

۱۵   چشمِ حرامخوارهٔ من دُزدِ حُسنِ تُست

ای جان سزایِ دُزدِ بَصَر میکُنی مکُن

۱۶   سر در کَش ای رفیق که هنگامِ گُفت نیست

در بیسریّ عشق چه سَر میکُنی مکُن

۱۷   غَیر از جمالِ مفخرِ تبریز شمس دین

گُر زآنکه بر دو کَون نَظَر میکُنی مکُن

---

۱۵ حرامخوارهٔ تو (BV). ای جان برایِ دُزدِ نَظَر میکُنی

۱۷ شمس آلدین (V).   (L).

Thou art denying sweetmeats to one sick of abstinence;

Thou art making thy patient worse : do not so.

My lawless eye is a thief of thy beauty ;

O Beloved, thou tak'st vengeance on my thievish sight :
do not so.

Withdraw, comrade, 'tis no time for speech ;

In love's bewilderment why dost thou intrude thyself ?
do not so.

Except the beauty of Shamsi Dīn, the pride of Tabrīz,

If so be that thou throwest a glance upon (aught in) the
two worlds, do not so.

۳۸

Metre: رَمَلِ مُثَمَّنِ مخبونِ مقصور

[××--|∪∪--|∪∪--|∞∞××]

L.	خُنُك آن دم که نِشستیمِ در ایوانِ من و تو	۱
	بدو نقش و بدو صورت بیکی جانِ من و تو	
	رنگِ باغ و دمِ مُرغان بدهد آبِ حیات	۲
	آن زمانی که در آئیمِ بُستانِ من و تو	
	اخترانِ فَلَک آیند بنظّارهٔ ما	۳
	مه خُودرا بنُمائیمِ بایشان من و تو	
	من و تو بی من و تو جمع شَویمِ از سرِ ذوق	۴
	خَوش و فارِغ ز خُرافاتِ پریشانِ من و تو	
	طوطیانِ فَلَکی جُمله شِکَرخوار شَوَند	۵
	در مقامی که بخندیمِ بر آن سانِ من و تو	
	این عَجَبترکه من و تو بیکی کُنج اینجا	۶
	همِ در این دمِ بعراقیمِ و خُراسانِ من و تو	

―――――

BCLT

۱ خُنُك آن‌را (.L). بدو نفس (.L). ۲ زانك باغ (.L).

۵ شَکَرخوار (CT.). ندهد (.L).

XXXVIII.

Happy the moment when we are seated in the palace,
   thou and I,
With two forms and with two figures but with one soul,
   thou and I.
The colours of the grove and the voice of the birds will
   bestow immortality
At the time when we come into the garden, thou and I.
The stars of heaven will come to gaze upon us ;
We shall show them the moon itself, thou and I.
Thou and I, individuals no more, shall be mingled in
   ecstasy,
Joyful, and secure from foolish babble, thou and I.
All the bright-plumed birds of heaven will devour their
   hearts with envy
In the place where we shall laugh in such a fashion,
   thou and I.
This is the greatest wonder, that thou and I, sitting
   here in the same nook,
Are at this moment both in 'Irāq and Khorāsān, thou
   and I.

مضارع مُثَمَّنِ اخرَبِ مكفوفِ مقصور : Metre

$$[--\cup | -\cup-\cup | \cup--\cup | -\overset{\smile}{\sim}]$$

١   رفتم بكویِ خواجه و كُفتم كه خواجه كو   L.

كُفتا كه خواجه عاشق و مستست و كو بكو

٢   كُفتم فریضه دارم و آخِر نِشان دِهید

من دوستدارِ خواجه ام آخِر نَیَم عدو

٣   كُفتند خواجه عاشقِ آن باغبان شُدست

اورا بباغها تو بجو یا كِنارِ جو

۴   مستان و عاشقان پَیِ دِلدارِ خَود رَوَند

هر كس كه كُشت عاشق رَو دست ازو بشو

٥   ماهی كه آب دید نیاید بخاكدان

عاشق كُجا بمانَد در دَورِ رنگ و بو

٦   برفِ فُسُرده كو رُخِ آن آفتاب دید

خُرشید پاك خَوردش اكر هست تو بتو

BCLT

١ سرمست for مستست   (L). ٢   دوستِ خواجه (L)

٣ كُفتند كه (L) contra metr.   كه كُفتند contra metr.

۴ مُشتاق و عاشقان (C).   نیست عاشق (B³C):   رَو for او

٥ در درد و رنگ (B³).   (LT).

XXXIX.

I went to the Master's abode and said : 'Where is the
   Master ?'

He said : 'The Master is in love and intoxicated and a
   wanderer from place to place.'

I said : 'I have an obligation, at least give me a clue ;

I am the Master's friend : nay, indeed, I am no enemy.'

They replied : 'The Master is fallen in love with the
   Gardener ;

Seek him in gardens or on the bank of a stream.'

Frenzied lovers pursue the object of their love ;

If any one has fallen in love, go, wash thy hands of him !

The fish that has known water comes not to land :

How should a lover stay in the sphere of colour and
   perfume ?

The frozen snow that has beheld the face of yonder Sun,

Is swallowed up by the sun, tho' it be piled in drifts.

۷ خاصه کسی که عاشقِ سُلطانِ ما بُوَد

سُلطانِ بی نظیر و وَفادار و قندخو

۸ آن کیمیایِ بی حد و بی عد و بی قیاس

بر هر مِسی که بر زد زر شُد بارُجِعو

۹ در خواب شَو ز عالَم و از شش جِهت گُریز

تا چند گُول گُردی و آواره سو بسو

۱۰ ناچار می بَرندت باری باِختیار

تا پیشِ شاه باشدت اِعزاز و آبِ رو

۱۱ گُر زآنکه در مِیانه نبودی سرِ خری

عیسیٰت کشف گُردی اسرار مو بمو

۱۲ بستمِ رهِ دهان و گُشادمِ رهِ نِهان

رستمِ بیک فنینه ز سَودایِ گُفت و گُو

_____

۷ و (L.) قندخو (L.) om. before بامرِ او ۸ بارُجِعو for (L.)
اسرار ۱۱ (L.) تا پیش باشدت مهِ اِعزاز و آبِ رو ۱۰
بستمِ for بس ۱۲ (L.) فاش گُردی و عکسیست مو بمو
ز ننگِ فِتنه و سَودایِ (L.) نِهان for زبان (L.) om. (L.) و
گُفتگو (T.) (L.) ز سَودا و

Especially one who is the lover of our King,

A king peerless and faithful and sweet-tempered.

By that infinite alchemy, which none may compute or
conjecture,

Copper, as soon as it is touched, becomes gold at the
command, "*Return*".

Sleep the world away, and flee from the six dimensions;

How long wilt thou roam in thy folly and bewilderment
to and fro ?

Inevitably they will bring thee at last, with thy own
consent,

That thou mayst have honour and glory in the presence
of the King.

Had not there been an intruder in the company,

Jesus would have revealed to thee the mysteries, point
by point.

I have closed the passage of the lips, and opened the
secret way ;

I am free in one moment from the desire of speech.

۴۰.

Metre : [–×–ᴗ–|–ᴗ–ᴗ||–––ᴗ|–ᴗ–×] مُضارِعِ مُثَمَّنِ اخرَب

L.	در خانهٔ دل ای جان این کیست ایستاده	۱
	بر جایِ شه که بُجز شاه و شاهزاده	
	کرده بدست اِشارت کز من بِتو چه خواهی	۲
	مخمور می چه خواهد بُجز نُقل و جامِ باده	
	نُقلی ز دل مُعلّق جامی ز نورِ مُطلق	۳
	در خلوتِ هُوَ آلحق بزمِ ابد نهاده	
	ای بس دَغَل‌فروشان در بزمِ باده‌نوشان	۴
	هُش دار تا نَیُفتی ای مردِ نرمِ ساده	
	در حلقهٔ قلاشی زِنهار تا نباشی	۵
	چون غُنچه چشم بسته چون گُل دهان کُشاده	
	چون آینه است عالَم نقش کمال عشقت	۶
	ای مردُمان که دیدست جُزوی ز کُل زیاده	

BCL Lakh. T

۱ دل و جان (T). ۲ شاه شاهزاده (L). جُز جامِ لعل
باده (L). ۳ نُقلی ز مَی مُعلّق (L). جامی for جانی
(L). ۶ نقش for پیش (T). نرمِ for بزمِ ۴ (L).
ای مؤمنان (T).

XL.

O my soul, who is this, stationed in the house of the
 heart?

Who may occupy the royal seat save the King and the
 Prince?

He beckoned with his hand: 'Say, what do you desire
 of me?'

What does a drunken man desire except sweetmeats and
 a cup of wine?

Sweetmeats derived from the soul, a cup of the Absolute
 Light,

An eternal banquet laid in the privacy of "*He is the
 Truth*".

How many deceivers are there at the wine-drinkers' feast!

Take heed lest thou fall, O easy simple man!

Beware! do not keep, in a circle of reprobates,

Thine eye shut like a bud, thy mouth open like the rose.

The world resembles a mirror: thy Love is the perfect
 image;

O people, who has ever seen a part greater than the
 whole?

٧ چون سبزه شَو پیاده زیرا درین گُلِستان

دِلبر چو گُل سُوارست باقی همه پیاده

٨ هم تیغ هم کُشنده هم کُشته هم کُشنده

هم جُمله عقل کُشته هم عقل باد داده

٩ آن شه صلاحِ دین است کو پایدار بادا

دستِ عطاش دائم در گُردنم قِلاده

---

٨ هم تیغ بر کشیده هم کشته هم کشیده (L).
هم عقل (L). هم عقل ازو پیاده (CT). هم جُمله عشق
هم عقل (Lakh. T). باد داده (C). باده داده (B). باز داده

Go on foot, like the grass, because in this garden

The Beloved, like the rose, is riding, all the rest are
on foot.

He is both the sword and the swordsman, both the slain
and the slayer,

He is at once all Reason and brings Reason to nought.

That King is Ṣalāḥu'ddīn—may he endure for ever,

May his bounteous hand perpetually be a necklace on
my neck !

۴۱

Metre: مُضارِع مُثَمَّنِ اخرَب [– ∪ – ∪ | – – ∪ | – – ∪ | – – ∪ –]

V. ۱ دیدم نِثارِ خَودرا میکِشت کِردِ خانه

بر داشته رَبابی میزد یکی ترانه

۲ با زخمهٔ چو آتش میزد ترانهٔ خَوش

مست و خراب و دِلکش از بادهٔ شبانه

۳ در پردهٔ عِراقی میزد بنامِ ساقی

مقصود باده بودش ساقی بُدش بهانه

۴ ساقیّ ماهروئی در دستِ او سبوئی

از کُوشهٔ در آمد بِنهاد در میانه

۵ پُر کرد جامِ اوّل ز آن بادهٔ مُشعَّل

در آب هیچ دیدی کآتش زند زبانه

۶ بر کف نِهاد آنرا از بهرِ عاشقانرا

آنگه بکرد سِجده بوسید آستانه

XLI.

I saw my Beloved wandering about the house :

He had taken up a rebeck and was playing a tune.

With a touch like fire he was playing a sweet melody,

Drunken and distraught and bewitching from the night's
carouse.

He was invoking the cup-bearer in the mode of 'Irāq :

Wine was his object, the cup-bearer was only an excuse.

The beauteous cup-bearer, pitcher in hand,

Stepped forth from a recess and placed it in the middle.

He filled the first cup with that sparkling wine—

Didst thou ever see water set on fire ?

For the sake of those in love he passed it from hand
to hand,

Then bowed and kissed the lintel.

٧ بِستد نِگار از وَی اندر كشید آن مَی

شُد شُعلها از آن پَی بر رو و سر دوانه

٨ میدید حُسنِ خَودرا میگُفت چشمِ بدرا

نه بود و نه بیاید چون من درین زمانه

٩ شمسُ الحقِ جهانم معشوقِ عاشِقانم

هر دمِ بُوَد بپیشم جان و روان روانه

---

٧ شُعلهای (V).   مَی for پَی (T).   ٨ بیامد (T).

My Beloved received it from him, and quaffed the wine:
Instantly o'er his face and head ran flashes of flame.
Meanwhile he was regarding his own beauty and saying
    to the evil eye,
'There has not been nor will be in this age another
    like me.
I am the Divine Sun of the world, I am the Beloved of
    lovers,
Soul and spirit are continually moving before me.'

Metre : هَزَجِ مُثَمَّنِ اخرَب [ـ⏑⏑⏑ | ⏑⏑⏑⏑ | ⏑⏑⏑ | ⏑⏑⏑ـ]

V. ١   همرنگِ جماعت شَو تا لذّتِ جان بینی

در کویِ خرابات آ تا دُردکشان بینی

٢   در کَش قَدَحِ سَودا هل تا نشَوی رُسوا

بر بند دو چشمِ سر تا چشمِ نِهان بینی

٣   بِکشای دو دستِ خَود گر مَیلِ کِنارستت

بِشکن بُتِ خاکیرا تا رویِ بُتان بینی

۴   از بهرِ عجوزیرا چندین چه کَشی کابین

وَز بهرِ سِه نان تا کی شمشیر و سِنان بینی

٥   شب یار همی گَردد خشخاش مخَور امشب

بر بند دهان از خَور تا طعمِ دهان بینی

٦   نک ساقیِ بیجَوری در مجلسِ او دَوری

در دَور در آ بِنشین تا کی دَوران بینی

B³C Lakh. TV

٢ نشَوی شَیدا (V).   نِهان for جهان (C).   ٣ جویِ
حوری (CV).   وَز مجلسِ او (V).   شب باز ه (B³CV).   جِنان بینی (B³).   ٦ ساقیِ بی (B³CV).

XLII.

Make yourself like to the community, that you may feel
    spiritual joy ;
Enter the street of the tavern, that you may behold the
    wine-bibbers.
Drain the cup of passion, that you may not be shamed ;
Shut the eyes in your head, that you may see the
    hidden eye.
Open your arms, if you desire an embrace ;
Break the idol of clay, that you may behold the face of
    the Fair.
Why, for an old woman's sake, do you endure so large
    a dowry,
And how long, for the sake of three loaves, will you
    look on the sword and the spear ?
Always at night returns the Beloved : do not eat opium
    to-night ;
Close your mouth against food, that you may taste the
    sweetness of the mouth.
Lo, the cup-bearer is no tyrant, and in his assembly there
    is a circle :
Come into the circle, be seated ; how long will you regard
    the revolution (of time)?

٧ اینجاست رِبا بِنگر جانی دِه و صد بِستان

كُرگی و سگی کم كُن تا مِهر شبان بینی

٨ كُفتی که فُلانیرا بِبرید ز من دُشمن

رَو ترکِ فُلانی كُن تا هستِ فُلان بینی

٩ اندیشه مكُن اِلّا از خالقِ اندیشه

اندیشهٔ جان بِهتر كاندیشهٔ نان بینی

١٠ با وسعتِ ارضِ اللّه در حبس چه خُسپیدی

ز اندیشه گِرِه کم زن تا شرحِ جِنان بینی

١١ خاموش شَو از گُفتن تا گُفت بری باری

از جان و جهان بِگذر تا جانِ جهان بینی

---

٧ اینجاست رِبا نیکو (C).   ٨ نیست فُلان (C).

٩ اندیشهٔ جانان بِه (T).   بیست فُلان (B³CT).

١١ پری یابی (V).   تا گُفتِ پری یاری (B³).

از جانِ جهان بِگذر (TV).

Look now, here is a bargain: give one life and receive
 a hundred.

Cease to behave as wolves and dogs, that you may experience the Shepherd's love.

You said: 'My foe took such an one away from me':

Go, renounce that person in order to contemplate the
 being of Him.

Think of nothing except the creator of thought;

Care for the soul is better than feeling care for one's
 bread.

Why, when God's earth is so wide, have you fallen
 asleep in a prison?

Avoid entangled thoughts, that you may see the explanation in Paradise.

Refrain from speaking, that you may win speech here-
 after;

Abandon life and the world, that you may behold the
 Life of the world.

۴۴۳

Metre: رَمَلِ مُثَمَّنِ مشکول [‒∪‒∪|∪‒‒∪|∪‒‒∪|∪‒∪‒]

B².   ۱   خَبَریست نَو رسیده تو مگر خَبَر نداری

جِگَر حسود خون شُد تو مگر جِگَر نداری

۲   قَمَریست رو نموده پِر نور بر کشوده

دل و چشم وام بِستان ز کسی اگر نداری

۳   رسد از کمانِ پنهان شب و روز تیرِ پرّان

بِسپار جانِ شیرین چه کُنی سِپَر نداری

۴   مِس هستِیت چو موسَی نه ز کیمیاش زر شُد

چه غمست اگر چو قارون بِجوال زر نداری

۵   بدرونِ تُست مِصری که توئی شَکَرِستانش

چه غمست اگر ز بیرون مددِ شَکَر نداری

۶   شُدهٔ غُلامِ صورت بِمثالِ بُت‌پرستان

تو چو یوسُفی و لیکن سویِ خَود نَظَر نداری

BB⁹CLT

۳ بِسپار جان بتیرش (BCT).   ۴ که ز کیمیاش (L).
۵ شَکَرفشانش (T).

XLIII.

The knowledge has newly come : perchance you have no
knowledge.

The envious heart is bleeding : perchance you have no
heart.

The moon has revealed her face and opened her radiant
wings :

Borrow a soul and eyes from some one, if you have
them not.

Night and day comes a winged arrow from the hidden
bow.

Yield up your sweet life ; what can you do ? you have
no shield.

Has not the copper of your existence been changed, like
Moses, to gold by his alchemy ?

What matter tho' you have no gold in a sack, like
Qārūn ?

Within you is an Egypt, and you are its garden of sugar-
canes ;

What matter tho' you have no supply of sugar from
without ?

You are become a slave to form, like idol-worshippers ;
You resemble Joseph and yet you gaze not on yourself.

٧   بخُدا جمالِ خُودرا چو در آینه به بینی

بُتِ خویش هر تو باشی بکسی کُذَر نداری

٨   خِرَدا نه ظالِمی تو که ورا چو ماه کُوئی

ز چه روش ماه کُوئی تو مَثَر بَصَر نداری

٩   سرِ تُست چون چِراغی بِکْرِفته شش فتیله

همه شش ز چیست رَوشن اکَر آن شَرَر نداری

۱۰   تنِ تُست همچو اُشتُر که رَوَد بکعبهٔ دل

ز خری بحج نرفتی نه از آن که خر نداری

۱۱   تو بکعبه کَر نرفتی بکشاندت سعادت

مَکُریز ای فُضولی که ز حق مَفَر نداری

---

۸ طالِبی for ظالِمی (B³).   ۱۰ بَرَوَد (B³) contra metr.

۱۱ نکُشایدت (C).

By God, when you behold your own beauty in the
　mirror,

You will be the idol of yourself, you will not pass over
　to any one.

O Reason, art not thou unjust in calling him moon-like?

Wherefore dost thou call him moon? perchance thou
　hast no sight.

Your head is like a lamp containing six wicks :

How should all the six be alight unless you have that
　spark ?

Your body is like a camel which goes to the Ka'ba of
　the soul ;

You failed to go on the pilgrimage because of your ass's
　nature, not because you have no ass.

If you have not gone to the Ka'ba, Fortune will draw
　you thither ;

Do not flee, O babbler, for you have no refuge from
　God.

مُجتثِ مُثَمَّنِ مخبون :Metre
[ᵛ−ᵛ−|ᵛᵛ−−|ᵛ−ᵛ−|ᵛᵛ−˘]

T.	۱ دلا چه بستهٔ این خاکدانِ بر گُذرانی
	ازین حظیره بِرون پر که مُرغِ عالَمِ جانی
	۲ تو یارِ خلوَتِ نازی مُقیمِ پردهٔ رازی
	قرارگاه چه سازی درین نِشیمنِ فانی
	۳ بحالِ خُود نظری کُن بِرون بَرو سفری کن
	ز حبسِ عالَمِ صورت بمرغزارِ معانی
	۴ تو مُرغِ عالَمِ قُدسی ندیمِ مجلسِ اُنسی
	دریغ باشد اگر تو درین مقام بمانی
	۵ همیرسد ز سمٰوات هر صباح نِدایت
	که ره بری بِنِشانه چو گَردِ ره بِنشانی
	۶ براهِ کعبهٔ وَصلش ببین بهَر بُنِ خاری
	هزار کُشتهٔ شَوقند داده جان بجوانی
	۷ هزار خسته درین ره فرو شُدند و نیامد
	ز بویِ وَصل نسیمی ز کویِ دوست نِشانی

CTV

۱. حضیره (CV).   ۳ بِرون ز خَود (CV).

XLIV.

O heart, why art thou a captive in the earth that is
    passing away ?

Fly forth from this enclosure, since thou art a bird of
    the spiritual world.

Thou art a darling bosom-friend, thou art always behind
    the secret veil :

Why dost thou make thy dwelling-place in this perish-
    able abode ?

Regard thine own state, go forth and journey

From the prison of the Formal world to the meadow of
    Ideas.

Thou art a bird of the holy world, a boon-companion in
    the assembly of Love ;

If thou wilt remain here, 'tis a pity.

Every morning a voice comes to thee from heaven :

'When thou lay'st the dust of the way, thou win'st
    thy way to the goal.'

On the road to the Ka'ba of union, lo, in every thorn-
    bush

Are thousands slain of desire who manfully yielded up
    their lives.

Thousands sank wounded on this path, to whom there
    came not

A breath of the fragrance of union, a token from the
    neighbourhood of the Friend.

٨   بیادِ بزمِ وِصالش در آرزویِ جمالش

فُتاده بیخبرانند ز آن شراب که دانی

٩   چه خَوش بُوَد که ببویَش بر آستانهٔ کویَش

برایِ دیدنِ رویَش شبی بروز رسانی

١٠   حواسّ جُثّهٔ خَودرا بنورِ جانِ تو بر افروز

حواسّ پنج نماز است و دل چو سبع مثانی

١١   فرو خَورَد مه و خورشید و قُطبِ هفت فَلَکرا

سُهَیلِ جان چو بر آید ز سویِ رُکنِ یمانی

١٢   مجو سعادت و دَولت درین جهان که نیابی

ز بندگیش طلب کُن سعادتِ دو جهانی

١٣   حدیثِ عشق رها کُن که آن رهگُذرانست

تو بندگیِّ خُدا کُن بهَر قَدَر که توانی

١۴   ز شمسِ مفخرِ تبریز جو سعادتِ عُقبَی

که اوست شمسِ معارف به پیشگاهِ معانی

---

١٠   حواسّ خمسهٔ جانرا (T).   ١١   و om. before قُطب

(T).   حدیثِ عقل ١٣ (V).   که آن ره دِگُریست (V)

contra metr.   ١۴   که اوست شمسِ معانی فُزون ز شمس

(C).   مقرّب به پیشِ شمسِ معانی (V).   مکانی

In memory of the banquet of union, in yearning for his
  beauty

They are fallen bewildered by the wine thou knowest.

How sweet, in the hope of him, on the threshold of his
  abode,

For the sake of seeing his face, to bring night round
  to day !

Illumine thy bodily senses by the light of the soul :

The senses are the five prayers, but the heart is the
  seven verses.

The moon and the sun and the axis of the seven heavens
  are swallowed

By the Canopus of the soul, when it rises from towards
  the southern angle.

Look not in the world for bliss and fortune, since thou
  wilt not find them ;

Seek bliss in both worlds by serving Him.

Put away the tale of love that travellers tell ;

Do thou serve God with all thy might.

From the Sun who is the glory of Tabrīz seek future
  bliss,

For he is a sun, possessing all kinds of knowledge, on
  the spiritual throne.

۴۵

Metre: مُجتثّ مُثَمَّنِ مخبونِ مقصور

[∪ – ∪ – | ∪ ∪ – – | ∪ – ∪ – | ﹈ ﹈]

B³.   ۱   بیا بیا که نیابی چو ما دِگر یاری

چو ما بِجُمله جهان خَود کُجاست دلداری

۲   بیا بیا و بِهَر سوی روزگار مبر

که نیست نقدِ تُرا پیشِ غیر بازاری

۳   تو همچو وادیِ خُشکی و ما چو بارانی

تو همچو شهرِ خرابی و ما چو مِعماری

۴   بغَیرِ خِدمتِ ما که مشارقِ شادیست

ندید خلق و نه بیند ز شادی آثاری

۵   هزار صورتِ جُنبان بخواب می بینی

چو خواب رفت نبینی ز خلق دیّاری

۶   ببند چشمِ کژ و بر کُشای چشمِ خِرَد

که نفس همچو خر اُفتاد و حِرص افساری

B³CL Lakh.

۴ و ۴ om. before (B³) contra metr. همچون وادیِ ۳

ببند چشمِ خَود ۶ .(B³L) صورتِ حسنان ۵ .(B³) نه بیند

(L). چشمِ حسد (C). اُفتاده (B³).

XLV.

Come, come, for you will not find another friend like
me.

Where indeed is a Beloved like me in all the world?

Come, come, and do not spend your life in wandering
to and fro,

Since there is no market elsewhere for your money.

You are as a dry valley and I as the rain,

You are as a ruined city and I as the architect.

Except my service, which is joy's sunrise,

Man never has felt and never will feel an impression of
joy.

You behold in dreams a thousand moving shapes;

When the dream is past you do not see a single one of
the kind.

Close the eye that sees falsely and open the intellectual
eye,

For the senses resemble an ass, and evil desire is the
halter.

٧ ز باغِ عشق طلب کُن عقیدهٔ شیرین

که طبع سِرکه‌فروشست و غوره‌افشاری

٨ بیا بجانِبِ دارِ الشِّفایِ خالِتِ خویش

کز آن طبیب ندارد کُنزیر بیماری

٩ جهان مِثالِ تنِ بی‌سرست بی آن شاه

به پیچ گِردِ چنان سر مِثالِ دستاری

١٠ اگر سیاه نهٔ آینه مده از دست

که روح اینهٔ تُست جِسمِ زنگاری

١١ کُجاست تاجرِ مسعودِ مُشتری‌طالِع

که کُرمدار منش باشم و خریداری

١٢ بیا و فِکرتِ من کُن که فِکرتت دارم

چو لعلِ مِ، خری از کانِ من بخرباری

١٣ بیا و جانِبِ آنکس بَرو که پایَت داد

بدو نِگر بدو دیده که داد دیداری

ستّاری ٩ (B³). کُریز (B³). ٨ که هرکه فروشست ٧
for چِشمِ (L). اگر سِتاره نهٔ ١٠ (B³). دستاری for
که فِکرتت دارم (C). پیا و for بیاد ١٢ (B³L). جِسمِ
for که رو (B³). بیا جانِب (B³). ٣١ می خِر (CL).
بَرو (B³).

Seek sweet syrup in the garden of Love,

For Nature is a seller of vinegar and a crusher of un-
ripened grapes.

Come to the hospital of your own Creator:

No sick man can dispense with that Physician.

The world without that King is like a headless body:

Fold yourself, turban-wise, round such a head.

Unless you are black, do not let the mirror go from
your hand:

The soul is your mirror, while the body is rust.

Where is the fortunate merchant, whose destiny Jupiter
controls,

That I may eagerly trade with him and buy his wares?

Come, and think of me who gave you the faculty of
thought,

Since from my mine you may purchase an ass-load of
rubies.

Come, advance towards him who gave you a foot,

Look with all your eyes on him who gave you an eye.

۱۴ دو کف بشادیِ او زن که کف ز بحرِ وَیَست

که نیست شادیِ اورا غمی و تیماری

۱۵ تو بی دو گُوش شِنَو بی زبان بِگو با او

که نیست گُفتِ زبان بی خِلاف و آزاری

_____

۱۴ کف om. before ز بحر (B³).   ۱۵ دو om. (B³).

Clap your hands for joy of him, by whose sea the hand
(foam) is produced,

For his joy admits no sorrow nor affliction.

Listen without ears, speak to him without tongue,

Since the speech of the tongue is not without offence
and injury.

۴۶

رَمَلِ مُثَمَّنِ مخبونِ مقصور : Metre
[ᴗ ᴗ – – | ᴗ ᴗ – – | ᴗ ᴗ – – | ᴗ ᴗ –]

V.	در رُخِ عشق نِگر تا بصِفَت مرد شَوی	۱
	پیشِ سردان منِشین کز دمِشان سرد شَوی	
	از رُخِ عشق بجو چیزِ دِگَر جُز صورت	۲
	گاه آنست که با همرهِ همدرد شَوی	
	چون گُلوخی بصِفَت تو بهوا بر نشَوی	۳
	بهوا بر شَوی ار بِشکنی و گُرد شَوی	
	تو اگُر نشکنی آن کت بسرِشت او شِکَنَد	۴
	چونکه مرگُت شِکَنَد کی گُهَرِ فرد شَوی	
	برگ چون زرد شَوَد بیخِ تَرَش سبز کُند	۵
	تو فُغان میکُنی از عشق کزو زرد شَوی	

BCTV

۲ کار آنست (BCT). که با عشق تو همدرد شَوی (BT).
۳ همرِه و همدرد (V). بصِفَت تو for بصورت (T).
۴ چون for کی (C). بیخ و برش (V).

XLVI.

Look on the face of Love, that you may be properly a
man.

Do not sit with the frigid; for you will be chilled by
their breath.

Seek from the face of Love something other than beauty;

It is time that you should consort with a sympathetic
companion.

Since you are properly a clod, you will not rise into the
air;

You will rise into the air, if you break and become dust.

If you break not, He who moulded you will break you;

When death breaks you, how should you become a
separate substance?

When the leaf grows yellow, the fresh root makes it
green;

You are complaining of Love thro' which you become
pale.

٦   وَر بيائى بسر اى دوست درين مجلسِ ما

جاىِ تو صدر بُوَد در همه برخَورد شَوى

٧   وَر بمانى تو درين خاك بسى سالِ دِگُر

جا بجا بر كُذرى چون عددِ نرد شَوى

٨   شمسِ تبريز كَرَت در كَنِف خويش كشد

چون ز زِندان برهى باز در آن گُرد شَوى

چون عددِ فرد ٧   (BT.) وَز همگان فرد (C.) وَز همه ٦

(V.) باز در آن درد ٨   (T.) چون علفِ زرد (V.)

And, O friend, if you reach perfection in our assembly,

Your seat will be the throne, you will gain your desire in all things.

But if you stay many years more in this earth,

You will pass from place to place, you will be as the dice in backgammon.

If Shamsi Tabrīz draws you to his side,

When you escape from captivity you will return to that orb.

Metre: رَمَلِ مُثَمَّنِ مخبون [x–∪∪|–∪∪|–∪∪|–∪∪–] [∪∪––|∪∪––|∪∪––|∪∪–]

۱   V.   چو بشهرِ تو رسیدم تو ز من گوشه گُزیدی

چو ز شهرِ تو برفتم بوداعیم ندیدی

۲   تو اگر لُطف گُزینی و اگر بر سرِ کینی

همه آسایشِ جانی همه آرایشِ عیدی

۳   سببِ غَیرتِ تُست آن که نِهانی و اگر نه

همچو خورشید نِهانی و ز هر ذرّه پدیدی

۴   تو اگر گوشه بگیری نه چِنانکگوشهٔ میری

و اگر پرده دری تو همه‌را پرده دریدی

۵   دلِ کُفر از تو مُشَوَّش سرِ ایمان به مَیَت خَوش

همه‌را هوش رُبودی همه‌را گوش کشیدی

۶   همه کُلها گِرَوِ دَی همه سرها گِرَوِ مَی

تو همین‌را و همآن‌را ز کفِ مرگ خریدی

_____

TV

۱ گُردیدی for گوشه گُزیدی (V).   بوداعم دیدی

۳ همه خورشید (V).   ۴ و اگر پرده دریدی (V).

XLVII.

When I came to thy city, thou chosest a corner apart
  from me;
When I went from thy city, thou didst not look upon
  me to say 'Farewell'.
Whether thou choosest to be kind or inclinest to rancour,
Thou art all the comfort of the soul, thou art all the
  adornment of the feast.
The cause of thy jealousy is that thou art hidden or,
  otherwise,
While thou art revealed by every atom, thou art hidden
  like the sun.
If thou dwell'st in seclusion, art not thou the darling
  of the Prince?
And if thou rendest the veil, thou hast rent the veils
  of all.
By thee the heart of infidelity is confounded, by thy
  wine the head of faith is intoxicated;
Thou dost rob all of sense, thou dost draw all towards
  thee.
All roses are a prey to December, all heads a prey to
  wine:
Both these and those thou redeemest from the hand of
  death.

۷   چو وَفا نبوَد در کُل چه رَوی تو سویِ هر کُل

همه بر تُست تَوَکُّل که عِمادی و عمیدی

۸   اگر از چِهرهٔ یوسُف نَفَری کف بِبُریدند

تو دو صد یوسُفِ جانرا ز دل و عقل بُریدی

۹   ز پلیدی و ز خوبی تو کُنی صورتِ شخصی

که گُریزد بدو فرسنگ وَی از بویِ پلیدی

۱۰   کُنیَش طعمهٔ خاکی که شَوَد سبزهٔ پاکی

برَهَد او ز نجاست چو درو روح دمیدی

۱۱   هله ای دل بسما رَو بچراگاهِ خُدا رَو

بچراگاهِ سُتوران چو یکی چند چریدی

۱۲   تو همه طمع بر آن نِه که بر آن نیست اُمیدت

که ز نَومیدیِ اوّل تو بدین سوی رسیدی

۱۳   تو خمُش کُن که خُداوَندِ سُخن‌بخش بگُوید

که هم او ساخت در و قُفل و هم او کرد کِلیدی

و ۱۳ .(V) چند خریدی ۱۱ .(V) کف و عقل ۸

om. before قُفل (V).

Since in the rose there is no constancy, why do you
   approach every rose ?

On thee alone is reliance : thou art the stay and support.

If a few cut their hands on account of Joseph's face,

Thou hast bereft of soul and reason two hundred spiritual
   Josephs.

Thou mouldest of foul and fair the form of a man,

That he may flee two leagues from the odour of foulness.

Thou mak'st him a morsel of dust that he may become
   pure herbage ;

He is free from filth when thou hast breathed into him
   a soul.

Come, O heart, fare heavenward, fare to the divine pasture,

Since thou hast grazed awhile in the pasture of cattle.

Set thy whole desire on that whereof thou hast no hope,

For thou hast come thus far from original hopelessness.

Be silent that the lord who gave thee language may
   speak,

For as he fashioned a door and lock, he has also made
   a key.

۴۸

Metre: مُجتَثِّ مُثَمَّنِ مخبونِ مقصور

$$[\cup - \cup - | \cup \cup - - | \cup - \cup - | \overset{\smile}{-} \overset{\smile}{-}]$$

L.

بعاقبت بُبُریدی و در نِهان رفتی

عجب عجب بُکدامین رِه از جهان رفتی

۲ بسی زدی پر و بال و قفص در اِشکستی

هوا گِرِفتی و سویِ جهانِ جان رفتی

۳ تو بازِ خاص بُدی در وِثاقِ پیر زنی

چو طبلِ باز شنیدی بلامکان رفتی

۴ بُدی تو بُلبُلِ مستی میانهٔ جُغدان

رسید بویِ گُلِستان بِگُلِستان رفتی

۵ بسی خُمار کشیدی ازین خمیرِ تُرُش

بعاقبت بخرابات جاوِدان رفتی

۶ پَیِ نِشانهٔ دَولت چو تیر راست شُدی

بدآن نِشانه چو تیری ازین کمان رفتی

B³L Lakh.

۶ بدآن نِشانه بُریدی و زین (L.) ۲ جهان جهان (B³).

XLVIII.

At last thou hast departed and gone to the Unseen ;
'Tis marvellous by what way thou wentest from the
　　world.
Thou didst strongly shake thy wings and feathers, and
　　having broken thy cage
Didst take to the air and journey towards the world of
　　soul.
Thou wert a favourite falcon, kept in captivity by an
　　old woman :
When thou heard'st the falcon-drum thou didst fly away
　　into the Void.
Thou wert a love-lorn nightingale among owls :
The scent of the rose-garden reached thee, and thou
　　didst go to the rose-garden.
Thou didst suffer sore head-ache from this bitter ferment;
At last thou wentest to the tavern of Eternity.
Straight as an arrow thou didst make for the mark of
　　bliss ;
Thou didst speed like an arrow to that mark from this
　　bow.

٧ نِشانهايِ کژت داد این جهان چون غول

نِشان گُذاشتی و سويِ بینِشان رفتی

٨ تو تاجرا چه کُنی چونکه آفتاب شُدی

کمر چرا طلبی چونکه از میان رفتی

٩ دو چشمِ گُشته شنیدم که سويِ جان نِگری

چرا بجان نِگری چون بجانِ جان رفتی

١٠ دلا چه نادِره مُرغی که در شِکارِ شُکور

تو با دو پر چو سِپَر جانِبِ سِنان رفتی

١١ گُل از خِزان بگُریزد عجب چه شوخ گُلی

که پیشِ بادِ خِزانی خِزان خِزان رفتی

١٢ ز آسمانِ تو چو باران ببامِ عالَمِ خاك

بهَر سوئی بدویده بناودان رفتی

١٣ خموش باش تو از رنجِ گُفت و گُوی مُخُسپ

که در پناهِ چنان یارِ مِهربان رفتی

جانِبِ (.L) ببال و پر ١٠ (.L) سويِ جان نِگرد ٩

(.B³) شبان رفتی (.L) نگُریزد ١١ (.L) خِران خِران

(.B³) تو از و مکش ١٣

The world gave thee false clues, like a ghoul :

Thou took'st no heed of the clue, but wentest to that
which is without a clue.

Since thou art now the sun, why dost thou wear a tiara,

Why seek a girdle, since thou art gone from the middle?

I have heard that thou art gazing with distorted eyes
upon thy soul :

Why dost thou gaze on thy soul, since thou art gone
to the soul of Soul ?

O heart, what a wondrous bird art thou, that in chase
of divine rewards

Thou didst fly with two wings to the spear-point, like
a shield !

The rose flees from autumn—O what a fearless rose
art thou

Who didst go loitering along in the presence of the
autumn wind !

Falling like rain from heaven upon the roof of the ter-
restrial world

Thou didst run in every direction till thou didst escape
by the conduit.

Be silent and free from the pain of speech : do not
slumber,

Since thou hast taken refuge with so loving a Friend.

NOTES.

I.

اکَر تو عاشِقِ عشقْنی ۱—Love, implying loss of self-hood and by that means perfect union with the divine Beloved, is the living rock on which all mysticism is based.

حِيا—cf. the ḥadīs: اَلْحَيَاءُ يَمْنَعُ ٱلْإِيمَانَ, Shame hinders faith, and Redhouse's *Maṣnavī*, p. 115: Ḥusām-u'ddīn having publicly spoken in praise of certain individuals who bore an extremely bad character...complaint was made to Jalāl, who confirmed what Ḥusām had said, and remarked: "God looks only to man's heart. Those seemingly lewd fellows are really God-loving saints." Cf. also:

چو مردِ شرمِ و ناموسی چو مجنون فاش باید شُد

چنان مستوررا هرگِز نیابد کس بمستوری

(T. 93. 1).

Since you are moved by feelings of shame and honour, you must become manifest, like Majnūn;
One concealed as He is will never be found by concealment (continence).

رَوِش ۲—the Ṣūfī path (طریقت) whereby the pilgrim arrives at true knowledge of God.

ناموس—Greek νόμος (see Dozy's *Supplément aux Dictionnaires Arabes*, under نمس).

حديث—I have not been able to discover any tradition to this effect. Possibly the word is used here, as often, in a non-technical sense.

بصفا—sincerely, without prejudice.

مجنون ٣—literally, possessed by the جِنّ. Majnūn is the Orlando Furioso of eastern romance; in Persia the love of Majnūn and Lailā has long been a brilliant theme for poetry: mention may be made here of the masnavīs by Niẓāmī, Jāmī, and Hātifī. Majnūn represents the soul seeking union with God, who is the Beloved par excellence.

كُزين—Orientals regard lunacy as a special mark of divine favour.

Observe the assonance شَيدا شَيد مجنون جُنون. This figure, in which two or more words of like sound and derived (or at least apparently derived) from the same root are brought together, is called اشتِقاق, according to others تجنيسِ اشتِقاق.

ز زهر چشيد ٤—suffered the agony of separation from his Beloved. Cf. Hāfiz (I. 256. 2): زهرِ جُدائى چشاند.

فنا—self-annihilation 'which is attained by absorption in the glory of the Creator and by contemplation of the Truth' (Kitābu 'tta'rīfāt), 'to die spiritually, so far as the senses are concerned, during life' (Juan de la Cruz). See Whinfield's Masnavī, p. xxvi seq., with the passages there referred to, De Sacy's Pendnāmeh, p. liv, Gulshani Rāz, 334 seq., with Lāhijī's commentary, and cf. also Kor. II. 88: Desire death if ye are sincere, and the hadīs: مُوتُوا قَبْلَ أَنْ تَمُوتُوا, Die before ye die.

عنکبوت ٥—This may allude to an incident in the Prophet's flight from Mecca, when a spider spun its web across the mouth of a cavern where he had taken refuge, and thus caused his enemies to abandon their pursuit. 'Aṭṭār says (*Manṭiqu 'ṭṭair*, 14):

عنکبوتی را بحکمت دام داد

صدرِ عالَمرا درو آرام داد

He providentially gave a snare to the spider,
And therein rendered the Prince of the world secure.

رَبِّیَ ٱلْأَعْلَى—these words do not occur in the Kor'ān, but were probably suggested by Pharaoh's boast: أَنَا رَبُّكُمُ ٱلْأَعْلَى (Kor. LXXIX. 24). One of the Bāb's titles was حضرتِ رَبِّیَ ٱلْأَعْلَى (Browne's *Episode of the Bāb*, Vol. II. p. 229).

چگونه باشد ٦—what is earthly beauty compared with immediate vision of God?

أَسْرَى بِعَبْدِهِ لَيْلًا—Kor. XVII. 1. A full description and mystical interpretation of Mohammed's night-journey to heaven is quoted from Abū ʿAlī Ibn Sīnā (Avicenna) in the *Dabistān*, Vol. III. p. 177 seq. The second foot in this line is – – – instead of ◡ ◡ – –, and as a general rule, for two short syllables occurring together, even if they do not belong to the same foot, one long syllable may be substituted. Cf. note on XI. ١٠.

دواوین ٧—Arabic broken plural of دیوان, which is the name usually given to a collection of short poems, e.g. ghazals and qaṣīdas. As it seems unlikely that Waisa and Rāmīn formed the subject of any such collection, the term must be extended to include the maṣnavīs bearing this title by Niẓāmī ‘Arūẓī of Samarcand and Fakhru’ddīn Jurjānī, both of whom flourished under the Seljūqs. The former was a pupil of Mu‘izzī and one of the poets at Sultān Sanjar's court (479—552 A.H.).

وامق (lover) and عذرا (virgin) are the hero and heroine of the oldest poetical romance in Persian literature, by ‘Unṣurī (died 431 A.H.), which, like that of Waisa and Rāmīn, is said to have appeared in Pehlevī, under the Sāsānians, and to have been subsequently lost.

خوردنیست ٨—patiendum est. For this form see Platts, *Persian Grammar*, Part I. § 95.

دریا—wash away every stain of 'self' in the ocean of divine love.

پستی ٩—self-abasement, according to the proverb: سُمُوُّ ٱلْمَرءِ فِی ٱلتَّوَاضُع, Humility exalts a man.

مستی—ecstasy, loss of personal consciousness, produced by contemplation of the beauty of God. The torrent, furiously rushing along in its low channel, unites these qualities.

میانِ حلقهٔ عُشّاق الخ ١٠—among spiritual disciples you will attain the highest degree, if you serve him who is highest.

نگین—‘Omar Khayyām, having declared that Man is the final cause of creation, adds:

این دائرهٔ جهان چو انگشتریست

بی هیچ شکی نقشِ نگینش مائیم

This circle of the universe resembles a ring;
Unquestionably we are the signet engraved on its bezel.

(Quatrain 340).

Cf. also Hāfiz (II. 98. 3): سرحلقهٔ رندان, ringleader of the intoxicated.

حلقه بگوش حلقه—the play on حلقه and بگوش cannot be preserved in English.

نشین in this line may be referred either to God or to the پیر (Director) who is here Shamsi Tabrīz, and throughout the Dīvān it will be found, for the most part, impossible to distinguish between them.

۱۲ زیان کرد—cf. the common phrase سود نکرد, it was of no use. Latin and French have similar idioms (damnum facere and faire une perte).

۱۳ With this couplet cf. Hāfiz (III. 102. 6):

My heart is weary of hypocrisy and of the drum
  under the blanket ;
Come, let me raise my standard at the door of the
  wine-house.

دُهُل بزیرِ گلیم—do not conceal what is perfectly obvious, proclaim your love.

صحرا—the desert of Absolute Being, in which the phenomenal world is a mirage (*Gulshani Rāz*, 843) or the world itself. Cf.

صحرا چه بُوَد زمینِ امکان

کآنست کتابِ حق تعالَی (T. 114. 5).

What is the desert? This contingent universe,
Which is the book of God most High.

۱۴ بگوشِ جان—because they would be inaudible to the sensual ear.

خُنْبَدِ خَضْرا —the sky, which Orientals, perhaps owing to some optical peculiarity, often see as green (cf. Garcin de Tassy, *La poésie religieuse chez les Persans*, p. 24, note), or rather they consider blue and green to be merely varieties of the same colour. This metaphor is a favourite one with our poet. Cf. a passage from Browne's 'The Modern Traveller' quoted in Rosen's *Maṣnavī*, p. xx : The splendid Tekieh (or monastery) of Mewlawy dervishes (at Konieh) is the first among such buildings in the Turkish Empire, and is universally celebrated. Its *cupola covered with shining green tiles* is conspicuous from afar.

قبا ١٥ —the body, 'this fleshly dresse' (Henry Vaughan).

تو های و هوی فَلَك الخ —when the soul is no longer blinded by sensual desires and affections, it perceives that all phenomena are intoxicated and reeling with the wine of love. Cf. *Gulshani Rāz*, 825 seq.

مُنَزَّه ز زیر و از بالا ١٦ —illimitable, transcending Space.

آفتاب ١٧ —an allusion to Shamsi Tabrīz (شمس = sun, in Arabic).

خموش کردم ١٨ —so end a large number of these poems. Speech is only the prelude to silence : true worshippers are 'breathless with adoration' (cf. Whinfield's *Maṣnavī*, pp. 5, 261, 326).

II.

بیابانِ ما ١ —cf. note on I. ١٣. But this is rather the desert of Love, the راهِ پُر خون (*Maṣnavī*, 4. 7) which Hāfiz thought easy until he tried it, and then :

Whichever side I turned, new terrors lay;
Beware of this dark waste, this endless way!
Even in our dreams no end—pass, one by one,
A thousand stages, and 'tis scarce begun.

(I. 214. 7 seq.).

۲ جهان در جهان—this obscure phrase may refer (1)
to the different categories of being, i.e. the series of
emanations which connect the phenomenal world with the
Divinity (cf. Whinfield's *Maṣnavī*, p. 77), or (2) to Man,
who is a world within a world, the microcosm contained in
the macrocosm. See *Gulshani Rāz*, 140 seq. [in 144,
second miṣrā', read بِی یَبْصُر و بِی یَسْمَع, 'by me he sees
and by me he hears': the words are taken from the
tradition quoted on p. 15].

صورت—phenomenal appearance opposed to معنَی,
spiritual reality.

کُدامست الخ—when Man annihilates his lower nature
and divests himself of all that is not God, he no longer has
anything in common with the world of illusions around
him.

۳ بُریده سری—true Knowledge is attainable only by
فنا. Cf. Ḥāfiz, I. 534. 4:

How wonderful is the path of Love,
Where the headless one lifts up his head (is exalted).

and see note on XXXVII. ۱٦.

سوي مَیدانِ ما—cf.

بی دست و پا چو کُوئی سوي وَیثیمِ غلطان
چوکانِ زُلف مارا اینسو اینسو همیدواند

(T. 174. 6ᵃ).

Without head and feet, like a ball, we are rolling
 towards Him;

In this direction the bat of His curl is driving us on.

[For the mystical signification of زُلف see *Gulshani Rāz*,
763 seq. It is used here because its crookedness makes it
resemble the چوگان (polo-stick).].

٥–٦ — What if God should bestow on us the beatific
vision of eternal Truth, as He did, e.g. to Moses at Mt
Sinai?

زبانهاي مُرغانِ ما —a reference to Kor. xxvii. 16:
'and Solomon was David's heir, and he said, O people, we
have been taught the language of birds.'

٦ يك مُرغ —the hoopoe (هُدهُد) which Solomon sent
with a letter to Bilqīs, queen of Sheba (Kor. xxvii. 20–45).

طَوق —cf. the Arabic expression: طَوَّقَنِى نِعْمَةً, 'he
conferred upon me a permanent badge of favour' (Lane,
under طوق), and see xl. ٩, with note on قلاده. The ring-
dove is called in Arabic ذَاتُ ٱلطَّوق.

٧ امكانِ ما —when Not-being (عَدَم) reflects the
qualities of Being (حقّ) and thus loses to a certain extent
its own negative and phenomenal character, it receives the
name of امكان, Contingent being. This is the state of
Man, in whom the flesh and the spirit are forever at war.

٨ چگونه زنم دم —Ibnu'l Fārid says in his *Tā'iyya*
(36th beyt):

Thro' weakness I refrain from uttering many things
 (troubles);

By my tongue they shall not be recorded, altho', if I
 spoke, they would become less.

دمر زدن also means 'to speak,' and so possibly here.

این پریشان ما—adjective used as noun (see Vullers, under پریشن). It may however be translated : our distressed one, i.e. the soul. Cf. بمستانِ شُما = to your drunken eyes (Hāfiz, I. 4. 6).

چه—چه ٩—both—and.

چه کبکان چه بازان—great and small, high and low, go hand in hand to seek God. Hāfiz refers to the partridge being hunted by the falcon (I. 454. 9, and 532. 4), and this explains the reading of B, بازانِشان, their falcons, i.e. the falcons pursuing them.

کهستانِ ما—'the shining table-lands To which our God Himself is moon and sun' (Tennyson).

کیوانِ ما ٠١—Saturn, according to the Ptolemaic system, is lord of the seventh heaven.

عرش ١١—the ninth and highest heaven.

جولانِ ما—alluding to the سماع or mystic dance, which represents allegorically the harmonious movement of the spheres (see Whinfield's *Maṣnavī*, p. 182).

هواهاي عرش و فَلَك ١٢—a play on the two meanings of هوا, air and desire. Even Heaven, in so far as it rests upon a phenomenal basis, is an obstacle to union with the Absolute. Cf.

گر کعبه است و زمزم وُر جنّت است و کوثر
چون پرده گشت دلرا درهم درید باید
(T. 187. 2ᵃ).

Tho' the Kaʻba and Zamzam exist, and tho' Paradise
and Kauṣar exist,
Since they are a veil to the soul, you must tear the
veil asunder.

مپُرس ۱۳—I have abandoned with reluctance the
reading of L and V, بپُرس. If it be kept, we must
take دستان as the plural of دست and translate: Inquire
concerning us whose hands are crushed, i.e. whose state is
one of extreme weakness and humiliation.   Cf.

خَود دامنش نگیرد الّا شِکستهدستی

(T. 248. 4).   اکنون بُلند کُردم چون جَور کرد پستم
Indeed, none may grasp his skirt save with bruised hands:
Now that oppression has abased me, I become exalted.

صلاحُ الحق و دین ۱۴—for Ṣalāḥu'ddīn Zarkūb
(Goldsmith) see Redhouse's *Maṣnavī*, p. 110.

III.

اِستارهرا ۱—cf.

I hold converse nightly with every star
From desire of the splendour of thy moon-like face.
                                   (Ḥāfiz, II. 468. 5).

بتابَش ۲—the pointing تابِش is also possible.

دلبرِ خونخوارهرا ۳—for the cruelty of the Beloved
see Whinfield's *Maṣnavī*, p. 30 seq.   Grief and pain are
often synonymous with love in the language of mystics.

سو بسو کُشتم ۴—i.e. in the سماع (cf. Ibnu'l Fāriḍ,
Tā'iyya, beyt 434).

طِفِل دلو — cf. the same author (ib. beyts 435 and 436):

When it (the child) tosses about in longing for one
　　who shall sing it asleep, and yearns
To fly to its original home,
It is hushed by being rocked in its cradle
When the hands of its nurse set the cradle moving.

and

جان همچو مسیح است بکهوارهٔ قالب

(T. 291. 8). آن مریمِ بندندهٔ کهوارهٔ ما کو

The soul is like the Messiah in the cradle of the body;
Where is the Mary who fashioned our cradle?

ه ز گُریَهاش — scan *zi giryash* ($\smile - -$).

٧ خُمار — the relapse from ecstasy into consciousness.

ساقيا — the cup-bearer is God, who intoxicates all creation with the rapture of love (see *Gulshani Rāz*, 805 seq.).

نرگِس خمّارهٔرا — the final ه in خمّاره does not here
denote the feminine gender but has an intensive force
(see Wright's *Arabic Grammar*, Vol. I. p. 139). The word
is used adjectively = مست. Cf. چشمِ خمّارش (T. 200.
10ᵃ), and نرگِسدانِ خمّارش (T. 215. 1ᵃ).

IV.

٢ کُنجی بُدمِ من در نهان — this famous tradition,
which innumerable Sūfī poets and commentators have
illustrated and embellished (cf. especially a beautiful passage in Jāmī's *Yūsuf ū Zulaikhā*, p. 16), runs in Arabic:

كُنْتُ كَنْزًا مَخْفِيًّا فَأَحْبَبْتُ أَنْ أُعْرَفَ فَخَلَقْتُ ٱلْخَلْقَ لِكَىْ
أُعْرَفَ, I was a hidden treasure and I desired to be known,
so I created the creation in order that I might be known.

٣ آئينهٔ كردم عيان—every object reflects one or more
of the divine attributes, but Man, as the microcosm, reflects
them all. 'Man,' says Lāhijī (*Gulshani Rāz*, 141), 'is the
eye of the world, whereby God sees His own works.'

رويش دل و پُشتش جهان—the earthly part of Man is
compared to the back, his eternal attributes to the face of
a mirror. He is 'blackened on one side with the darkness
of Not-being in order to reflect Real Being' (Lāhijī on
Gulshani Rāz, 265).

٤ چون كاه جُفتِ كُل بُوَد—straw is mixed with
clay to form a kind of stucco or mortar (كهگِل). Unless
you are pure clay, i.e. entirely purged of self, the divine
image reflected in your heart will be blurred and incom-
plete.

٥ شيره نگردد مَى الخ—cf. T. 353. 8–9, and

در خُمِّ جهان همچو عصيريد گِرِفتار

چون نيك بجوشيد ازين خُمِّ بدر آئيد
(T. 197. 11).

Ye are imprisoned like grape-juice in the jar of the
world ;
Ye will come forth from this jar, when ye are well
fermented.

٦ زين سان كه رفتى آمدى—i.e. you return to me
no better than when you entered the world.

ما آلآيِ —suggested perhaps by the verse which runs as a refrain through Kor. LV. : فَبِأَيِّ آلَآءِ رَبِّكُمَا تُكَذِّبَانِ.

اين كيمياي نادِره ٧ —the transforming influence of divine grace.

كاه = مسرِا in beyt ٣٣, whatever in Man's nature is false and unessential.

اين آفتاب ٨ —Shamsi Tabrīz.

فَيض —the perpetual raying out or emanation of the Absolute : hence grace, inspiration.

بِنشست عيسَى بر خرى ٩ —St Matthew, ch. xxi. Jesus mounted on the ass represents the soul degraded by contact with the body. Cf.

عيسِي مريَمِ بفَلَك رفت و فرو ماند خرش

من بزمين ماندمِ و شُد جانِبِ بالا دلِ من

(T. 268. 8ᵃ).

Jesus, son of Mary, went to heaven and his ass re-
    mained below ;
I remain on the earth but my spirit has flown to
    the sky.

See Whinfield's *Masnavī*, p. 85, and 'Attār, *Mantiqu 'ttair*, 621.

باد صبا —in allusion to the quickening breath of Jesus, whom Moslems call روحُ ٱلله (cf. Kor. IV. 169). Hāfiz has مسيحانَفَسى (I. 228. 3), and عيسَى صبا, of the Spring (I. 540. 1).

سر ساز همچون آبِ جو ١٠ —see note on I. ٩, and cf.

بر روی و سر چو سَیل دوان تا بجوی دوست

(T. 137. 2).

Running on face and head, like a torrent, to join the
river of the Friend.

and

آب شَوَم سجده کُنان تا بـتُگلستان برسم (T. 256. 5ᵃ).

I become water, bending low in prayer, that I may
reach the rose-garden.

عقل, the intellectual faculty, involving the separation
of the thinker from the object of his thought, and therefore
dualistic, is constantly opposed to عشق, the spiritual faculty
(intuition, illumination, inner light) which attains the truth
by transcending thought.

بقا—eternal life in God, only to be gained through
annihilation of self : بقا بعد أَلفنا.

فراموش ۱ ۱—here used as a noun, cf. پریشان, II. ۸.

تا محو الخ—see the passage from Ghazzālī quoted by
Tholuck (*Ssufismus*, p. 3) and translated by Whinfield on
Gulshani Rāz, 411. Cf.

خَود ثنا کُفتن ز من تركِ ثناست
کاین دلیلِ هستی و هستی خطاست

(*Masnavī*, 7. 23).

'Tis blasphemy to praise Him : I proclaim
My 'self' extant, and 'self' is mortal shame.

V.

چَمَنی ۱—cf. Song of Solomon, ch. iv. 12 seq., and
Jāmī's *Bahāristān*, p. ۰۹ :

What care tho' mine be all the loss, tho' veiled
　　The glory and dark the vision of my desire?
He Beauty's garden is; there gathers one
　　A rose, and one with bleeding hands a briar.

نِثار—sweetmeats and small coins which are thrown among the bystanders at a wedding and on other festal occasions.

۱۴ دِر زاهدیْ شِکستم—in a state of ecstasy (حال). Cf.

$$بی پای طواف آریم کُرد در آن شاهی$$

$$کاو مستِ اَلَست آمد بِشکست در مارا$$

(T. 129. 11ᵃ).

Let us without feet make the holy circuit round the
　　door of that King,
For he has come intoxicated with "*Am I not?*" and
　　broken our door.

See for بی پای note on II. ۳, and for اَلَست note on IX. ۹.

بیقرار—spent in seeking God and devoted to the sleep-less passion which he inspires.

۵ بِدُعایِ او—the prayer of the perfect spiritual man is identical with the divine will. یاری and the pronominal suffix in خُداش refer to the same person, probably Shamsi Tabrīz.

کَه بخونِ ماست تِشنه—see note on III. ۳.

۶ مانِدن—from مانَد.

چنكِ زُهره—for the simile, see note on XVI. ۲۲. The sign of Zuhra or Anāhīd, the celestial Venus, is in the third heaven. She leads the starry choirs to music. According to the legend Zuhra, a mortal woman, was beloved by two angels, Hārūt and Mārūt, whom she beguiled to tell her ' the ineffable name,' and by means of this talisman gained admission to heaven. See Mīrkhwānd's *Rauzatu 'ṣṣafā* translated by Rehatsek, Vol. I. p. 75 seq. and Sale's note on Kor. II. 96.

كُسِستهتار — for then all earthly discords will be drowned in the divine harmony.

حلاوتِ غمش ۷—cf. Ḥāfiẓ (II. 252. 3):

Thine eye hath wrought my ruin, but so my love
Send it, a thousand welcomes to the woe!

غمش includes the sorrow of the soul caused by her passionate longing to be united with God, and also the pains which he inflicts either as a probation or as the result of jealousy (see note on xxv. ۱۲).

چه عروسیست در جان ۸—see Whinfield's *Maṣnavī,* p. 34, where the poet makes an apology for calling God by this name.

نگار—the ornamental design traced with henna on the hands and feet of a bride.

تنِ تیره ۱۰—because it is عَدَم (Not-being).

جهانِ تن—cf.

جهانِ عقل چو روم و جهانِ طبع چو زنگ
میان هر دو فُتاده است كارزار و جهاد

(T. 164. 3).

The world of Intelligence is like Rūm (white) and the world of Nature like Æthiopia (black);
Strife and warfare has fallen out between them.

بچهار عُنصُر ۱۱—see note on VIII. ٤.

VI.

تلخی ۱—like بلاي نفی in *Gulshani Rāz*, 402, the mortification of all desires, whether sensual or intellectual. True spirituality (to quote Juan de la Cruz) seeks in God the bitter more than the agreeable, prefers suffering to solace, would rather lack all good for God's sake than possess it, is better pleased with dryness and affliction than with sweet communications: knowing that in this it follows Christ and denies self, instead of peradventure seeking self in God, which is against Love.

فقر—Mohammed said: اَلْفَقْرُ فَخْرِى, Poverty is my pride, and again اَلْفَقْرُ سَوَادُ الْوَجْهِ فِى الدَّارَيْنِ, Poverty is blackness of face (dishonour) in both worlds (see his own explanation of the inconsistency in Malcolm's *History of Persia*, Vol. ii. p. 268, note). The Sūfīs have given these sayings a mystical turn. فقر becomes poverty of 'self,' i.e. self-annihilation, and by سَوَادُ الْوَجْهِ they mean the darkness which is nothing but excess of light betokening the proximity of Being (cf. *Gulshani Rāz*, 123 seq.). 'I tell you, by the eternal Truth, that ye are not rightly poor while ye have a will to perform the will of God, or any desire of God and eternity; for the poor man is he who wills, knows, and desires nothing' (Eckhart, *Deutsche Mystiker*, Vol. ii. p. 281).

كُنْجِ روان—according to the *Burhāni Qāṭi'* this is 'the name of Qārūn's treasure: it is said to be in perpetual motion under the ground.' For Qārūn (Korah) see note on XLIII. ٤.

آنچه نبُودست وهم الخ ۲—cf. 1 Corinthians, ch. ii. 9: Eye hath not seen, nor ear heard, neither have entered into the heart of man, the things which God hath prepared for them that love him.

قبله—the Moslem turns his face in prayer towards the Ka‘ba, the mystic directly to God.

نعمت—اغانی in the next line suggests the emendation نغمت (sweet voice, melody). نغمت, however, does not seem to occur, and the change from نغمه, as the word is commonly written in Persian, to نعمت, is less easy.

آرد او—for this repetition of the pronoun cf. XXXVI. ٠.

گرچه نخوانی—even if thou dost not call me into thy presence.

اغانی—Arabic broken plural of اُغْنِیَّةٌ from the root غنی.

در رکعاتِ نماز الخ ٥—cf. T. 231. 9ᵃ seq.

اگر نه رویِ دل اندر برابرت دارم
من این نماز حسابِ نماز نشمارم
ز عشقِ رویِ تو من رو بقبله آوردم
و گرنه من ز نماز و ز قبله بیزارم ٬

Unless I have the face of my heart towards thee,
I deem prayer unworthy to be reckoned as prayer.
If I turned my face to the *qibla*, 'twas for love of thine;
Otherwise, I am weary both of prayer and *qibla*.

سبع مثانی—there are various interpretations of these words: the most probable is that which makes them refer to the seven verses of the opening Sūra of the Kor'ān (اَلْفَاتِحَه).

٧ Perhaps it is better to regard this couplet as complete in itself, and translate:

If a never-ceasing bounty should offer kingdoms
And lay the universe before me, thou art still my
    hidden treasure.

For گنج نهانی see note on IV. ٢.

٨   عشقِ فُلانی —the love of God.

١٠   cf.—عُمر اوانیست

باطنِ ما چو فَلَک تا یابد مُستغنی است

گرچه روزی دو سه در نقش و نِثارِ بشریم

کوزها دان تو صُوَررا و ز هر شربتِ فِکر

همچو کوزه همه هر لحظه تِهی ایم و پُریم

شربت از کوزه نروید بُوَد از جایِ دِگَر

همچو کوزه ز اُصولِ مددش بیخبریم

(T. 252. 2).

Our celestial spirit is free to eternity,

Tho' for a short while we have the shape and figure
of man.

Know that phenomenal forms are pitchers: with draughts
of the Ideal,

Like a pitcher, we all are being filled and emptied
continually.

The draught is not derived from the pitcher, it comes
from another source;

Like the pitcher we are ignorant of the springs which
replenish it.

اوانی—sing. إنآء.

cf.—بی تو چه کار آیدم الخ

عُمر که بی عشق رفت هیچ حِسابش مگیر

آبِ حیات است عشق در دل و جانش پذیر

(T. 203. 13).

Prize not at all life that has passed without love;

Love is the Water of Life: receive it in thy heart
and soul.

رنج اوانی—the tribulation which the soul suffers in the world.

مرا—cf. note on ٤. But رنج اوانی مرا may be construed together = رنجی که مرا از اوانی است.

امان ١١—نماند هیچ امانی مرا—literally : not even an امان (cry for quarter) remained to me, i.e. for love's sake I was prepared to sacrifice all. Prof. Bevan suggests that امانی here may be the plural of اُمْنِیَّة, object of desire. هیچ followed by a plural is found in Khāqānī (500—582 A.H.). According to the *Bahāri 'Ajam* (Vullers, under هیچ) this use is rare and archaic. But a stronger argument, to my mind, against taking امانی in the sense proposed is the occurrence, which can hardly be accidental, of ایمن in the next line.

مدد ١٢—this term is employed by Jalālu'ddīn to denote the perpetual replenishment of the phenomenal world by a succession of emanations from the Absolute.

جانِ جهانی—as God is all, and all is God, he who is absorbed in the divine essence (مجذوبِ مُطلق) becomes identical with it. Hence the أَنَا ٱلْحَقّ, I am God, of Manṣūr Ḥallāj and the سُبْحَانِی, Praise be to me !, of Bāyazīd. And this is what our poet means when he says, e.g.:

هم دُزدِ عیّاران منم هم رنجِ بیماران منم
هم ابر و هم باران منم در باغها باریده ام
(T. 258. 4).

I am the theft of rogues, I am the pain of the sick,
I am both cloud and rain, I have rained in the gardens.

گوهرِ معنَی اوست الخ ۱۳—at first sight these words seem to defy the rules of grammar. Obviously the sense is: جان و دلم پُر از گوهرِ معنَی او شُده است, and this can be obtained from the text only by treating گوهرِ معنَی او پُر as a compound adjective. In such formations پُر is usually prefixed, but cf. 'Attār, *Manṭiqu 'ṭṭair*, 525 :

چاه چون بِشنود آن تابش نبود

لاجرم خون پُر شُد و آبش نبود

او سگِ کو کُفت—a play on او, He (God), and او or عَو, the sound of a dog's bark.

ثالث—alluding to the doctrine of the Trinity (see Kor. IV. 169, with Sale's note, v. 77).

ثانی—as in the Magian religion.

بروح جسم نکرد اِلتِفات ۱۴—during this life the body is conscious of the soul's superiority, but not in the divine presence, for then it is non-existent.

تبریزرا ۱۵—the poet puns on the double meaning of تبریز : (1) the city of that name, and (2) manifestation (from Arabic بَرَّزَ), with a reference to کُشت عیانی.

VII.

می ۱—this is perhaps the most frequent of the inexhaustible images under which Oriental writers represent beauty.

ندیدش فَلَك بخواب—a not uncommon metaphor to

signify what is incapable of being conceived. Cf.

$$آن شَكَريرا كه مِصر هيچ نديدش بخواب$$

(T. 219. 6ª).

آتشى كه نميرد هيچ بهب آب—cf. Song of Solomon, ch. viii.
7 : 'Many waters cannot quench love.'

خراب ۲—'a man of true self-abandonment must be
unbuilt from the creature' (Suso, quoted in Vaughan's
Hours with the Mystics, Vol. I. p. 271). And Meister
Eckhart says : forasmuch as thou hast despoiled and
denuded (verwüestet) thyself of all attributes, God must
needs enter wholly into thy being and faculties, as it is
written : 'the voice crieth in the wilderness (wüeste).'
Let this eternal voice cry in thee, as it willeth, and be
empty (wüeste) of thyself and of all things (*Deutsche
Mystiker*, Vol. II. p. 22).

مير شرابخانه ۳—see note on III. ٧.

ندا رسد ۴—cf. Eckhart quoted above.

پياله—Greek φιάλη.

بر كَنَد الخ ٥—cf.

$$بام خانه چون حِجابست از جمالِ آفتاب$$
$$با كلندِ عشقِ حق زوتر فرو كن بامرا$$

(T. 116. 4).

The roof of the house is, as it were, a veil over the
sun's beauty.
Make haste to demolish the roof with the mattock of
divine love.

مرا بياب ٦—i.e. 'you cannot find me : the drop is lost
in the ocean.'

خُرشيد ٧—Nominativus pendens, cf. x. ٢.

دلهاي چون سحاب—the izāfat is affixed because چون
سحاب is equivalent to an adjective. Cf. سمرقند چو قند,
sweet Samarcand (*Maṡnavī*, 8. 19).

VIII.

مردِ خُدا ١—the perfect Sūfī.

سير بُود بی كباب—in accordance with the tradition:
اَلْجُوعُ طَعَامُ اللّٰهِ يُحْیِی بِهِ أَبْدَانَ الصِّدِّیقِین, Fasting is
the food of God whereby he revives the bodies of the
sincere.

واله و حَیران ٢—see note on I. ١٠.

شاه بُود ٣—i.e. in the spiritual world. Cf. Ḥāfiz
(I. 366. 6):

> Despise not thou the poor who Love obey ;
> Unbelted monarchs, crownless kings are they.

The same idea is found in a poem by Abū 'l ‘Atāhiya
(*Transactions of the Ninth Congress of Orientalists*, Vol. II.
p. 114) to which Prof. Bevan has drawn my attention :

> If thou seekest the most noble of all mankind,
> Behold a king in beggar's garb !

كنج بُوَد در خراب—it is a well-known Oriental fancy,
that treasures guarded by inviolable talismans lie buried in
the ruins and remains of ancient splendour, e.g. the site of
Persepolis.

٤ Bodies are composed of the four elements, earth,
water, fire, and air. The ‘man of God,’ casting off this
phenomenal vesture, which does not belong to his true
essence and which only veils the divine principle within
him, ‘breaks through to the Oneness.’ Cf.

در آبِ و در خاكِم در آتش و در بادم

این چار بگِردِ من امّا نه ازین چارم

(T. 235. 5).

I am in water and earth and fire and air;
These four around me, yet of these four I am not.

and

از آب و آتش نیستم وَز بادِ سركش نیستم

خاكِ مُنقّش نیستم من بر همه خندیده ام

(T. 258. 6).

I am not of water nor fire, I am not of the froward
      wind;
I am not moulded clay: I have mocked (transcended)
      them all.

بحر بُوَد بی كران ٥—he is absorbed in the Sea of
Absolute Being.

بارد دُر بی سحاب—he can perform miracles, because
his will is identical with the divine Will. The metaphor
is drawn from the notion, found in Pliny, that the oyster
is impregnated by rain-drops, which in due course become
pearls. Cf. *Gulshani Rāz*, 568 seq., Sa'dī's *Būstān*, p. 230.

دارد صد ماه و چرخ ٦—mystics dwell in the spiritual
universe, of which the visible one is a faint inglorious reflection, 'solemque suum, sua sidera norunt.'

عالِم از ٧—scan | – – – |. Any short syllable may be
lengthened before ١. Cf. I. ٦, VI. ١٢, ١٥, etc.

نیست فقیه از كِتاب—see note on IV. ١٠. Mere learning
will never enable a man to know God. 'Mind is nothing
but disease, And natural health is ignorance,' i.e. inspiration.

زآن سویِ كُفرست و دین ٨ —the Truth is independent of outward forms: it shines as brightly in the
tavern as in the mosque or the church; moreover, the
religion of the heart, which alone has value, is not the
monopoly of any particular creed. In reality all creeds
are one. Cf. a curious passage (T. 54. 3ᵃ):

این زمان و آن زمان بَیضه است و مُرغی كاندر اوست

مُظلِم و اِشكسته‌پر باشد حقیر و مُستهان

كُفر و ایمان دان درین بَیضه سفید و زرده‌را

واصِل و فارِق میانشان بَرْزَخٌ لَا یَبْغِیَان

بَیضه‌را چون زیرِ پرِّ خویش پرورد از كَرَم

كُفر و دین فانی شُد و شُد مُرغِ وَحدت پرفِشان

This world and that world are the egg, and the bird
    within it
Is in darkness and bruised of wing, contemptible and
    despised.
Regard unbelief and faith as the white and the yolk
    in this egg,
Between them, joining and dividing, "*a barrier which
    they shall not pass.*"
When He hath graciously fostered the egg under His
    wing,
Infidelity and religion disappear: the bird of Unity
    spreads its pinions.

چه خطا و صواب —the Sūfī adept is above law. Whatever he does proceeds directly from God, just as a flute
produces harmonies or discords at the will of the musician.

عَدَم ٩ —the created world, which considered *per se* is

Not-being, although it may be said to exist as a manifestation of the Creator.

عالیرِکاب—cf. Wordsworth's 'trailing clouds of glory
do we come From God who is our home.' But Jalālu'ddīn
refers to the second birth of dying to the world and
absorption in the Divinity.

هست نِهان ۱۰—Jāmī, in the *Nafaḥātu 'l Uns*, p. 20
seq., asserts on the authority of the *Kashfu 'l Mahjūb*,
that there are 4000 saints 'unacquainted with each other
and ignorant of their exalted state, who are always hidden
from themselves and others.'

مَنْ طَلَبَ وَ جَدَّ وَجَدَ ,cf. the ḥadīṣ : بجوی و بیاب—
he who seeks earnestly shall find.

IX.

This ghazal was sent by the poet Sa‘dī to Shamsu'ddīn
Hindī, prince of Shīrāz, who had asked him ' to select the
best ode, with the most sublime thoughts, that he knew of
as existing in Persian, and to send it to him for presenta-
tion to the great Khān of the Moguls' (Redhouse's *Maṣnavī*,
p. 28).

عزمِ تماشا کراست ۱—not as Redhouse : 'to witness
our departure who'll be found?' تماشا, like تفرّج, is the
term applied to a walk taken for diversion or recreation.

ما بفَلَك بوده ایم ۲—see note on XVII. ۱.

وَز مَلَك افزونتریم ۳—a ḥadīṣ attributed to 'Alī says
that angels have knowledge, but not lust and anger, beasts
anger and lust, while man has all three. Therefore if man
subdue lust and anger, and strive to attain perfect knowledge, he is above the angels, who attain perfection, as it

were by instinct, without any choice or conscious volition.
The text of the ḥadīs, with a commentary, will be found in
the *Magnavi*, 336. 5, and for a discussion of the whole
subject see *Akhlāqi Jalālī*, p. 23 seq., where the following
lines are quoted :

آدمی‌زاد طُرفه معجونیست

از فرشته سرِشته و حَیوان

گر کُند مَیلِ این شَوَد کم از این

وَر کُند قصدِ آن شَوَد به از آن

Angel and beast Man's wondrous leaven compose:
To these inclining less than these he grows,
But if he means the angel, more than those.

عالَمِ خاك از کُجا الخ ع٤—a variation of the well-
known verse :

چه نِسبت خاكرا با عالَمِ پاك

کُجا......کُجا is a very common idiom, to express
contrast.

جوان ٥—i.e. flourishing.

دادنِ جان كارِ ما—cf. Ḥāfiz (i. 476. 7) :

Not here, O Ḥāfiz, thou should'st timidly deny
The lover's lightest duty, for love's sake to die.

مُصطَفَی—'the Chosen one': Mohammed, whom the
Sūfīs identify with Universal Reason (عقلِ كُلّ), the first
emanation from the Absolute. See *Gulshani Rāz*, 19.

وَالضُّحَی ٦—Kor. XCIII. 1.

مه شكافت ٧—a famous miracle of the Prophet's.

کُداست—because her light is borrowed from the sun.

در دلِ ما الخ ۸ —referring to the dissolution of personality in the divine effulgence. 'The fissure of the moon typifies nothing else but renunciation of the external for the internal' (*Dabistān*, Vol. III. p. 201).

کز...چشمِ تو زآن سو چراست —lit., 'wherefore is thine eye on the side further from...?'

اَلَست ۹ —the words اَلَسْتُ بِرَبِّكُم, Am I not your Lord? (Kor. VII. 171), were addressed by God, as the commentators inform us, to all future generations of men, who were drawn forth from the loins of Adam in the shape of small ants. They answered بَلَى, Yes, and thus acknowledged God's right to judge their actions and to punish their sins. Such is the interpretation of Mohammedan orthodoxy. The Sūfīs, while accepting it in the main, lay more stress on the love, less on the power and vengeance, of God. It was the Beloved who claimed authority over the assembled souls (not insects), and love was the obligation which they avowed. Hence phrases like مست اَلَست (note on v. ٤). Cf. Ibnu 'l Fāriḍ, *Tā'iyya*, beyt 156 :

'Twas given me to draw nigh to Her on a day that
    had no yesterday ;
I saw Her when I made the covenant in the first
    moment of my existence.

کشتیِ قالب شکست —their bodies were effaced in the glory of the divine presence.

باز چو کشتیِ شکست —i.e. in death.

دریايِ جان ۱۰ may be understood either as Universal Soul (نفسِ کُلّ), which comprehends all particular souls, or as Absolute Being (see *Gulshani Rāz*, 562 seq.). But these alternatives are only different aspects of the One.

دُريمِ ‎ ‎—or—بدريا دُريمِ ‎ ‎؟ The double preposition is common in older Persian.

مَوجِ پياپَى—the continual efflux of Being by which phenomena are renewed. Cf.

عالَمِ جان بحرِ صفا صورتِ قالِب كَفِ او

بحرِ صفارا بِنگر چنك درين كف چه زدى

هيچ قرارى نبُوَد بر سرِ دريا كف‌را

زآنكه قرارش ندِهد جُنبِشِ مَوجِ مددى

كف همگى آب شَوَد تا بكنارى بَرَوَد

زآنكه دورنگى نبُوَد در دلِ بحرِ احدى

(T. 354. 9ᵃ).

The world of soul is a pure sea, whereof bodily form is
    the foam.
Contemplate the pure sea; why have you plunged your
    hand into the foam?
The foam never rests on the surface of the sea,
Because the motion of the replenishing wave does not
    allow it to rest.
All the foam becomes water, that it may reach the shore,
Because there is no bicolority in the heart of the ocean
    of Unity.

۱۲—۱۳—a figurative description of حال (ecstasy).

۱۳—this couplet is مُسَجَّع, i.e. it contains three middle rhymes in addition to the end-rhyme.

صورتِ تصویرِ الخ ‎١۴‎ — referring to such allegories as we find, e.g. in Jāmī's *Salāmān ū Absāl*, where Shāhi Yūnān typifies the First Intelligence (عقلِ کُلّ) and Prince Salāmān the soul of Man, while خردِ پیر will correspond to the Sage, who is above them both.

این همه روپوشهاست — a 'veil' is whatever prevents union with the Deity. "Some one said to Junaid (ob. 297 A. H.): 'I find that the shaikhs of Khorāsān recognise three species of veils; the first is human nature (خلق), the second is the world, and the third is concupiscence (نفس).' 'These,' answered Junaid, 'are veils on the hearts of the vulgar; the elect are veiled otherwise, namely by regarding works, by seeking future recompense for them, and by considering the favour of God'" (Jāmī, *Nafaḥātu 'l Uns*, p. 92).

درِ سر و چشمِ شُماست ‎١۵‎ — see note on XVII. ١١.

هست شُمارا دو سر ‎١۶‎ — all visible objects are but shadows of their archetypes in the Ideal world.

‎١٧‎ That phenomena derive from the Ideal what partial existence they possess is shown by the myriads of سرهایِ پاك ریخته در زیرِ خاك, i.e. of those who have annihilated self and embraced death in order to gain perfect union with the Ideal. Cf. note on II. ٣.

‎١٩‎ مشك, water-skin, is opposed to خُمِّ مَی, wine-jar, as Reason, logic, scientific method, to Love, illumination, intuitive knowledge.

سقا — for 'cup-bearer' in the translation read 'water-bearer.' The word usually has a tashdīd : سقّا, but may be scanned as an iambus whenever the metre requires it (cf.

T. 211. 4, 277. 8, 304. 5ᵃ, 307. 4ᵃ). So صَیاد instead of
صَیّاد (R. 190. 7). Conversely, a tashdīd is sometimes added
(see note on XXIII. ᵉ).

۲۰ نورِ تو الخ—although the rays of the sun of Being
are diffused and woven through creation, yet the sun itself
must be distinguished from the objects which vanish as
soon as its rays are withdrawn.

X.

۲ سزایِ آنکه الخ—lit. 'the punishment of him who
lives without thy face—is there a worse (punishment) than
that?'

زیستن aorist of زِیَد.

بدتر = بَتَر. In the second miṣrā' there is a play on the
double meaning of سزا.

۳ حوادث—phenomena, the outward shows of things.

بآشنا ... آشنایِ تو نیست—I have noted this ambiguous
use of آشنا in the following passages of the Dīvān : T. 82. 4,
83. 5, 96. 2ᵃ, 100. 3ᵃ, 162. 8ᵃ (cf. also Hāfiz, I. 392. 3, II.
510. 6). The words are not connected by derivation.

۴ بقا ندارد عالَمِ الخ—see VIII. ۹, note.

٥ رُخِ تُرا—the pun is obvious.

٦ خاك بر سرِ جانی—i.e. 'woe befall it!' Orientals
throw earth upon their heads as a sign of mourning.

۷ مُرغان—we shall often meet with this comparison of
the soul to a bird.

در هواي تو—see II. ١١, note.

خام ٨—a novice in the mysteries of divine love, opp. to پُخته.

سوخته آتِش بلا—cf. with the use of the iẓāfat to denote agency expressions like 'born of a woman.' بلا is love regarded as a probation.

نظامى ١٠—Niẓāmī (535—5 **A.H.**) composed, while yet a young man, the mystical **poem** entitled *Makhzanu 'l Asrār*, but his fame rests mainly on four great romances, *Khosrau ū Shīrīn, Lailā ū Majnūn, Iskandar-nāma*, and *Haft Paikar*. See Bacher, *Niẓāmī's Leben und Werke*, Ouseley's *Notices of Persian Poets*, p. 43, and the *Encyclopaedia Britannica* under 'Niẓāmī.'

آنکه بنظم ميگويد—probably Lailā.

XI.

باقِر ١—Persian is exceedingly rich in these prepositional adjectives, and their number might be increased to almost any extent.

با اين همه ٣ = nevertheless, cf. Italian 'con tutto ciò,' and Spanish 'con todo eso.'

به پيشِ وصالش مُكَدَّرست—see the explanation of سَوَادُ الْوَجْه, VI. ١, note, and cf. the passages quoted from Dionysius the Pseudo-Areopagite and Ludovic Blosius in Vaughan's *Hours with the Mystics*, Vol. I. pp. 287—290.

دهان‌باز ۴—the nīmfatḥa (ă) is not pronounced after ن preceded by a long vowel, unless that vowel is a diphthong, e.g. کُون, xv. ۳, but the older poets do not always observe this condition.

اَللّٰهُ أُكبَر—an exclamation of astonishment.

دل یافت دیدهٔ الخ ٥—this is the oculus cordis described by Hugo of St Victor: 'an eye within...one that beholds at once the past, the present, and the future; which diffuses through all things the keen brightness of its vision; which penetrates what is hidden, investigates what is impalpable; which needs no foreign light wherewith to see, but gazes by a light of its own, peculiar to itself' (Vaughan, *Hours with the Mystics*, Vol. I. p. 305).

دل و دیده پرور—a compound adjective (noun + aorist stem).

چاکرنوازیست ٦—Man is a plaything of the Deity: the favours which he receives are not the reward of merit, for whatever in him is good belongs to God.

در هوای تو ۷—cf. x. ۷.

هوا زو مُنَوَّرست—the pure soul is a mirror reflecting and radiating the divine sunbeams.

هر کس که بی مُراد شُد الخ ۸—cf. *Maṣnavi*, 232, 23:

I recognise another class of the saints
Who, closing their mouths, refrain from prayer.
On account of the contentment which these exalted ones
    command
Endeavour to avert what is decreed they hold unlawful.
They take an especial delight in what is decreed;
It is infidelity for them to seek escape.

Cf. the 'sainte indifférence' of the French Quietists, and

Eckhart in *Deutsche Mystiker*, Vol. II. p. 623 (translated by Vaughan, *Hours with the Mystics*, Vol. I. p. 152).

Nothing can fall out contrary to the desire of him who desires nothing: he may answer, like the darvīsh whom Bahlūl asked how he fared (*Masnavī*, 233, 3):

> I fare as one by whose majestic will
> The world revolves, floods rise and rivers flow,
> Stars in their courses move; yea, death and life
> Hang on his nod and fly to the ends of earth,
> His ministers of mourning or of joy.

٩ هر دوزخی الخ—referring to the ḥadīs: On the day of resurrection when some shall enter Paradise and others Hell, whoever has in his heart so much faith as a millet-seed, God will command that he be taken from the fire and cast into Kauṣar.

او فُتاد—it is impossible to decide whether the poet wrote this or اوفتاد, the older form of اُفتاد.

cf.—که عشق تو کوثرست

ای دل ار آبِ کوثرت باید

(T. 202. 13). آتشِ عشقِ را تو کوثر گیر

O heart, if thou must needs have the water of Kauṣar,
Deem Kauṣar to be the fire of love.

١٠ پایَم نمی رسد بزمین—the soul in her longing 'spernit humum fugiente penna.'

دست بر سرست—this gesture denotes sorrow and despair, cf. 'Aṭṭār, *Manṭiqu 'ṭṭair*, 215, 864; Ḥāfiz, II. 76. 1; 'Omar Khayyām, Quatrain 76. دست بر سر گرفتن or نهادن also means ' to salute.'

وَرِد احمر ۱۲—cf. Burns:

> O my love's like a red red rose
> That's newly sprung in June.

که آن – کآن ۱۵, which some MSS. read, is inadmissible. Two short syllables, namely, the last of the second and the first of the third foot, coalesce and make one long syllable (see I. ٦, note). It may be laid down as an invariable rule that when the second foot in Muzāri' is $|-\cup--|$ instead of the normal $|-\cup-\cup|$, the third foot becomes $|--\cup|$. Cf. XIII. ٦, ۱٤, ۱٥ ; XXXIX. ٤, ٥, ۸, etc.

کز قمران من اقمرم : اقمرست—cf. T. 70. 2ᵃ.

XII.

هر نقش را الخ ۱—this is the Platonic theory of Ideas. Cf. *Maṣnavī*, 32, 7 :

> When waves of thought from Wisdom's sea profound
> Arose, they clad themselves in speech and sound.
> The lovely forms a moment's sparkle gave,
> Then fell and mingled with the falling wave.
> So perish all things fair, to re-adorn
> The Beauteous One whence all fair things were born.

دل بد مدار—like بدل مشو ۲ (Hāfiz, II. 498. 4).

مَیَندیش for مندیش ۵.

٦—۱۰.—the evolution of Man. Cf. a fine passage in the *Maṣnavī* (278. 8, translated by Whinfield, p. 159) :

> از جمادی مُردم و نامی شُدم
> وَز نما مُردم بحَیوان سر زدم

مُردم از حَیوانی و آدم شُدم

پس چه ترسم کی ز مُردن کم شُدم

حملهٔ دیگر بمیرم از بشر

تا بر آرم از ملائك بال و پر

وَز مَلَك هم بایدم جُستن زجو

کُلُّ شَیْءٍ هالِك إِلّا وَجْهَهُ

بارِ دیگر از مَلَك قُربان شَوَم

آنچه اندر وَهم نآید آن شَوَم

پس عَدَم گُردم عَدَم عَدَم چون ارغنون

گُویدم كاِنّا إِلَیهِ راجِعون

آمدستی ٦—see Platts, *Persian Grammar*, Part I. § 98.

بَرو در آن یَم ١٠—lose your individuality in the Absolute.

عُمانست—the sea of 'Omān is the southernmost of three —the others are the بَحْرُ الفارس and the بَحْرُ اَلبَحْرَین— known collectively as the Persian Gulf.

وَلَد ١١—see VI. ١٣, note, and cf.

منم عیسَی خَوش‌خنده که عالَم شُد بمن زنده

ولی نِسبت ز حق دارم من از مریَم نمیدانم

(T. 255. 2).

I am sweet-smiling Jesus by whom the world is revived,
But my lineage is from God: I know nought of Mary.

XIII.

١ شِعار—the inner garment, opp. to دِثار.

نابوده به—this terse construction is very frequent, cf.
Ḥāfiz (I. 350. 2): دردم نِهُفته به, 'tis best to hide my woe,
and Sa‘dī, *Gulistān*, p. 24 : خوابش بُرده به, 'tis best that
sleep should overtake him.

cf.—بودنِ او غَیرِ عار نیست

نیست شَو نیست از خَودی زیراك
بتّر از هستیَت جِنایت نیست
(T. 139. 12ᵃ).

Become nought, nought from selfhood, because
There is no crime worse than thy being.

٢ بر—برِ یار, originally a substantive meaning 'breast,'
'side,' is used with the iẓāfat as a preposition = beside,
towards. It must be distinguished from the preposition
بر = up, on, etc., which is prefixed to verbs.

٣ هر كاو الخ—Man proposes, but God disposes,
therefore freewill is absence of self-will. See XI. ٨, note.

٥ مجاز = (استعاره,)' مُستعار, lit. 'used as a metaphor (استعاره),'
(profane) contrasted with حقیقی (divine). The subject
understood is غَیرِ این, i.e. all except love.

٦ معشوقِ مُردهرا—the world, which Ḥāfiz (I. 80. 7,
II. 232. 8) likens to a γυνὴ πολυάνωρ. In the second miṣrā‘
كنار = (a) bosom, (b) limit.

٧ مدد—see VI. ١٢, note.

٨ آن گُل كه از بهار بُوَد الخ—the celestial Rose

and Wine, unlike their counterfeits on earth, are wholly
free from defect : which is Not-being.

٩ نظّاره‌گر—for the tashdīd see XXIII. ٠, note.

درین راه—see I. ٢, note.

فی—هیچ مرك بَتَر ز انتظار نیست—cf. the proverb :
آلتَّاخیر آفات, 'in delay are calamities.' Procrastination
in love implies a lack of devotion, for as Sa‘dī says
(*Gulistān*, p. 21):

فرقست میانِ آن که یارش در بر

با آن که دو چشمِ انتظارش بر در

How blest is he who folds the loved one to his breast,
O'er him whose waiting eye still on the door doth rest !

The Sūfī must live in the present, regarding neither
yesterday nor to-morrow, but absorbed in the 'eternal Now'
of divine energy. Cf. Whinfield's *Maṣnavī*, p. 6, note on
ابْنُ آلْوَقْت.

١٠ بر نقد قلب زن الخ—a play on قلب, which means
'heart,' and also 'adulterated coin.'

گَرت گوشوار نیست—'if you are not a slave' i.e. of a
base disposition. Among Orientals a ring in the ear is
the badge of servitude (cf. حلقه بگوش = thrall). The
phrase corresponds to اگر قلب نیستی in the preceding
line.

١١ بر اسپ تن الخ—this metaphor explains itself.
Let the soul refuse to be led astray by the senses, that she
may soar up to God on the wings of love.

اندیشها ۱۲ —not only worldly thoughts, but also intellectual apprehensions and all operations of the mind.

چون ساده شُد ز نقش الخ ۱۳ —when the soul has thoroughly purified and emptied herself of sensible forms and images, she will be transformed to the pure and simple light and there dwell in a state of perfection. This light is always ready to be communicated to the soul, but cannot pour in so long as she is masked and hampered with natural forms and veils (Juan de la Cruz). Cf.

روح چو از مِهرِ کِنارت گِرِفت

روح شَوَد پیشِ تو جُمله نُقوش (T. 74. 9ª).

When the spirit lovingly embraces thee,
  In thy presence all images become spirit.

سادهروی —one who has no hair on his face, effeminate. Cf. the use of 'glaber' in Latin (Catullus, LXI. 142, etc.).

کورا ز راستگوئی الخ ۱۴ — Kor. XXXIII. 53:

وَٱللَّهُ لَا يَسْتَحْيِي مِنَ ٱلْحَقِّ, and God is not ashamed of the truth.

ز تمیز ۱۵ —i.e. by being cleaned. Cf.

آینهات دانی چرا غمّاز نیست

زآنکه زنگار از رُخش مُمتاز نیست

(*Maṣnavī*, 5. 8).

Dost thou know why from the mirror glancing rays are
  furnished not?
'Tis because the rusty surface, where they strike, is burnished not.

کورا غُبار نیست —but cf.

جان چو آئینهٔ صافی است برو تن کُردست

حُسن در ما ننماید چو بزیرِ کُردیم

(T. 238. 11ª).

The soul resembles a clear mirror: the body is dust
upon it;

Our beauty is invisible, since we are under the dust.

کین رازدار آمد الخ ۱٦—the heart cannot reveal the
bewildering rapture of divine knowledge, whereas the
mirror is a tell-tale (غمّاز).

XIV.

This poem affords an example of the rhetorical artifice
called جواب و سُوال, Question and Answer.

جوشی ۲—i.e. with fervid love.

جَرَحَ ٥ گُواه جرحست—cf. the Arabic expression:
جَرَحَ ٱلشَّهَادَة he (the judge) invalidated the testimony (see Lane
under جرح).

تردامن—like دامن آلوده (cf. Jeremiah, ch. ii. 34). In
T. 310. 6ª the word is used in its literal sense:

چشمِ عُشّاق ز چشمِ رُخِ تو تردامن

By the eye of thy countenance the eyes of lovers are
fringed with tears.

عدلند—for the adjectival force cf. ترازو عدلست, the
balance is just, and see Lane under عَدْلُ.

غرامت—the ordinary meaning is 'penalty,' 'forfeit,'
but according to the *Ghiyasu 'llughat* it sometimes
= پشیمانی, 'shame,' 'contrition.' Thus بی غرامت may
be translated 'having no cause for shame,' i.e. 'innocent.'

٨ قَيصر—the Arabicised form of Cæsar.

٩ آن ملامت—worldly censure, which is apt to produce backsliding. Cf. Hāfiz, II. 496. 6 :

> I said, 'They blame my fond pursuit of thee;
> Who ever loved and lived from slander free?'

١٠ ره سلامت—cf. the proverb (Freytag, Vol. I. p.
14): إِنَّ ٱلسَّلَامَةَ مِنْهَا (ٱلدُّنْيَا sc.) تَرْكُ مَا فِيهَا, Salvation
from the world is to renounce the things of the world.
But the poet, be it remarked, does not value زُهد except
as a means (رو) of gaining the ultimate knowledge of God
which only union can give. Cf.

> زُهد اندر كاشتن كوشيدنست
>
> معرِفت آن كِشترا روئيدنست
>
> (*Maṣnavī*, 541, 5).

> Striving to sow is abstinence,
> Making the seed grow is knowledge.

١١ آفت—see notes on III. ٣, V. ٧, X. ٨.

استِقامت—Jurjānī (*Kitābu 'tta'rīfāt*, p. 19) gives three
definitions of this word. The last is: 'continuance, the
non-preference of any thing to God.' Here, I think, it
signifies the permanent spiritual condition (مقامر), which
never 'deviates into sense,' opposed to the momentary
state of exaltation (حال).

١٢ This beyt occurs in Hāfiz, II. 496. 3, where the
first miṣrā' reads :

> هرچند كآزمودمر از وَى نبود سودمر

The proverb will be found in Freytag, Vol. II. p. 730.

XV.

The uncontracted rhyme, ‏انه است‎ —, where however the ‏ه‎ is elided in pronunciation, does not appear in any of the MSS. except V.

Lines ‏۱‎—‏۶‎ give an allegorical picture of the Temple of Love.

‏چغانه‎—the *Burhāni Qāṭi'* describes this instrument as 'a piece of wood resembling a weaver's comb (‏مُشته‎), split at one end and adorned with bells.'

‏این صورتِ بُت الخ‎ ‏۲‎—indifference of religions is a cardinal Sūfī doctrine. All forms and objects of worship are regarded as 'broken lights' of the One Being: hence idolatry is essentially unification (*Gulshani Rāz*, 867), and the sincere idolater more praiseworthy than the orthodox hypocrite. Cf. the following quatrain (T. 365. 5):

‏در بُتکده تا خیالِ معشوقهٔ ماست‎

‏رفتن بطوافِ کعبه از عینِ خطاست‎

‏گر کعبه ازو بوی ندارد کُنش است‎

‏با بوي وصالِ او کُنش کعبهٔ ماست‎

While my loved phantom dwells in the pagoda's bound,
'Twere mortal sin, should I the Ka'ba compass round.
The Ka'ba is but a church, if there his trace be lost;
The church my only Ka'ba, while he there is found.

‏که در کُون نگنجد‎ ‏۳‎—alluding to the ḥadīs: ‏لَا یَسَعُنِی أَرْضِی وَلَا سَمَائِی وَلَٰکِن یَسَعُنِی قَلْبُ عَبْدِی الْمُؤْمِنِ‎, My earth and heaven contain me not, but the heart of my believing servant contains me.

‏همه فعل و بهانست‎—i.e. these names are wholly meta-phorical.

۴ این خانه طلسمست —because it protects a 'hidden treasure' (cf. the last beyt and see notes on IV. ۲, VIII. ۳). Prof. Bevan proposes to take the words in a different sense: 'this house is under a charm' and therefore dangerous to one who should imprudently violate its sanctity (see Ṭabarī, p. 829, Nöldeke, *Geschichte der Sasaniden*, p. 38). طلسم is probably the Greek τέλεσμα.

(T. مخمور ز بادهٔ شبانه —this may = مستِ شبانست 299. 8ᵃ), or مخمور از شب گُذشته, which I prefer.

۵ بیت و ترانست —love is expressed in music and song. The *Maṣnavī* opens with an invocation to the reed-flute (نای). Cf. Rousselot, *Les Mystiques Espagnols*, p. 298, note.

۸ بجانِ تو —as the value of an oath depends upon the dignity of its object, the Persians, who are born flatterers, swear by you or something of yours, e.g. بقبرِ پدرت, by thy father's grave, بمرگ خودت, by thy death (the greatest possible calamity), etc.

۹ This couplet describes the dazzling effect of divine beauty.

۱۰ زهره —see v. ۶, note.

۱۱ سرِ زُلفِ تو — phenomena which veil God are likened to the tresses with which a coquette conceals her face. The poet means to say that, when the internal mirror is cleansed from 'self,' the illusion of plurality disappears.

۱۲ زنان دست بُریدند — Kor. XII. 31: 'and she (Zulaikhā) said (to Joseph), "Come forth to them." And when they beheld him they marvelled at him and cut their hands and said, "God forbid! this is not a man, but an exalted angel."' By cutting their hands the women showed that they had lost their senses and were absorbed in the Beloved.

تاریك بُوَد الخ ۱۴ —cf. the story (Whinfield's *Masnavi*,
p. 47) of the lover who came to his friend's house and
sought admittance. 'Who is there?' ''Tis I.' 'Then
begone.' After a year he returned and being asked the
same question replied, ''Tis thou who art at the door,'
whereupon his friend received him, saying, 'There is no
room for two "I's" in one house.' See also XIII. ۹, note.

دوكَانست ۱۵ —unity is incompatible with the existence of the fleshly nature (هوا).

در بیشهٔ شیران رَو ۱۶ —engage in the 'Greater Warfare' against the passions, each one of which is a شیر باطن
or moral lion (*Masnavi*, 37. 4). Cf. Redhouse's *Masnavi*,
p. 101 seq. Juan de la Cruz (p. 180) in his commentary on
stanza XX. of the *Cántico Espiritual*, l. 2, 'Leones, ciervos,
gamos saltadores,' explains 'leones' as 'the fierceness and
violence of the irascible faculty,' and again (stanza XXXVI.
last line, 'Entremos mas adentro en la espesura') he
says (p. 207): 'Hence this thicket (espesura), which the
soul desires to enter, may very properly be understood to
mean the throng and multitude of troubles and tribulations,
entrance into which is desired by the soul, because nothing
delights and profits it more than suffering.' Some may
prefer to take در بیشهٔ شیران رَو as meaning: Join the
ranks of fearless lovers (cf. *Masnavi*, 37. 12: 'the true lion
is he who conquers himself'), and this interpretation agrees
better with آنجا in beyt ۱۷.

پس در وَهمِ تو الخ ۱۷ —you invest the dark wood of
sensuality with imaginary terrors; it is not so formidable
as you suppose. The love and mercy of God will enable
you to overcome every danger.

> Avert thy face from fancy, by the code
> Of Love convicted, whether fancy's slave
> Or foul idolater, of equal crime.　　　(Jāmī.)

Cf. the verses (*Maṣnavī*, 6. 8; Redhouse, p. 6, l. 34 seq.)
in which imagination is described as governing all human
actions:

نیست‌وَش باشد خیال اندر جهان

تو جهانی بر خیالی بین روان

بر خیالی صُلحِشان و جنگِشان

بر خیالی نامِشان و ننگِشان

XVI.

٣　The طبل باز is used to startle water-fowl, which,
as they fly into the air, are attacked by a hawk (*Bahāri
'Ajam*). According to a gloss on the *Maṣnavī*, 'when
the huntsman wishes to call his bird back, he beats a
drum: the hawk, having an affection for the drum, returns
speedily' (بهوای آن مُعاودت کُند).

٥　دفع کُفتن—to repulse. Cf. ترک کُفتن, to abandon.

٦　مُژدهٔ رَیحانم آرزوست—an allusion to Kor. LVI.
87–88: 'and if he be of those who draw nigh unto God,
he shall enjoy peace and bounty (رَیحان) and a garden of
pleasure.'

٧　آن نان و آبِ چرخ—the petty doles of Fortune,
contrasted with divine beneficence.

نهنگ—نهنگم is the crocodile, or, generally, any large

fish. For عُمَّان see XII. ١٠, note, and for what may be called the 'metrical' tashdīd, XXIII. ٠, note.

٨ وا أَسَفَاهَا—Kor. XII. 84: 'and he (Jacob) turned from them and cried, "O how I grieve for Joseph!"' (يَا أَسَفَى عَلَى يُوسُفَ).

٩ آوارِكِّي كُوه الخ—cf. Sa'dī, *Gulistān*, p. 62:

Since God was my sole occupation, I ran
To bare crags and moors undiscovered of man.

١٠ This couplet probably refers to Shaikh Najmu'ddīn Kubrā (see his life in Jāmī's *Nafaḥatu 'l Uns*, pp. 480—487), who was murdered by the Moguls (كُفَّارِ تتار) in the year 618 A.H. 'At the moment of his martyrdom he had seized the forelock of an infidel, and after his death ten men could not release it from his grasp. Some say that in the following lines Maulānā Jalālu'ddīn Rūmī alludes to this event and his (spiritual) relationship to the Shaikh':

(۱) مَا از آن مُحتشمانیم كه ساغر گيرند
نه از آن مُفلسْكان كه بُز لاغر گيرند

(۲) بِيَكى دست مَى خالِص ايمان نوشند
بِيَكى دست دِگر پرچم كافر گيرند

The ode from which these beyts are taken begins in T at p. 164. 6ª. They are not immediately connected: (١) is 164. 6ª, and (٢) 165. 1. As we are chiefly concerned with (٢), I add to my translation the beyt (164. 12ª) which precedes it in T.

We are of the lords who lift the goblet,
Not of the beggars who grasp at a lean goat.

Make fast the door and give us wine, for the hour is
    come
When the sallow-cheeked receive crimson wine.
With one hand they quaff the pure wine of faith,
With the other they grasp the forelock of an infidel.

Thus (٢) corresponds exactly to the first miṣrā‘ of ١٠. For
پرچمِ کافر we have جامِ باده, and for مَیِ خالصِ ایمان
(the dark tresses of the Beloved are called ‘ infidel’ because
they veil his unity) زُلفِ یار. The reference to Najmu'ddīn
is confirmed by the fact that Sulaimān Khān, the Bābī,
recited this couplet (یك دست جامِ باده الخ) at his execution. See Browne's *Episode of the Bāb*, Vol. ii. p. 334.

رقصی—cf. Hāfiz, i. 470. 5 :

Come, let us under the sword go merrily dancing to-
    gether ;
    Fortunate he at the last whom thou, Beloved, hast
        slain !

١١ شیرِ خُدا—‘Alī. It is noteworthy that our poet,
notwithstanding his Sunnī prepossessions, should have left
more than one eloquent ode to testify his admiration for
the Shī‘ite chief. The language of the following extract
is quite similar to that habitually used by Sūfīs in praising
Mohammed :

‘Alī existed since the world assumed a form,
‘Alī existed since the beginning of space and time.
'Twas for ‘Alī's sake that Man was worshipped by
    the angels :
Man was like a *qibla* and ‘Alī was the object of
    worship.

'Alī was Adam and Seth and Job and Enoch
And Joseph and Jonah and Hūd.

(T. 174. 2, 4, 5.)

Cf. the poem (T. 6. 1 seq.) which is the exordium of the
first Dīvān. 'Alī's bravery was never doubted, and he is
therefore fitly joined with Rustam, the national hero of
Persia. Both stand here as types of the divine perfection.

دستان—for the story of Zāl, see *Shāhnāma*, Vol. I.
p. 131 seq. This name was given to Zāl by the Sīmurgh,
his legendary foster-nurse, who explains it (*ib.* p. 138):

I called thee Dastāni Zand
Because thy sire wrought with thee deceit (دستان)
and guile.

١٢　cf.—در دستِ هر که هست الخ

این بهار و باغِ بیرون عکسِ باغِ باطِن است

یك قُراضه است این همه عالَمِ و باطِن هست کان

(T. 54. 10).

This outward spring and garden is the reflexion of the
garden spiritual;
All this world is a filing, and the spiritual is the mine.

١٣　عقیقِ خُرد—i.e. earthly goods, Mammon. لرزان
describes the sparkling lustre of the stone.

١٤　پُر شِکایت—زین خلقِ الخ is here a noun = com-
plainant, but if we read

زین خلقِ پُر شِکایت گِریانم و ملول

it becomes an adjective qualifying خلق. For the scansion,
in this case, see XI. ١٠, note.

زاري ٍ مستانم ٖ آرزوست—cf. notes on v. ٧, l. ٩.

فرعَون ١٥—Pharaoh is to Moses as خیال (imagination) to حقیقت (divine truth).

ظُلم—suggesting ظُلمت (darkness), and hence appropriately followed by نور in the second miṣrāʻ.

یافت ١٦—the abbreviated form of یافته. As a rule, the past participle retains final ه except in some compounds. Cf. e.g. خواب آلود, خُدا داد, پاکزاد.

ز رشك ِ عام ١٧—not 'because of vulgar envy' (as in the text), but 'because I am jealous of the crowd.' The sentiment is that of Horace: Odi profanum vulgus et arceo.

دی شَیخ با چراغ الخ ١٨—this anecdote of Diogenes the Cynic (اَلْکَلْبی) is found in the *Lives of the Philosophers* by Diogenes Laertius, whose words are: λύχνον μεθ' ἡμέραν ἅψας περιῄει λέγων "ἄνθρωπον ζητῶ" (ed. C. G. Cobet, p. 142). It is told at greater length in the *Maṣnavī*, p. 459. 15 seq.; Whinfield's *Maṣnavī*, p. 257. Mīrkhwānd (*Rauẓatu 'ṣṣafā* translated by Rehatsek, Vol. II. p. 279 seq.) gives a short notice of Diogenes and quotes a number of his sayings. The variant نامِزاج means 'ill-tempered.'

که—کز often introduces a speech, without any preceding verb, such as پُرسیدن or گُفتن.

خُود کار ِ من الخ ١٩—cf. VI. ١١.

پنهان ز دیدها ٢٠—as the past participle in Persian has both an active and a passive signification, دیده is the seeing eye as well as the object seen.

آن آشکار صُنعت ِ پنهان — cf. *Maṣnavī*, 118. 5:

کارکُن در کارگه باشد نِهان

تو بَرو در کارگه بینش عیان

کار چون بر کارکُن پرده تنید

خارج آن کار نتوانیش دید

The Worker is hidden in the work-shop;
Enter the work-shop and behold him face to face.
Since a veil is drawn over the Worker by his work,
Apart from his work you cannot see him.

(The 'work-shop,' as the poet proceeds to explain, is عَدَم,
Not-being, and 'enter the work-shop' = annihilate self.)

٢١ کُو—perhaps an imitation of the Koranic قُل.

٢٢ cf.—من خَود ربابِ عشقم

من چنگِ تو ام بر هر رگِ من

تو زخمه زنی من من تنتنم (T. 236. 3).

I am thy lute, on every vein (chord) of mine
Thou strikest the quill, and I vibrate.

And the beautiful lines of the Silurist:

> Thus doth God key disorder'd man,
>   Which none else can,
> Tuning his breast to rise or fall;
> And by a sacred, needful art
>   Like strings stretch every part,
> Making the whole most musical.

یایِ فاعل the—عشقم ربابی است the ی in ربابی is یایِ فاعل
(ی of the agent), not the یایِ وَحدت. Translate: 'Love
is my rebeck-player.' ربابی in this sense is found again

(T. 335. 3ᵃ). See a description and drawing of the rabāb in Lane's *Modern Egyptians*, Vol. II. p. 70 seq.

عُثمان—the Caliph 'Othmān was famous for his personal beauty, and may therefore, like Joseph, represent symbolically the divine Beloved. 'Othmān's name occurs in 'the apostolical succession of saints and prophets' (*Maṣnavī*, 121. 11 seq.; Whinfield, p. 73 seq.). But why should it be used here in connexion with the rabāb? I can only suggest that نغمهٔ عُثمان may have been the name of a particular tune called, perhaps, after some contemporary musician.

من هُدهُدم الخ ‏٢٥—see II. ٦, note.

XVII.

With this magnificent ode, which has been admirably rendered in English verse by Professor Falconer (Forbes's *Persian Grammar*, p. 159), the reader should compare two poems of Henry Vaughan, entitled 'The Search' and 'The Dwelling-place' (Vol. I. pp. 33 and 241 of the Muses' Library Edition). Unfortunately the text is not found in any of the MSS. which I have consulted except V ; that given by Forbes (p. ٣٨) agrees with R.

من آن روز بودم الخ ‏١—referring to the pre-existence of the soul (cf. the ḥadīs : أَنَا نَبِيٌّ وَ آدَمُ بَيْنَ آلْمَاءِ وَ آلطِّينِ, I was a prophet when Adam was water mingled with clay). In the beginning 'God was, and there was nought beside him.' The first thing created was the soul of man (أَوَّلُ مَا خَلَقَ آللَّهُ رُوحِى), which lived and moved and had its being in God : mankind were ψυχαὶ καθαραὶ καὶ νοῦς

συνημμένος τῇ ἀπάσῃ οὐσίᾳ, μέρη ὄντες τοῦ νοητοῦ, οὐκ ἀφω-
ρισμένα οὐδ' ἀποτετμημένα, ἀλλ' ὄντες τοῦ ὅλου (Plotinus,
quoted by Ritter and Preller, 6th Ed. p. 509). The Dīvān
is full of passages affirming the soul's original purity,
lamenting its fallen state in the world, and bidding it 'flow
back to the burning fountain whence it came.' Cf. with
this beyt:

پیش از آن کاندر جهان باغ و رز و انگور بود

از شرابِ لا یزالی جانِ ما مخمور بود

ما ببغدادِ ازل لافِ أَنَا ٱلْحَقّ میزدیم

پیش از آن کاین دار و گیر و نُکتهٔ منصور بود

پیش از آن کاین نقشِ دل بر آب و گِل مِعمار شُد

در خراباتِ حقایق عَیشِ ما معمور بود

(T. 185. 2ᵃ).

Ere there was garden and vine and grape in the world,
Our soul was intoxicated with immortal wine.
In the Baghdād of eternity we proudly were proclaiming
    "I am God"
Before the tumult and mystery of Manṣūr.
Ere this image of the spirit became a builder on water
    and clay (the body),
Our life was founded in the tavern of celestial truths.

(For Manṣūr Ḥallāj cf. VI. ١٢, note, and see Herbelot's
Bibliothèque Orientale under Hallage, Ibn Khallikān,
Vol. I. p. 423, Jāmī's *Nafaḥātu 'l Uns*, p. 168, 'Aṭṭār's
Tadhkiratu 'l Auliyā in Tholuck's *Blüthensammlung*, pp.
310—326. He was executed at Baghdād in 309 A.H.)

اسما—'and He taught Adam the names of all things'
(Kor. II. 29).

۲ ز ما شُد الخ —i.e. Man was the final cause of creation. Cf. the ḥadīs̱: لَوْلَاكَ لَوْلَاكَ مَا خَلَقْتُ ٱلْأَفْلَاكَ, But for thee, but for thee, I had not created the heavens.

كَآنجا من و ما نبود —cf. Jāmī's *Yūsuf ū Zulaikhā*, p. 16:

> In solitude, where Being signless dwelt,
> And all the Universe still dormant lay
> Concealed in selflessness, One Being was
> Exempt from ' I '- and ' Thou '-ness, and apart
> From all duality.
>
>   (Translated by Mr E. G. Browne.)

۳ زُلف —phenomena. See note on xv. ۱۱.

۴ چلیپا — Arabic صلیب.

۵ بُتخانه —a centre of Hindoo idol-worship.

دَیر —a Magian fire-temple.

۷ کوهِ قاف —according to popular belief, this mountain, which Oriental geographers have localised in Caucasus, is five hundred parasangs high, and encompasses the whole earth. It is the fabled haunt of the dīvs and perīs, as well as of the

عنقا —or Sīmurgh, a mysterious bird, perhaps identical with Sindbād's Roc (رُخ), by which the Sūfīs (e.g. 'Aṭṭār in the *Manṭiqu 'ṭṭair*) often represent the unknown God. See Lane's *Arabian Nights*, Vol. III. p. 91, and Muṭarrizī's commentary on أَغْرَبَ مِنَ ٱلْعَنْقَاءَ (Ḥarīrī, Vol. II. p. 678), the text of which, accompanied by a translation, will be found in Garcin de Tassy's *Les Oiseaux et les Fleurs*, p. 218 seq.

از ابن سيناش حال ۹ —the pronominal suffix belongs to حال. Abū 'Alī Ḥusain Ibn 'Abdullāh Ibn Sīnā (Avicenna) was born near Bokhārā (370 A.H.), and soon became celebrated for his researches in science, medicine, and metaphysics. As the champion of free-thought against dogma, he gave great offence to the 'ulamā, who accused him of blasphemy. He concluded an adventurous and somewhat Bohemian life, at the age of fifty-eight, in his patron's gaol. Consult for further information Herbelot's *Bibliothèque Orientale* under Sina, Ibn Khallikān, Vol. I. p. 440, and the article 'Avicenna' in the *Encyclopaedia Britannica*.

قَابَ قَوْسَيْن ۱۰ —'then he (Gabriel) approached (the Prophet), and drew nigh, until he was at the distance of two bow-lengths, or nearer' (Kor. LIII. 8–9). But the Sūfīs interpret the passage as signifying the approach of Mohammed himself to the divine presence.

مَنْ عَرَفَ نَفْسَهُ ۱۱ —cf. the ḥadīs: اندر دل خويشتن عَرَفَ رَبَّهُ, He who knows himself knows his Lord (and see xv. ۳, note). The idea, common to all mystics, of the immanence or indwelling of God in the soul, is by Jalālu'ddīn and other Sūfī writers pushed forward unfalteringly to the inevitable conclusion :

دلا جُستيم سر تا سر نديدم در تو جُز دلبر

مخوان اى دل مرا كافر اگر گويَم تو خَود اوئى

(T. 331. 2ª).

O heart, we have searched from end to end : I saw in thee nought save the Beloved.

Call me not infidel, O heart, if I say, 'Thou thyself art He.'

آنانکه طلبتگارِ خُدائید خُدائید

حاجت بطلب نیست شُمائید شُمائید

چیزی که نکردید کُم از بهرِ چه جوئید

کس غَیرِ شُما نیست کُجائید کُجائید

(T. 188. 6ª).

Ye who in search of God, of God, pursue,
Ye need not search, for God is you, is you!
Why seek a something which was missing ne'er?
Save you none is, but you are—where, O where?

بِجُز شمسِ تبریز الخ ١٢—as subject and object, lover
and Beloved, are really identical (cf. T. 331. 2ª, above),
love itself cannot be predicated of any being except the
One, symbolised here by Shamsi Tabrīz.

XVIII.

میریزد و میروید ١—just as the existence of the
phenomenal world is renewed every instant by a fresh
influx from the fountain of Being, there is in the soul
also a perpetual ebb and flow of divine grace. Cf.

پَیمانه ایست این جان پَیمانه این چه داند

کز پاك میپذیرد در خاك میرساند

در عشقِ بیقرارش پَیمودنست کارش

از عرش میستاند بر فرش میفشاند

(T. 177. 8).

This soul is a measure: how should the measure know
That it is receiving of spirit and conveying to dust?
Its task is to measure in restless love,
Taking from heaven above, scattering o'er earth below.

از خاك بروَيد سر ٢—'a new life is born.' So Hāfiz
says, alluding to spiritual regeneration (I. 430. 3):

Authority for union with thee is given to any one
Who under thy sword continually receives a new head,
    like the candle.

Cf.

زِهی خورشیدِ جان‌افزا که یك تابش چو شُد پَیدا

هزاران جانِ اِنسانی بروَید از گِلِ تیره

                                        (T. 93. 12).

Welcome, soul-producing sun! When a single ray of
    thine hath appeared,
Thousands of human souls shoot forth from black
    (barren) clay.

No doubt the poet had in his mind, if not before his eye,
the sudden growth and blossoming of spring flowers:
hence سر. بروَید is the natural antithesis to پائی.

    This seems the most probable explanation of a rather
enigmatical phrase. Other passages, however, suggest that
the meaning may be: Why, for the sake of one poor life,
lose Him, whose love has claimed so many victims that he
cannot take a step without a severed head (cf. II. ٣)
starting up at his feet?

جان داند و جان داند ٣—perhaps a reminiscence
of 'Omar Khayyām, Quatrain 401:

او داند او داند او داند او.

Cf.

$$\text{آن چیز که دارد او او داند و او داند}$$
(T. 161. 2ᵃ).

خانه ٥—خانهٔ جان .i.e

کز رخت بپردازم—in order to become devoid of 'self.'
Cf.

$$\text{رختی که داشتیم بیَغما ببُرد عشق}$$
$$\text{از سود و از زیان و ز بازار فارغیم}$$
(T. 146. 11).

Love carried off as plunder the chattels which we
    possessed;

We are independent of profit and loss and market.

میکاهم—cf. v. ٦, and

$$\text{رها کُن تا که چون ماهی کُدازانِ غمش باشم}$$
$$\text{که تا چون مه نکاهم من ز مه زآن پس نیَغزایم}$$
(T. 246. 1).

Let me, like the moon, melt away in anxious love
    of him;

For until I wane like the moon, I cannot wax more
    than the moon thereafter.

(T reads بیَغزایم; if this be correct, we must also read
بکاهم.)

افزوید—the grammars do not mention this anomalous
form. Only two other examples are known to me, viz.
نفرسوید and نیَغزوید, which occur as rhymes (T. 167.
1 seq.).

همان ارزد الخ ٦—here the pɔet would seem to have
anticipated Walpole's maxim that every man has his price:
he means to say that the worth of a man is higher in

proportion to the excellence of his ideal. Cf. Eckhart
(*Deutsche Mystiker*, Vol. II. p. 199): 'The words of
Augustine, "Man is what he loves," are to be understood
in this way. If he loves a stone, he is a stone; if he loves
a man, he is a man; if he loves God—I dare not say more,
for if I said that he would then be God, ye might stone
me.' Freytag (Vol. III. p. 644) gives a proverb to the
same effect: قَدْرُ ٱلرَّجُلِ عَلَى قَدْرِ هِمَّتِه, the dignity of a
man depends upon the height of his aspiration. The view
of Jalālu'ddīn himself is plainly expressed in the following
beyts:

بر هرچه همیلرزی میدان که همآن ارزی

زین روی دلِ عاشق از عرش فُزون باشد

(R. 64. 2).

> Know that your value is equal to the object for which
> you are quivering with desire;
> On this account the lover's heart is higher than the
> empyrean.

(Cf. the ḥadīs quoted by Whinfield on *Gulshani Rāz*, 214).

جُنبِش هر ذرّه باصلِ خَود است

هر چه بُوَد مَیلِ کسی آن شَوَد

جان و دل از جذبهٔ مَیل و هَوَس

همصِفَتِ دلبر و جانان شَوَد

(T. 184. 10).

> The motion of every atom is toward its origin;
> A man comes to be the thing on which he is bent.
> By the attraction of fondness and yearning the soul
> and the heart
> Assume the qualities of the Beloved and the soul of
> souls.

XIX.

This poem is a metaphorical description of the mystic's journey to and in God (see *Gulshani Rāz*, 288 seq.).

١ ماه يكی —the Beloved.

٢ مرا بربود —i.e. transported me out of 'self.' The first stage is فنا, return from phenomenal to Absolute Being.

٥ (٩ .IX) كِشتیِ وجودم —like كِشتیِ قالب.

٦ In the second stage of his journey (بقا) the pilgrim abides in God and experiences with Him the differentiation of Unity into plurality.

موج بزد بحر آن —God revealed himself by successive emanations. For موج see IX. ١١, note.

خِرَد —Universal Reason, the first emanation.

افكَند در آوازه —proclaimed the majesty of its Maker.

٧ كرد كفی —He created phenomena. Cf. the passage, T. 354. 9ᵃ seq., quoted on p. 225.

٨ الخ جِسم كفِ پاره هر —outward form is an illusion which dissolves at the command of God.

٩ تبریز الحق شمس —see XVII. ١٢, note. Vision and union are not to be grasped by intellectual effort. They are acts of grace.

XX.

مكش تو چو تيرش ا —he who seeks God must not rely on his own exertions, but rather allow himself, wisely passive, to be swept along by the unseen current of divine energy in which all finite existences are flowing backwards to their original source. Cf.

جذبهٔ شاخِ آبرا از بیخ تا بالا کشید

همچنانکه جذبه جانرا بر کشد بی نردبان

(T. 54. 1).

The bough's attraction drew the sap from root to summit,
Even as attraction draws the soul upward without a ladder.

که یك جذبِ حق به ز صد کوشِش است

نِشانها چه باشد برِ بی‌نِشان

(T. 282. 9ᵃ).

Since one impulse from God is better than a hundred efforts,
How should there be clues to Him who has no clue?

چو عنکبوت ز دوده لُعابِ اندیشه

دِگر مباف که پوسیده پود و تار بُوَد

چو تو نگوئی گُفتِ تو گُفتِ او باشد

چو تو نبافی بافنده کِردِگار بُوَد

(T. 181. 4ᵃ).

Weave no more with soot, like the spider, a web of care
Wherein both woof and warp are rotten.
While thou art silent, His speech is thy speech;
While thou weavest not, God is the weaver.

چو مُرغِ گُمانت ٥ —quick as the flight of fancy.

یقین —truth known intuitively and not depending on logical demonstration.

این و آن ٦ —phenomena, plurality.

ز عشقِ کُل ٧ —see XI. ۱۲, note.

که گُفت نیز نتابی ٨ —as it seems uncertain whether the construction نتابی گُفت is admissible, I now prefer to read نتانی, the shorter form of نتوانی.

آن فُلان —cf. VI. ٨.

XXI.

شیوَه آموزد ۱ —surpasses in coquetry.

بجادوئی —cf. Ḥāfiz, I. 218. 1: فریبِ چشمِ جادویَت, and III. 376. 1:

May thine eye, schooled in Babylonian magic,
Never, O Lord, forget its enchantments!

بر دوزد —for the meaning 'shut' cf. Niẓāmī, Iskandar-nāma, 55. 9: گُشاده دل و دیده بر دوخته, and for the interpretation 'fascinate' cf. the use of چشم بند (Vullers, sub voc.). There may be an allusion to the practice of sorcerers, who deprive a man of sleep by making his effigy in wax (که از مومِ خود خوابرا دوختند, Iskandar-nāma, 58. 18), sticking it while hot into his eye, and uttering a charm over it (Clarke's Sikandar-nāma, p. 46). Possibly, however, the literal sense of بر دوختن is 'pierce' (see e.g. a passage from the Anvāri Suhailī in Spiegel's Chresto-

mathia Persica, p. 39, ll. 17—19), and the frequent comparison of glances to arrows supports this view.

باری ۲—once, once for all. It modifies or restricts a statement بهمه حال, القِصّه, like (برای تقلیل وانحصار), and بهر حال.

نیامیزد—in Arabic prosody the long vowels و and ی, when they form the ridf, are treated as rhymes. Persian poets do not avail themselves of this liberty. The present examples are perhaps unique.

هلا رو بر رسن‌بازی ۴—the heart entangled in the Beloved's tresses typifies (1) Man bewildered and held captive by worldly illusions (see xv. ۱۱, note), and (2) as here, the lover spell-bound in contemplation of the mysterious beauty of God. For the simile of زُلف and رسن cf. T. 90. 5:

رسنِ زُلفِ تو گر زآنکه درین دامِ اُفتد

صد دل و جان بزند دست بهر پیچ و شِکن

If the rope of thy tress should fall into this snare (pit),
A hundred hearts and souls would clutch every loop and
twist.

کجا پروانه تا سوزد—where is one who will devote his life for love's sake? Sa'dī has a delightful version of this allegory (*Būstān*, p. 224 seq.).

زو ۵—short for زود. Cf. بو for بُوَد in the phrase بو که.

چنبر شَو—I have translated these words literally in order to preserve the play on چنبر and رسن, which occurs again (T. 70. 6ª, 340. 10ª). چنبر is (1) a ring or hoop such as acrobats use in performing their feats, (2) a ringlet

چنبر زُلفش, Hāfiz, III. 216. 2). چنبر شُدن is equivalent
to كِرِفتار شُدن, i.e. to be made captive, and this, probably,
is the meaning which the poet himself attached to the
words, although he must have been conscious of their
double ambiguity.

شكيفتن از چيزى -- نشكيبى از آتش = to bear patiently
the want of anything, like the Arabic صَبَرَ عن شَىْءٍ.

آبِ حيات—the Fountain· of Life in the Land of
Darkness. Nizāmī tells how. Alexander, guided by the
prophet Khizr, sought it in vain (Clarke's *Sikandar-nāma*,
p. 798 seq. Cf. Semelet's *Gulistān*, p. 144).

XXII.

خواجه—Sanā'ī is also distinguished by the titles of
شَيخ and حكيم.

سنائى—Abū 'l Majd Majdūd ibn Ādam Sanā'ī, the
first great poet of Sūfiism, began his career at the court of
Sultān Ibrāhīm, the Ghaznavite. Stung by the chance
words of a half-witted buffoon, he abjured the society of
princes and applied himself to solitary meditation. His
chef-d'œuvre, the *Ḥadīqatu 'l Ḥaqīqat* (finished in 535 A.H.),
which formed the model for the *Manṭiqu 'ṭṭair* of Farīd-
u'ddīn 'Aṭṭār and the *Maṣnavī*, ran the gauntlet of theo-
logical censure until its orthodoxy was certified by a
special decree. Sanā'ī died in 545 A.H. (see Ethé's *Catalogue*). The date 576 A.H., given by Daulat Shāh, is
erroneous. Further details will be found in the *Encyclo-
pædia Britannica* under 'Sanā'ī,' Ouseley's *Notices of
Persian Poets*, p. 184, and Jāmī's *Nafaḥātu 'l Uns*, p. 693.

۲—۳ شانه, آب, کاه, and دانه are metaphors of the perishable phenomenal element in Man.

۵ جان و خِرَد—human soul and reason, regarded as the embodiment of their Universals (جانِ کُلّ and عقلِ کُلّ), emanate directly from, and eventually are re-united with, Absolute Being. Observe the different scansion of سوی in each miṣrā'.

٦ مَی دُردِ...صاف—the divine principle pervading 'this muddy vesture of decay.'

۷ جانِ کُلّ—جانِ دُومرا که ندانند خلق (see note on عقلِ کُلّ, جان و خِرَد, above), the Neo-platonic πνεῦμα as is λόγος, which may be ranked among the few items of popular ignorance that we have not yet parted with. Cf. Whinfield's *Maṣnavī*, p. 148, note 3.

٨ درسفر—in the upward progress of the soul from the Many to the One.

مروزی و رازی—these are opposing types: spirit and flesh, Being and Not-being.

مَرْوُ ٱلشّاهجان—so called to distinguish it from مَرْوُ ٱلرّود, was before the Moghul invasion a large and flourishing city in Khorāsān, peculiarly important because of its vicinity to the northern frontier. Rai (Rhages) is said to have rivalled Bāghdād in magnificence: its site near Teherān is now covered with ruins (see a résumé of its history in Brugsch's *Reise nach Persien*, Vol. I. p. 233).

Concerning the anomalous formation of مروزی and رازی cf. Wright's *Arabic Grammar*, Vol. I. p. 153 D, Ibn Khallikān, Vol. I. p. 7.

The *Masnavī* (11. 18 seq.) offers a striking parallel to this passage :

مؤمنان را بُرد باشد عاقبت

با مُنافق مات اندر آخرت

گرچه هر دو بر سرِ یك بازِیند

لیك باهم مرغزی و رازِیند

هر یکی سوي مقامِ خَود رَود

هر یکی بر وفقِ نامِ خَود رَود

Victory falls to the believers at last,
The hypocrites have death in the next world.
Although both parties are engaged in one game
Yet, as regards one another, they are natives of Marv
        and Rai (i.e. far asunder).
Each goes to his own place,
Each fares according to his name.

The edition of the *Masnavī* (Bombay, 1863), which I have used throughout, agrees with B in reading مرغزی for مروَزی. The word is correctly explained in the margin : مردُمِ منسوب بشهرِ مرو. Doubtless it is a dialectical variety of the common form. Others (cf. the *Burhāni Qāti'* under لاش and the *Būstān*, p. 345, l. 5 of the commentary) derive it from مرغز, the locality of which they are candid enough to leave *in nubibus*.

رومی—روم is a general term for the territories of the Byzantine Empire.

٩ خانهٔ خَود الخ—cf. Shelley's

Dust to the dust : but the pure spirit shall flow
Back to the burning fountain whence it came.

اطلس—old, outworn. The term is generally used of a garment, and it may be so here. But see below.

مُرد—plural of اَمُرَد. On consideration I prefer the variant بُرد, which enables us to give اطلس the meaning commonly attached to it in Persian, viz. satin. Translate: How should satin accompany (match) a garment of wool? If مُرد be retained, we must render اطلس by 'worn out apparel.' The translation 'an old man' is not, I think, justified.

چون نُقَط ١٠.—cf. Niẓāmī, *Iskandar-nāma*, p. 504, l. 15:

ز پرگارِ آن حلقه مدهوش ماند

در آن حلقه چون نُقطه خاموش ماند

He was amazed at the compass of the circle (of nobles round the king);

In that circle he remained silent, like the (central) point.

'A silent (closed) mouth is compared to a point. Some explain this simile by the fact that a point is incapable of partition, or because beauties make their mouths small when they are not speaking. Khān Ārzū says: نُقطه means a cipher (صفر), and we know from arithmetic that, while the other figures have numerical value, a cipher is nought. Accordingly نُقطهگویا and خاموش are synonymous' (Commentary ad loc.).

Cf. also

نُقطهٔ دل بی عدد ١و گردِش است

گُفتِ زبان جُز یك پرگار نیست

(T. 73. 2ᵃ).

---

¹ T. om. و contra metr.

The heart is the point (in the centre) without number
    or motion;
Speech of the tongue is only the compass (circumference).

مَلَك — مَلِك is a possible reading.

XXIII.

۶ صُقّه—see Lane under صف, and for the jingle with
صفا cf. I. ۳, note.

ه گُشت فنا—passive of گرد فنا, which is a compound
transitive verb. This usage may sometimes lead to misapprehension. E.g. in the lines of Sa'dī (*Gulistān*, p. 33):

ناسزائی‌را چو بینی بختیار
عاقلان تسلیم کردند اختیار

Mr Platts, taking اِختیار as the object of کردند تسلیم,
translates:

If thou see an unworthy man fortunate
(Thou wilt also see that) the wise have resigned authority.

تسلیم, however, as the context shows, is the object of
اِختیار کردند, and the second miṣrā' should be rendered:

The wise (in such a case) adopt resignation.

نظّاره—the tashdīd is written metri causā.   Cf.

(Jāmī)   هر سو یِی نظاره سر بر کرده از دیوارها

which Rückert (*Grammatik, Poetik, und Rhetorik der
Perser*, p. 108) translates correctly:

Die überall, um zu schauen, das Haupt heben über die
    Mauern.

Pertsch's statement (ibid.), that 'nur das letzere (نظاره)

heisst das Zuschauen, das erstere (نظّاره) dagegen die Zuschauer,' is not in accordance with the facts. Cf. قطّاره (xxxvi. ٢, note).

جُزْ خُدا نکرد — cf. xix. ٣—٤. None have vision of God but he who can say with Manṣūr, 'I am God' (vi. ١٢, note).

آن چِراغ ٦ — referring, probably, to the sun. Cf. Kor. xxv. 62.

چون این بهم رسید الخ — cf. *Maṣnavī*, 21. 1 :

There is no 'two,' unless you are a worshipper of form:
Before Him who is without form all becomes one.
When you regard form, you have two eyes;
Look on His light, which is single.
Necessarily the eye, when it falls on One,
Itself is one: 'two' is out of sight.
The light of the two eyes cannot be divided
When a man's eye is fixed upon His light.

٧ In beyt ٦ the poet used a metaphor implying dualism. He now corrects himself by affirming that all apparent difference is the manifestation of divine unity.

بیانست و مغلطه — translate rather: 'is mere explanation and error.' بیان is often opposed to عیان as inferential to intuitive knowledge.

برشك نور رُخش — God was jealous of his hidden beauty and desired to display it (cf. iv. ٢, note).

وَالضُّحَى — these words introduce and give their name to the 93rd Sūra of the Kor'ān. They express here the revelation of God in the phenomenal world.

cf. ٨ الخ خَیّاط روزگار

از بقا گردون قبائی بر قدِ یك تن ندوخت

خِلعتی بس فاخر آمد عُمر عَیش کوتهیست

(Jāmī).

Fortune never stitched on any one's stature a garment
of permanence;
Life is a very splendid robe: its fault is brevity.

چاك نکرد = قبا نکرد.

XXIV.

٣ بدامِ دیو — the variant دوغ, meaning literally
'butter-milk,' is used, as appears from this passage, in the
secondary sense of 'deception.' Cf. the phrase دوغ خَوردن =
غَلَط خَوردن.

٤ جِنان — plural of جَنّة. Owing to the absence of
vowel points in the MSS. we cannot determine whether
جَنان or جِنان has greater authority here. جَنان, however, is a word seldom met with in Persian.

٦ لَحَد — an oblong trench, where the corpse is de-
posited, in the side of a grave.

٧ بدلنهٔ انسان — cf.

دانهٔ دل کاشته زیرِ چنین آب و گُلی

تا بهارت نرسد او شجری می نشَوَد

(T. 163. 12ª).

The seed of the spirit, sown beneath this water and clay
(the body),
Becomes not a tree until it reach Thy spring.

٨ چاه—Kor. XII. 15.

٩ در جَوّ لامکان—cf. I. ١٤ for a similar division of the MSS. between جَوّ and جَوف.

XXV.

٣ شبِ غریب—probably we should render: 'On the strange night...thou wilt escape.'

آوازِ آشنا—lit. 'the Beloved's voice.' I have slightly modified the translation in order to bring out the contrast between غریب and آشنا. In the following miṣrā' مار and مور form one of those assonances, like شر و شور below, which are so pleasing to the Persian ear.

٥ خُمارِ عشق—خُمار—خَمّار for خُمّار (cf. IX. ١٩, note) would make the meaning plainer.

٦ بگیرانند—'on allume.' The poet regards death as a spiritual resurrection.

٨ گِرِفته دو گُوش خَود از بیم—cf. Kor. II. 18: 'they put their fingers in their ears because of the crashing thunder, for fear of death.'

نفخهٔ صور—Kor. LXIX. 13.

٩ عینِ ناظِر و منظور—complete union involves the identification of subject and object (see notes on IV. ١١, XXIII. ٦; *Gulshani Rāz*, 123 seq., 139 seq.).

١٠ آن شر و شور—the bewildering variety of phenomena by which Being is manifested.

احَوَلی ١١ —seeing double, dualism.　Cf. *Masnavi*,
12. 14 :

كُفت اُستاد احوَلی‌را كاندر آ

رَو بِرون آر از وُثاق آن شیشه‌را

چون درونِ خانه احوَل رفت زود

شیشه پیشِ چشمِ او دو مینمود

كُفت احوَل زآن دو شیشه تا كُدام

پیشِ تو آرم بكُن شرحی تمام

كُفت اُستاد آن دو شیشه نیست رَو

احوَلی بُگذار و افزون‌بین مشَو

كُفت ای اُستا مرا طعنه مزن

كُفت اُستا زآن دو یكرا بر شِكن

چون یكی بشكست هر دو شُد ز چشم

مرد احوَل كُردد از مَیلان و خشم

A master said to one who squinted, 'Come in,
Go and fetch that bottle from its place.'
When the squint-eyed man made haste to enter the house,
There seemed to be two bottles before his eye.
'Which of those two bottles,' said he,
'Shall I bring to you? Give me a clear explanation.'
'There are not two bottles,' replied the master, 'go,
Cease to squint and do not see more than one.'
'O master,' he said, 'rebuke me not.'
Said the master, 'Break one of those two.'
When one was broken, both vanished from sight;
'Tis lust and anger that make a man see double.

چشمِ احوَل (1) = چشمِ بد and (2) the 'evil eye'
(see Lane's *Modern Egyptians*, Vol. I. p. 315).

۱۲ بصورتِ بشرم الخ—referring to the doctrine of
حُلول (Incarnation), and particularly to the incarnation of
God in Christ. The Sūfīs distinguish between حُلول and
اتِّحاد. Cf. *Maṣnavī*, 439. 2 :

این انا هو بود در سرِّ اى فضول

ز اتِّحادِ نور نز راهِ حُلول

This 'I am He' was mystical, O babbler,
Expressing union with the Light not by way of incarnation.

عشق سخت غیور—it is high treason against the
majesty of Love to suggest that He, who is a pure spirit,
can ever dwell in a mortal body. Cf. Whinfield's *Maṣnavī*,
p. 29, and the ḥadīs there quoted : "Verily Saʿd is a
jealous man, and I am more jealous than he, and God is
more jealous than I, and of His jealousy He prohibits 'all
pollutions both outward and inward'" (Kor. vi. 152).

۱۳ صورت—چه جاى صورت in this line = the Platonic
ἰδέα. How is it possible, asks the poet, for Man, wrapt
up as he is in phenomenal attributes, to reflect even a
glimpse of the divine archetype? Cf.

لَیلَى و مجنون عجب هر دو بیك پوست درون

آینۀ هر دو توئى لیك درونِ نمدى

(T. 279. 12ᵃ).

A marvel! Lailā and Majnūn both under a single coverlet!
Thou art the mirror of both, but thou art muffled in felt.

تو‌صدتو, fold, has in modern Persian become a preposition meaning 'inside.'

آینه جان‌—فلكِ اضافت for the see Platts, *Persian Grammar*, Part I. § 29.

جُستندی ۱۴—this and ندیدئی in the next miṣrāʻ belong to the Past Conditional (Platts, *ibid.* § 97). The Present Conditional, which is not mentioned by Platts, occurs several times in the Dīvān and forms the rhyme of a ghazal (T. 337. 12ᵃ) beginning:

ره بنمودمی بتو گر همثی نه جانمی

دیده شُدی نشانِ من گر نه که بی نشانمی

كنده—خندق Arabicised. When Saʻdī fell into the hands of the Franks, he was set to work in the fosse of Tripoli (در خندق طرابُلُس—*Gulistān*, p. 62).

یك كور—a beggar who has lost his sight. Kings and blind men, says Dumas, are born deceivers.

غمّازخانه ۱۵—a compound noun, like غسّال‌خانه, wash-house.

Cf. دهان ببسته و غمّاز.

ز طنّازی شكوفه لب كُشاده است

بغمّازی زبان بسته است سَوسن (T. 47. 9ᵃ).

The blossom has opened its lips in pleasantry,
The lily has closed its mouth in coquetry.

غمّاز also means 'tell-tale' or, as an epithet of light, 'ray-scattering' (see XIII. ۱۰, note).

غیرِ اهل ۱۶—the uninitiated.

اهلِ جُمله—these words bear a double sense: (1) all
that is worthy, (2) all people.

راز شُد ز من مستور—I, as an individual, am non-
existent: God is the totality of Being, and therefore of
Knowledge.

مشرق ١٧—cf. xvi. ٢٠.

كَوكبهٔ فتح—فتح (pl. فتوح and فُتوحات) is employed
by the Sūfīs to denote all kinds of extraordinary favours
which God bestows upon the spiritual adept.

رايتِ منصور—alluding probably to Manṣūr Ḥallāj (the
title of Shāh or Sultān is often usurped by famous 'men
of the Path'). Cf. منصورِ من = my soul (T. 57. 5) and
بادهٔ منصوری, mystical wine, opp. to بادهٔ انگوری (T. 112. 3).
As regards رايت cf. Ibn Khallikān, Arabic text (Ed.
De Slane), p. 357, l. 1:

وَبَدَتْ رَايَةُ ٱلْوَفَا بِيَدِ ٱلْوَجْدِ وَ نَادَى أَهْلُ ٱلْحَقَائِقِ جُولُوا

And the banner of fulfilment was displayed by the hand of
    ecstasy,
And the champions of Truth gave the signal to charge.

In the *Maṣnavī* (542. 16; Whinfield, p. 301) Jalālu'ddīn
illustrates his doctrine of manifestation *per contraria* by
the metaphor of two standards, a white and a black, which
are set up in successive periods, e.g. Adam and Iblīs, Abra-
ham and Nimrod, Moses and Pharaoh.

XXVI.

از كِنارِ خويش ا—'self' refers here, not, as it
commonly does, to Man's phenomenal individuality, the

cheating mask which prevents him from seeing things as
they are, but to the divine spark or spirit which dwells
within him and cannot die. This is the true 'self.' Cf.
XVII. ۱۱, note, and Kor. L. 15: We (God) are nearer to
him than the jugular vein.

۲ باغ عشق بودم—the preposition is more usually
omitted with verbs of motion, as in XXII. ۹.

مهر او الخ—cf. XXXIII. ۲.

روان شُد جویبار—i.e. I wept for joy. Cf. Hāfiz, ۱.
64. 3:

چندان گریستیم که هر کس که بر گُذشت

در اشکِ ما چو دید روان گُفت کین چه جوست

۳ خندان—full-blown. Arabic poets employ ضَحَك
and تَبَسَّم in the same sense.

هستی—cf. XIII. ۸, note. هستی signifies here Contingent or Phenomenal Being.

ذو الفقار—the famous sword given by Mohammed to
'Alī, here used figuratively = death, corruption.

۵ آن سروِ ما—the Beloved (سرو = و خوشقدِ. شاهدِ
قامت).

دست برهم زد—in ecstasy. The words may also be
translated 'rustled its leaves' (see Vullers under دست
and کف).

۷ این عددرا—referring to آتشهایِ برهم in the last
beyt.

گُنجیدن—from گُنج.

پنج و چار —the five senses and the four elements.

صد هزاران سیب شیرین الخ ۸ —plurality is a phantom
(cf. XXIII. ٦, note). This illustration recurs in the *Maṣnavī*
(21. 5):

گر تو صد سیب و صد آبی بشمری

صد نماید یك شَوَد چون بغشری

بی شُمارِ حرفها ۹ —never mind the parts: look at the
whole. Cf.

بر اهلِ صورت شُد سُخُن اِجمالها تفصیلها

بر اهلِ معنَی شُد سُخُن تفصیلها اِجمالها

(T. 116. 4ᵃ).

With men of form the word is: Synthesis by analysis;
With men of spirit the word is: Analysis by synthesis.

این نُطق در دل —the language of the heart is—silence.
See I. ۱۸, note.

سادهرنگی —

'Life, like a dome of many-coloured glass,
　Stains *the white radiance of eternity*.'

(Shelley).

The same thought is found in Schiller's epigram, entitled
"Licht und Farbe":

Wohne, du ewiglich Eines, dort bei dem ewiglich Einen!
　Farbe, du wechselnde, komm freundlich zum Menschen
　　herab!

Cf. with this passage the following lines (T. 332. 10ᵃ):

روح یکی دان و تن كُشته عدد صد هزار

همچو كه بادامها در صِفَتِ رَوغنی

چند لغت در جهان جُمله بمعنى يكى

آب يكى كُشت چون خابِئها بشكنى

جان بفِرستد خبر جانِبِ هر با نظر

چونكه بتَوحيد تو دل ز سُخُن بر كنى

Deem the soul a unit and the body a hundred thousand
　　numbers,

Even as almonds in the form of oil.

How many words are there in the world! Yet all are
　　essentially one;

Water becomes one when you break the jars.

The soul sends intelligence to every person of insight

When by acknowledging Unity you pluck away your
　　heart from speech.

(فاعِلِ حقيقى) اصلِ كار—God is the only real agent

Cf. Whinfield's *Masnavī*, pp. 15, 78, 91, 242.

XXVII.

This poem is headed in T. : فى صِفَةِ ٱلْمُسافِرة.

چو قطره الخ—cf. VIII. ٥, note. ع

وَطَنِ خويش— the sea (of Absolute Being).

بازآمد—as a rain-drop.

مُصطَفَى—see note on IX. ٥. ٠

رفت جانِبِ يَثرب—on the occasion of his departure
(هِجره) from Mecca, A.D. 622. يَثرب is the older name for
the city which obtained at this time the honourable desig-
nation of مدينةُ ٱلنّبى, or briefly, Medīna.

سَفَرِ كُزين در خويش ۷ —introrsum ascende. Cf. the
ḥadīs̲: He who knows himself knows his Lord.

چو كانِ لعل الخ —for the idea that rubies are coloured
by the sun cf. Ḥāfiz, I. 46. 8 :

Thy curving lip reveals that rubies borrow
Their lustre from the world-enlightening orb.

'When the ruby, coming white from the mine, is dipped
in fresh blood (تازه قانلی جگره) and exposed to the sun,
it turns red' (Sūdī, Commentary, *ad loc.*).

پَذيرا شَو —lit. 'become recipient of' (see Platts,
Persian Grammar, Part I. § 92).

زخويشتن الخ ۸ —cf. XXVI. ۱, note.

خاك كُشت معدنِ زر —the earthly nature is transmuted by self-annihilation into the pure spiritual essence,
which is its real and everlasting self. Cf. IV. ۷.

XXVIII.

شبان ۱ —this is not an irregular plural, but is composed of ان + شب‍, the contracted form of the adverbial
suffix, ‍انه. Cf. شبانه‌روز and شبانروز = νυχθήμερον.

خانهٔ دل —although دل and جان are often used
synonymously by mystical writers, it is convenient in
translating to keep a separate word for each.

پُر همه نقشست ۲ —because the soul is the mirror of
God, in whom all images are contained.

شمعِ چِگِل —the radiant beauty of thy face illumines
even Chigil in Turkistān, the home of beauty.

محرم‎ ۴—literally, 'one who enjoys free access to the حَرَم‎.' Hāfiz calls the soul صَيدِ حَرَم‎ (I. 178. 2).

بِحِل‎—ب‎ + Arabic حِلّ‎. The text is uncertain here. Perhaps we should read بُكُن‎ and take بِحِل کردن‎ in its ordinary sense: to forgive. With مُكُن‎, it must mean: to make common property, to desecrate. Notice the word-play; حِلّ‎ and حرم‎ are opposites in Arabic.

سرِ زُلف‎ = سرِ رِشته‎—داد سرِ رِشته بمن الخ‎ ۵, the tip of the Beloved's curl, enwinding the amorous soul and leading it towards him (cf. XXI. ۴, note). Hāfiz says:

بی کُفت و گوی زُلفِ تو دلرا همی کشد

با زُلفِ دلکشِ تو کِرا روي کُفت و گوست

(I. 64. 5).

Thy curl is ever drawing the heart silently;
Who hath power to speak (quarrel) with thy heart-ravishing curl?

Cf. ib. I. 116. 4; I. 676. 3.

بکش تا بکشم‎—'respect the bond (IX. ۹, note): be faithful in love, and I will not fail.' Cf. Hāfiz, I. 386. 2:

گرت هواست که معشوق نگسلد پيمان

نگاه دار سرِ رِشته تا نگه دارد

If it is thy desire that the Beloved should not break the covenant,
Keep thy end of the thread that he may keep his end.

هم بکش و هم مگسل‎—see XX. ۱, note, and cf. Jāmī's *Bahāristān*, p. ۱۰, ll. 16—21; Hāfiz, II. 450. 6.

٦ خِرگَهِ جان—the Turkmāns are a people of tent-dwellers: hence the metaphor.

٧ تُرُش مصلحتم—literally, 'I am harsh in a good cause, or affair.' The use of the izāfat is remarkable; it seems to be imitated from the Arabic construction in cases like مَحْمُودُ ٱلسّيرَة (Wright's *Arabic Grammar*, Vol. II. p. 221). For the poet's view of the probationary and corrective purpose of suffering—τῷ πάθει μάθος—cf. Whinfield's *Maṣnavī*, p. 90 seq., 114, 295.

٨ كه منم—egoism, by asserting the reality of the phenomenal self, involves the denial of Unity. There is a proverb, مَنْ قَالَ أَنَا وَقَعَ فِى ٱلْعَنَا, Whoever says 'I' falls into trouble (Freytag, Vol. III. Part I. p. 424). Cf. xv. ١٤, note, and Hāfiz, II. 258. 8:

بیا و هستیِ حافظ ز پیشِ او بر دار

که با وُجودِ تو کس نشنَوَد ز من که منم

Come, lift the mask of my being from before me;
Let none, while thou art, hear me say, 'I am.'

٩ صلاحِ دل و دین—see II. ١٤, note.

صورتِ آن تُرک—a type or manifestation of divine beauty.

صورتِ دل—the soul is identified with God. Cf. note on XVII. ١١.

XXIX.

١ لُطف چو شکر—for the izāfat see VII. ٧, note.

تعال—'come' is perhaps an adequate rendering. Cf. Lane under علا.

اِرْجِعِی ۳ —Kor. LXXXIX. 28: اِرْجِعِی إِلَى رَبِّكِ رَاضِیَةً مَرْضِیَّةً, (O soul), return to thy Lord, well-pleased and well-pleasing. Cf.

شَهِ من كُفت این مجنون بجُز زنجیرِ زُلفِ من
دِكَر بندی بنپذیرد تو خویِ او نمیدانی
هزاران بند بر درّد بسویِ دست ما پرّد
إِلَیْنَا راجعون كَردد كه او بازیست سُلطانی

(T. 343. 11ᵃ).

Said my King: 'This Majnūn (the soul) will accept no
    gyve
But the chain of my tress; thou knowest not his nature.
He will break a thousand gyves, he will fly to our hand,
He will be "*to us returning*," for he is a royal falcon.'

طبل —see XVI. ۳, note. According to Kaempfer (*Amoe-nitates Exoticae*, p. 743 seq.) 'طبلِ باز, i.e. tympanum falconum, parvulum est, aeneum, in appendicem productum, reticuloque densissime munitum.' He adds that it is carried by kings and nobles on the left side of their saddles.

صوفی ۴ —this word has been erroneously connected with صفا, صفّه, and σοφός. It is derived from ضوف, wool. Cf. the phrase, لَبَسَ ٱلصُّوفَ, he donned the wool, i.e. devoted himself to a monastic or contemplative life, and see the article 'Ṣūfī' by T. Nöldeke, Z.D.M.G., Vol. XLVIII. p. 45.

جان‌بخشی ۵ —cf. Hāfiz, I. 184. 5:

از روان‌بخشیِ عیسَی نزنمِ پیشِ تو دم
زآنکه در روح‌فزائی چو لبت ماهِر نیست

and *Masnavī*, 370. 13 :

كارِ من سربخشى و بيخويشى است
كارِ شاهنشاهِ ما سربخشى است

'Tis my business to yield up life unselfishly,
To bestow life is the business of our King of kings.

cf.—قفس ٦

مُرغِ باغِ مَلَكوتمِ نَيَمِ از عالَمِ خاك
دو سِه روزى قفسى ساخته اند از بَدَنمِ

(T. 256. 7).

I am a bird of the heavenly garden : I belong not to the
earthly sphere ;

They have made, for two or three days, a cage of my
body.

پاى ماجان and صفّ نعال, otherwise called
كفشكن, is the lowest part of the room, beyond the
carpet, where visitors remove their shoes on entering ;
the least honourable place, where people of the humbler
sort stand (Browne, J. R. A. S., 1895, p. 806). It is also
a place of penance and humiliation. The darvīsh who has
committed a fault must stand here on one foot, holding his
left ear in his right hand, and his right ear in his left,
until the Director (پير) allows him to go. صَدْرُ ٱلجَلَال is
contrasted with صَفُّ ٱلنَّعَال in a passage from the *Kitábi
Aqdas* of Bahá 'ulláh (*ib.* p. 808).

ز كودكى الخ ١٠—cf. I Corinthians, ch. xiii. 11 :
' When I was a child, I spake as a child, I understood as
a child, I thought as a child, but when I became a man,

I put away childish things.' Commenting on this text
Juan de la Cruz remarks (*Subida del Monte Carmelo*, p. 41):
Objects of sense and the knowledge derived from them are
the occupation of a child; and therefore, if the soul will
attach itself to these and refuse to forsake them, it will
never cease to be a little child, and it will always speak
and think of God, as a child does, because, fixing its
attention on the outward sensible husk, which is the child,
it will never reach the spiritual essence, which is the perfect man. See also Law, *The Spirit of Love*, p. 140 (quoted
in *Characters and Characteristics of William Law* by Alex.
Whyte, D.D., p. 127).

١١ جُوالِ بِشكاف—جُوالِ, جُوال, a sack, is used metaphori-
cally to denote the human body.

١٢ راست بِدَست—on the day of judgement the
righteous will receive the book, wherein their actions are
recorded, in their right hand. Cf. Kor. XVII. 73; LXIX.
19—26; LXXXIV. 7—12.

این نامه—Cf.

کتابِ حِس بدستِ چپ کتابِ عقل دستِ راست

ترا نامه بچپ دادند بیرون ز آستانستی

(T. 59. 8ª).

In thy left hand the book of sense, the book of reason
in thy right;
Had the scroll been put into thy left, thou wouldst be
outside the threshold.

تو بستان نامه از چپّم بدستِ راستم در نه

تو ثانی کرد چپرا راست بنده ناتوانستی

(T. 59. 12ª).

Do thou take the scroll from my left hand and lay it in
    my right;
Thou canst make the left right: thy servant would not
    be able.

خِرَدرا ١٣ —ħuman reason (see IV. ١٠., note).

١۴ Observe the jingles: روان, spirit, روان, moving;
and كُنج; نالیدن from منال from Arabic نال, and منال,
رنج.

XXX.

٢ دلِ من الخ —alluding to the ḥadīs: قَلْبُ ٱلْمُؤْمِنِ
بَيْنَ ٱلْإِصْبَعَيْنِ مِنْ أَصَابِعِ ٱلرَّحْمٰنِ يَقْلُبُهُ حَيْثُ يَشَآء, the
heart of the believer is between the two (first and second)
fingers of the Merciful; He turneth it wheresoever He
pleaseth. Cf. Whinfield's *Maṣnavī*, p. 242 seq.

٦ در آن خُمّی الخ —the world resembles a dyeing-
vat in which the soul is coloured (i.e. blackened by associ-
ation with Not-being). Cf.

بیرنك فرو رفتم در عشقِ تو ای دلبر

بر كش تو ازین خُمّر تا رنكِ دِگَر گیرم

(T. 250. 3ª).

Without hue I descended in desire of thee, O Beloved;
Draw me forth from this vat that I may take another
    hue.

For رنك see XXVI. ٩, note.

٨ The mystic is alternately rapt to the shining heights
of vision and plunged in the dark abyss of separation:
these opposite states, resulting from the conflict of Being

and Not-being, are to him what faith and infidelity are to common men. Cf. Saʻdī, *Gulistān*, Book II. Story 9.

زِ جَیب و آستینم ۹ —the bosom of the shirt serves as a pocket, and loose money is often carried in the sleeve.

XXXI.

'The purpose of negation of self is to clear the way for the apprehension of the fact that there is no existence but the One' (Whinfield's *Maṣnavī*, p. 284). 'I am nought' means 'God is all.' Cf. Vaughan, *Hours with the Mystics*, Vol. I. p. 95. To this poem, one of the most splendid and sublime productions of his genius, Jalāl'uddīn has written a counterpart, scarcely less astonishing, the burden of which is echoed in Emerson's lines:

> I am owner of the sphere,
> Of the seven stars and the solar year,
> Of Caesar's hand and Plato's brain,
> Of Lord Christ's heart and Shakespeare's strain.

(See a version in English: *Dabistān*, Vol. I. p. clxvi and in German: Von Hammer, *Schöne Redekünste Persiens*, p. 191. The original text does not occur in any of the editions or MSS. used by me.)

کُبر ۱ —a Magian.

نه از خاکم الخ ۳ —cf. VIII. ٤, note.

بُلغار ٤ —for 'Bulgaria' in the translation read 'Bulghār.' This town was situated on the Volga, about 100 miles south of Kazan (see *Géographie d'Aboulféda* by Reinaud and Guyard, Vol. II. Part I. p. 324 seq.; Mouradja D'Ohsson, *Des Peuples du Caucase*, p. 73).

سقسین —there were two cities of this name, one on

the borders of China, and the other, evidently referred to here, in the land of the Khazars, who occupied a vast and ill-defined territory, extending at different periods from the Crimea to the Caspian Sea (D'Ohsson, *Des Peuples du Caucase*, p. 190 seq.; *Géographie d'Aboulféda*, Vol. II. Part I. p. 286, and note 2; Qazvīnī, *Kosmographie*, ed. Wüstenfeld, Part II. p. 402).

عِراقِ عَرَبی and عِراقِ عَجَمی‎ ,Irāqs' two the—عِراقَین‎.
The former, also called Jibāl and Kūhistān, is the great central province of western Persia, and is bounded on the east by Khorāsān, on the north by Māzanderān, Ghīlān, and Ādharbaijān, on the west by Ardilān and Lūristān, on the south by Khūzistān and Fārsistān. 'Irāqi 'Arabī lies between the Tigris and the Euphrates, and stretches westward to the borders of the Syrian desert.

فِردَوس‎ 5 —Greek παράδεισος (but see Lane under فردس‎).

رِضوان‎—the angel who has the keys of Paradise.

مَن از جانِ جانانِم‎ 6 —when every trace of finite existence is swept away, the Infinite remains.

یا هو‎ 8 —'O He' (Jahve, Jehovah), one of the most familiar darvīsh-cries.

یا من هو‎—'O He who is.'

رِندی و قَلّاشی‎ 9 —spiritual rapture and ecstasy.

cf.—اگُر در عُمرِ خُود الخ‎ 10

گُر برآرند یك نَفَس بی دوست

دلق و تسبیحِشان شَوَد زُنّار   (T. 26. 7).

If they pass one moment apart from the Beloved,
Their mantle and rosary become a Christian girdle
(they are guilty of infidelity).

‏اگر دست دهد مرا‏—i.e. ‏اگر دستم دهد الخ‏ ‏۱۱‏.
‏دست دادن‏ = to come to hand, to accrue. The subject is
‏دمی‏.

‏همی‏—here in its original meaning = ‏همیشه‏. For the
sentiment cf. Hāfiz, I. 710. 4.

‏۱۲‏ ‏نباشد هیچ دستانم‏—this may be translated : 'I
have no device.'

XXXII.

‏۲‏ ‏آتش تو‏—the celestial fire of love.

‏بو لهب‏—'Abdu 'l Uzzā, surnamed Abū Lahab (father
of flame), was the uncle and bitter enemy of Mohammed,
who denounced him as follows : 'The hands of Abū Lahab
shall perish and he shall perish. Neither his wealth shall
profit him, nor what he hath gained. He shall enter into
the flaming fire' (‏نَارًا ذَاتَ لَهَبٍ‏). See Kor. CXI. with Sale's
notes.

‏۳‏ ‏دریچهٔ دل‏—cf.

‏دوری ز تن لیک از دلم در پیش رویت روزنست‏
‏زآن روزن دزدیده همچون مه پیامت میکنم‏
(T. 261. 12).

From the body thou art far, but in my heart, fronting
thy face, is a window ;
Thro' that secret window, like the moon, I am
sending thee a message.

'The soul resembles this window, in which is ever being reflected, or rather is dwelling, the divine light of the all-pervading presence of God' (Juan de la Cruz, *Subida del Monte Carmelo*, p. 23).

For the exact signification of دریچه see *Gulistān*, translated by Platts, p. 7, note.

نِثار ۴ —v. ۱, note.

ای دو دیده ۵ —a term of endearment. So ای نورِ هر دو دیده (Hāfiz, II. 502. 1 ; 512. 7).

عجم—properly, all who are not Arabs, then specially, the Persians. Cf. the double sense of βάρβαρος.

باده ۶ —see *Gulshani Rāz*, 805 seq.

ای مادر و پدرِ تو ۷ —cf.

چون پدر و مادر عقلست و روح

هر دو توئی چون شَوَم اندر تو عاق

(T. 224. 8).

Reason and Soul are as father and mother ;
Thou art both : how should I be disobedient towards thee ?

در خود طلب ندیدم ۹ —see XVII. ۱۲, note, and cf.

خود است جُمله طالِب و ما همچو سایها

این گُفتگویِ ما همئی گُفتگویِ دوست

(T. 137. 3).

We are even as shadows, He is all who seek,
Lo, by Him is spoken every word we speak !

عاشقانرا جُستجو از خویش نیست

در جهان جوینده جُز او بیش نیست

(T. 150. 4ᵃ).

فضل و ادب رها کُن ۱۰ —VIII. v, note.

تا تو ادب نخواندی —read بخواندی, and translate:
'Since thou hast taught me culture, I know no culture but
thee.' For this meaning of خواندن cf.

بخواندهای مُعَلّم تمام بُگذاشتم

مُعَلّم آنچه نخواندست من ز بر دارم

Tho' all my teacher's lessons are forgot,
I have by heart whate'er he left untaught.

خواندن, like قَرَأ in Arabic, is originally 'to read with
a musical intonation,' 'to chant.' Ben Jonson supplies an
interesting parallel in *The Fox*, Act II. Scene 1 :

> that vulgar grammar,
> Which he that cried Italian to me, taught me.

جُز تو ادب ندیدم —Shakespeare, Sonnet LXXVIII :

> But thou art all my art, and dost advance
> As high as learning my rude ignorance.

ادب is a difficult word to translate. Jurjānī (*Kitābu 't-
ta'rīfāt*, p. ۱٤) defines it as 'the knowledge by which
one is guarded from committing any kind of fault.' Cf.
Nafaḥātu 'l Uns, p. 52, l. 17 ; p. 104, l. 16 ; p. 159, l. 6 ;
p. 320, l. 7.

XXXIII.

بکه چشم باز دارم ۲ —these words may also mean :
'in whom shall I have hope again ?'

منم آن که الخ ٤ —translate : 'Am I one whose
heart...?' i.e. ٤I am not one whose love admits of cure.' Cf.

خُدای پهلویِ هر درد داروئی داده

چو دردِ عشق قدیمست ماند بی ز دوا ۱

(T. 9. 13).

God hath given a physic for every pain ;
Since the pain of love is old (eternal), for it no
remedy hath been found.

XXXIV.

صورتگرِ نقّاشم ۱ —the human mind, by the necessity
of its nature, cannot form any idea whatsoever except
through the medium of symbols, images, and impressions.
All these, whether sensual or spiritual, partake of Not-
being, and therefore veil and obstruct the divine light.
See on this subject Juan de la Cruz, *Subida del Monte
Carmelo*, Bk. II. Ch. 12.

هر لحظه بُتی سازم —as regards the educative value
of 'forms' cf. Whinfield's *Masnavi*, p. 76, p. 270. 'Beholding in many souls the traits of the divine beauty, and
separating in each soul that which is divine from the taint
which it has contracted in the world, the lover ascends to
the highest beauty, to the love and knowledge of the
Divinity by steps on this ladder of created souls'
(Emerson).

چون نقشِ تُرا بینم الخ ۲ —the divine idea effaces all
others and fills the soul.   Cf. XIII. ۱۳, note.

۳   In what terms can I describe thee?   As the spirit
of love, or the foe of reason, or the destroyer of earthly
imaginations?

چون بوی تو دارد جان ۴ —cf. XVIII. ۳.

هر خون که ز من روید ٥—every drop of my blood, that thou sheddest (cf. دلبر خون‌خواره‌را, III. ۳), as it sinks into the earth proclaims its union with thee.

با مهر تو همرنگم—Unity is called a sea of blood (*Gulshani Rāz*, 499) 'because of the continual annihilation in it of its waves, viz. phenomena and plurality.'

خانهٔ آب و گِل ٦—the body.

XXXV.

صد پرده الخ ۱ — see IX. ۱٤, note.

از نَفَس گُسستن ... از قَدَم بُریدن ۲—to renounce self (فنا) and to travel abidingly in God (بقا), which are the beginning and end of the mystical journey (see notes on XIX. ۲ and ٦; *Gulshani Rāz*, 307 seq.). In the *Bahāristān* (p. ۱۰, l. 16 seq.) faith is defined as کندن و پَیوستن, i.e. 'to sever the heart from created things and unite it with God.'

نادیده گِرفتن این جهانرا—cf. ۳

تو مبین جهان ز بیرون که جهان درونِ دیده است

چو دو دیده‌را ببستی ز جهان جهان نماند

(T. 164. 3ᵃ).

Look not on the world from outside, for the world is within the eye;

When you shut your eyes to the world, the world remains not.

مر دیدهٔ خویش‌را ندیدن—this misrā' allows of another

interpretation, viz. 'not to see your own eye,' whence all
objects derive their unreal existence.

در کوچهٔ سینها دویدن ٥ —'introrsum ascendere.'
کوچه is the diminutive of کو.

cf.— ز کُجاست این طپیدن ٦

مُرغِ دلم میطپید هیچ سُکونی نداشت

مسکنِ اصلیش دید یافت درو ساکِنی

(T. 340. 3ᵃ).

Returning to its ancient nest
My restless fluttering soul had rest.

ای مُرغ —x. ۷, note.   ۷

بگو زبانِ مُرغان —use the language of mystics, speak
in parables. For the allusion to Solomon see II. ٦, note.

بکارخانه بودم ٨ —in the presence of, and not yet
separated from, the divine artificer. Cf. note on XVII. ۱.

تا خانهٔ آب و گِل بزیدن —see XXXIV. ٦, note.
According to an ḥadīs, 'He kneaded the clay of Adam
forty days.'

خانهٔ صُنع ٩ —the phenomenal world.

می کشیدند ۱۰ —because the soul was reluctant to
enter the world, and hated the body in which it was
doomed to captivity.

چون گُویَم —this simile may have been suggested by
the words چون پای نماند : the epithet بی پای , footless,
is frequently applied to a ball. The personal suffix belongs
to صورتی کشیدن. As regards the scansion of this
miṣrā' see XI. ۱۰, note.

XXXVI.

كوچ كردن‎ —to decamp, to migrate. ١

قطّارها‎ —the tashdīd is required by the metre. See notes on IX. ١٩, XXIII. ٠. ٢

حلالی خواستن از کسی — از ما حلالی خواسته‎ means: asking a person to make such and such a thing lawful to the asker, i.e., according to the context, either to give him permission to act in a certain manner, or to release him from all obligations which he may have incurred with respect to the person addressed. Here the camel-driver begs to be excused for having disturbed the travellers' repose.

Prof. Bevan suggests that (جلال pl. جُلّ) جلالی‎, which is found in one of the MSS., may be the correct reading. In this case we must imagine the saddle-cloths to have served as blankets; at dawn the sārbān comes to reclaim his property.

Cf. — چه خُفته اید ای کاروان‎

چرا ز قافله یك كس نمیشَوَد بیدار‎

که رختِ عُمرِ زکی باز میبَرَد طرّار‎

چرا ز خواب و ز طرّار می نیازاری‎

چرا از آنکه خبر میدهد کشی آزار‎

تُرا هر آنکه بیازُرد شَیخ و واعظِ تُست‎

که نیست مهرِ جهانرا چو نقشِ آب قرار‎

(T. 26. 12).

Why is no one in the caravan awake,
When the cutpurse is bearing away the baggage of pure life?

Why art thou not troubled by sleep and the cutpurse,
Why art thou aggrieved by him who gives thee warning?
He who troubles thee is thy shaikh and monitor,
Saying, 'The world's dowry, like a reflection in water,
    has no permanence.'

(Probably مِهرِ جهان, the worldly sun or the love of the
world, is a better reading, on account of نقشِ آب.)

شمعهاي سرنگون ۴ — Cf. Shakespeare, Sonnet XXI.:
'those gold candles fixed in heaven's air.'

— خلقی

    And yet as angels in some brighter dreams
      Call to the soul when man doth sleep,
  So some strange thoughts transcend our wonted
      themes
      And into glory peep.   (Henry Vaughan.)

عجب حاليست ، عجب — adjectival, as in the phrase, عجب.

۵ تا چند آب ريزد دولابِ آسمان — چرخِ دولابی (T. 62.)
هفت آسمان = هفت دولاب (Lakh. 29. 1). (12ª).

آمد گُران خوابی تُرا — 'our birth is but a sleep and a
forgetting.' The same idea is developed in a passage of
singular beauty (*Maṣnavī*, 385. 22 ; Whinfield's *Maṣnavī*,
p. 217):

کرچه خُفته گُشت و ناسی شُد ز پیش

کی گُذارندش در آن نِسیانِ خویش

باز از آن خوابش ۱ببیداری کشند

که کُنَد بر حالتِ خَود ریشخند

¹ The text has بینداری.

که چه غم بود آنکه میخوردم بخواب

چون فراموشم شُد احوالِ صواب

چون ندانستم که آن غم و اعتلال

فعلِ خوابست و فریبست و خیال

همچنین دُنیا که حُلمِ نائِم است

خُفته پندارد که این خود قائِم است

تا بر آید ناگهان صُبحِ اجل

وا رهد از ظُلمتِ ظنّ و دغل

For the repetition of تُرا to complete the rhyme, cf. VI. ٤.

ای پاسبان ٦—Shakespeare, Sonnet LXI. :

It is my love that keeps mine eye awake,
Mine own true love that doth my rest defeat,
To play the watchman ever for thy sake.

خُفته نشاید—Cf. the analogous construction of به with
a participle, XIII. ١, note.

جهانِ حامله الخ ٧—this world is passing away and
in its death-throes will bring forth the world without end.

تو گُل بُدی و دل شُدی ٨—Cf. XII. ٦—١٠; *Paradise
Lost*, Bk. v. 479 seq.

اندر کشاکشهای او الخ ٩—in the sweet anguish of
love, which 'carries a Man out from himself, as insufficient
to be his own Good, towards Good without him' (Norris,
Theory and Regulation of Love, p. 18).

توبه شِکستن ۱۰ —by repentance the poet means renunciation of love.

اگر زمین بسراسر بروید از توبه
بیک دم در آن همهرا عشق بِدرَود چو گیا

(T. 9. 11).

If the whole world should burgeon with repentance,
Love in a moment will reap it all like grass.

Cf. 'Omar's rebuke to the Harper (Whinfield's *Maṣnavī*, p. 34).

این ذرّها لرزاندلان —*Gulshani Rāz*, 165 :

Each atom doth invisibly enshrine
The deep-veil'd beauty of the Soul divine.

۱۱—۱۳ These lines are addressed to the sober worldly man whose heart, devoid of warmth and sincerity, is satisfied with mere observance and ceremonial; who has nothing but contempt for raptures, ecstasies, and illuminations; to whom it is incredible that religion should ever rise to a passion or become an 'affaire du cœur.'

ریشخند رخنهجه ۱۱ ای ریشخندِ—ریشخند is (1) laughing-stock, (2) mocker. In my translation I have given it the former sense, but the second is equally appropriate. Cf. افسوسها میداشتی below. رخنهجه seems to be an ἅπαξ λεγόμενον.

ده—سالارِ ده is the old Persian dahyāush (land, province). Like شهر, it has lost in men's mouths even the memory of its birthright.

دیئی ۱۳ —your soul, which should reflect the truth, is obscured by pride and self-will. Cf. *Maṣnavī*, 176. 9 :

زنگِ تو بر توت ای دیكِ سیاه

كرد سیماي درونت‌را تباه

Thy rust, coat on coat, O black kettle,
Has corrupted thy interior aspect.

۱۴ cf. Hāfiz, I. 276. 3 :—در من كسی دیگر بُوَد

در اندرونِ منِ خسته‌دل ندانم كیست

كه من خموشم و او در فُغان و در غَوغاست

۱۵ خَوشم چون گُلستان—the quietist is at peace
with all men. Cf. XI. ۸, note.

۱۶ این سو جهان آن سو جهان الخ—Man is the
meeting-point of two worlds : on one side the baser elements of his nature attach him to the shows and apparitions
of mortality, but in virtue of his 'divine spark' he passes
beyond them into the spiritual universe, and knocks at the
door of Being.

۱۷ كو ناطِقِ اخرس بُوَد—whose love is too deep for
utterance. Cf. I. ۱۸, note.

XXXVII.

۳ تو در جهان غریبی الخ—cf. IX. ۲۰, note. God is
foreign to the world, yet never absent from it, i.e. He at
once transcends and pervades all phenomenal existence.
Cf. *Nafaḥātu 'l Uns*, p. 183, l. 2.

~ دُزویده—the participle is used adverbially.

۶ سِپَر میکنی—'why defend your constancy by words,

when you break it in deed?' But I am inclined to believe
that سپَر کردن here = سپردن, trample under foot.

پایگاه‌—v synonymous with صفِّ نعال (XXIX. v, note).

از وُجود‌—from the state of manifestation to that of
occultation.

کوُرهٔ ۱۰‌—this reading, which involves a very slight
change, is due to Prof. Bevan. کوره, being comparatively
a rare word, would readily become کوزه : we may dis-
regard the evidence of MSS. in such cases, where the
ductus litterarum is identical, and the pointing rests, as is
likely, on the caprice or hasty conjecture of the scribe.

چو زر‌—yellow (زرد) is the hue of paleness in the East,
as in Italy. Cf. saxum quoque palluit auro (Ovid, *Meta-
morphoses*, XI. 110), luridus, lūteus pallor, etc.

عقیلهٔ عُشّاق ۱۳‌—I have erred in my translation of
this line. عقیله seems to admit two meanings in Persian,
(1) =شریف و نفیس, excellent and choice (Sūdī on Hāfiz,
III. 28. 2) and (2), like عِقال =پابند, shackle, tether,
according to a marginal gloss on *Maṣnavī*, 60. 10:

چون که عقلِ تو ۱عقیله مردُم است
آن نه عقل است آن که مار و کژدُم است

Since thy reason is the fetter of mankind,
'Tis a snake and a scorpion, but not reason.

Cf.   بگذر از لافِ عقل و فضل که هست
عقل اینجا عقیله فضل فُضول (Jāmī).

---

۱ For عقیله, by اِضافت, فلکِ.

Cease to boast of your reason and learning:
Here reason is a shackle, and learning a folly.

$$\text{اُشترِ دیوانهٔ سرمستِ من}$$

$$\text{سِلسلهٔ عقل دریدن گِرفت}\quad(\text{T. 140. 4}).$$

My frenzied intoxicated camel (the soul)
Began to rend reason's tether.

It appears from these passages that the correct translation of the first miṣrā' in the text is:

Since thou canst not endure a shackle for lovers,
i.e. if thou desirest that none who seek union with thee
shall be hindered and trammelled in their search, why then
dost thou make Reason no better than a blind guide?

$\text{سزای دُزدِ بَصر میکُنی}$ ۱۵ —viz. by withdrawing the
light of thy countenance.

در بیسریِّ عشق ۱۶ —'headlessness,' in mystical language, is equivalent to self-annihilation, utter absorption
in the divinity. Cf.

$$\text{بر من نیست من و ما عَدمیم بی سر و بی پا}$$

$$\text{سرو دل ز آن بنهادهٔ که سر از یار بر آرم}$$

$$(\text{T. 265. 2}^{a}).$$

In me is no 'I' and 'We' (personality), I am Nought,
without head and without feet;
I have sacrificed head and soul to gain the Beloved.

(Cf. the phrase, $\text{سر از خویش بر آوردن}$, to recover one's
senses.)

گر چُنانکه and گر ز آنکه ۱۷ occur frequently in
poetry instead of the simple گر.

XXXVIII.

بیکی جان ا—cf. the lines attributed to Manṣūr Ḥallāj (*Ibn Khallikān*, Arabic text, Ed. De Slane, p. 217, l. 1):

$$\text{أَنَا مَنْ أَهْوَى وَ مَنْ أَهْوَى أَنَا}$$

$$\text{نَحْنُ رُوحَانِ حَلَلْنَا بَدَنَا}$$

$$\text{فَإِذَا أَبْصَرْتَنِى أَبْصَرْتَهُ}$$

$$\text{وَ إِذَا أَبْصَرْتَهُ أَبْصَرْتَنَا}$$

I am he whom I love, and he whom I love is I;
We are two souls dwelling in one body.
When thou seest me, thou seest him,
And when thou seest him, thou seest us both.

آبِ حیات ۲—XXI. ٦, note.

اختران فلك الخ ۳—so Tennyson:

> the summer night that paused
> Among her stars to hear us; stars that hung
> Love-charmed to listen.

بعراقیم و خراسان ٦—our souls, united with the omni-present deity, are no longer subject to the laws of Space and Time.

XXXIX.

خواجه ا — the allusion in beyt ٦ (آن آفتاب) points to Shamsi Tabrīz, and not another of the poet's spiritual teachers.

فریضه دارم ۲—cf.

بر عاشقان فریضه بُوَد جُستجوی دوست

(T. 137. 2).

Lovers are bound in duty to seek the Beloved.

آن باغبان ۳—the Keeper of the garden of created things, i.e. God.

ماهی که آب دید الخ ۵—this metaphor represents the soul as remembering her heavenly origin (XVII. ۱, note), and scorning the world.

بماند—بمانُد would be contra metr. See note on XI. ۱۰.

دَور رنگ و بو--the earth, where all is fleeting and unsubstantial.

آن آفتاب ٦—cf. IV. ۸, note.

پاك خوردش—'utterly consumed it.' Cf. the English use (archaic or slang) of 'clean': e.g. clean gone out of mind.

اگر هست تو بتو—the manifold phenomenal attributes, which envelop and benumb the soul, melt away like snow in the sunbeams of divine beauty. Cf.

فُسُرده ماند یَخی کآن بزیرِ سایه بُوَد

ندید شعشعهٔ آفتاب تابانم

تبسّمِ رُخِ خورشید هر یَخی که بدید

بخویش بالد و گوید که آبِ حَیوانم

(T. 240. 13).

The ice that remains in the shade is frozen:
It saw not the brilliance of my glowing Sun.
All ice that has seen the smile of the Sun's face
Grows itself again, and says, 'I am the Water of Life.'

٧ خاصه کسی الخ —these words are connected with

عاشق کجا بماند الخ in beyt ٥.

٨ آن کیمیای بی حد الخ —cf. IV. ٧, note.

مسی ... زر شُد —IV. *ibid.*, XXVII. ٨, note.

اِرْجِعُوا—بارْجِعُو is found several times in the Kor'ān, but I do not think that the poet had any of these passages in his mind. Probably the reference here is to Kor. LXXXIX. 28, which is a favourite Sūfī text (see XXIX. ٣, note).

٩ در خواب شَو ز عالَم —let the senses sleep that the soul may awake. Cf. Hāfiz, I. 220. 7 :

بر دوخته ام دیده چو باز از همه عالَم

تا دیدهٔ من بر رُخِ زیبای تو بازست

I have shut mine eye, like a falcon, to all the world,
Since my (inward) eye is open to thy beauteous coun-
    tenance.

هر شبی از دامِ تن ارواح‌را

میرهانی میکنی الواح‌را

میرهند ارواح هر شب زین قَفَس

فارِغان بی حاکِم و محکومِ کس

شب ز زِندان بیخبر زِندانیان

شب ز دَولت بیخبر سُلطانیان

١ کندن نُقوش‌را از الواح = کندن الواح‌را. Cf. eradere genas (Propertius, IV. 8. 26).

نی غمر و اندیشهٔ سود و زیان

نی خیالِ این فُلان و آن فُلان

حالِ عارِف این بُوَد بیخواب هم

کُفت یَزدان هُمْ رُقُودٌ زین مرم

خُفته از احوالِ دُنیا روز و شب

چون قَلَم در پنجهٔ تقلیبِ رَبّ

(*Masnavī*, 14. 4).

Spirits every night from the body's snare
Thou freest, and makest the tablets clean (by erasing all
　　sensual impressions).
Spirits are set free every night from this cage,
Independent, neither ruled nor ruling.
At night prisoners forget their prison,
At night kings forget their power.
There is no sorrow, no brooding over gain and loss,
No thought of this person or that person.
This is the state of the mystic, even when he is awake:
God hath said, "(Thou would'st deem them awake) while
　　they slept[1]." Flee not from this[2].
He is asleep, day and night, to the affairs of the world,
Like a pen in the controlling hand of the Lord[3].

شَش جِهَت—the world is regarded as a cube, and its
six sides or faces are: before and behind, right and left,
above and below.

---

[1] Kor. xviii. 17.

[2] Alluding to the words, لَوَلَّیْتَ مِنْهُمْ فِرَارًا, verily thou would'st
have turned from them and fled (*ibid.*).

[3] Cf. xxx. ٣, note.

سِرِ خری ١١ (رَأسُ آلحِمار)—this expression (in Arabic رَأسُ آلحِمار)
is applied to one whose presence in a company creates
embarrassment and checks the flow of conversation. The
poet means to say that, while 'self' exists, the highest
knowledge is unattainable.

رِه نهان ١٢—the supernatural way of 'illumination'
and 'intuition.' See XI. ٥, note.

XL.

در خانهٔ دل الخ ١—see XV. ٣, note.

هُوَ آلحَقّ ٣—Kor. XXII. 6.

دغلفروشان ۴—impostors in the guise of spiritualists
(بادهنوشان). Cf. Maṣnavī, 12. 7 :

رویِ هر یك مینگر میدار پاس

بو که گردی تو ز خِدمت بوشِناس

چون بسی اِبلیس آدمروی هست

پس بهر دستی نشاید داد دست

Look on every one's face, and keep watch :
It may be that by devotion you will grow familiar with
　　　the scent (of Truth).
Since there are many devils with human features,
'Tis wrong to give your hand to every hand.

قلاشی ٥—drunken revelry. For the dropping of the
tashdīd cf. IX. ١٩, note.

چون آینه است عالَم الخ ٦—each atom of Not-being
reflects a divine attribute : the sum of these reflected rays
of Being is 'the perfect image' of God.

‫جُزوی ز کُل زِیاده‬ — cf. *Gulshani Rāz*, 635 :

‫وُجود آن جُزو دان کز کُل فُزونست‬

‫که مَوجودست کُل وین بازکُونست‬

Regard Absolute Being as the part which is greater than
the whole,

For the whole is actual being—and this is absurd (contrary
to rule).

Lāhijī says, 'Absolute Being, ‫وُجود‬, by the individualisa-
tion, ‫تَشَخُّص‬, and phenomenalisation, ‫تَعَیُّن‬, which occur
to it, gets the name of ‫مَوجود‬, actual being, and therefore
‫وُجود‬ is a part of every ‫مَوجود‬; for ‫مَوجود‬ is ‫وُجود‬ plus
‫تَعَیُّن‬. Absolute Being, again, is greater than its whole
because it contains all ‫مَوجود‬' (*ibid.*, Whinfield's note).

‫چون سبزه شَو پِیاده‬ ۷ —be lowly and obedient.　Cf.

‫سبزه پِیاده کُشته سَمَن یَک کُل شُده‬

‫اندر رِکابِ کُل چو غُلامان و کُل سُوار‬

(R. 76. 12).

‫تِیغ کشنده‬ ۸ —i.e. ‫کُشنده‬.

‫هَمِ عقل باد داده‬ —Reason is annihilated in the mystical
union of the soul with God. ‫باد داده‬ stands for ‫بِباد داده‬.
Cf. ‫که خواهد باد دادن سر‬ (T. 94. 3).

‫نِعْمَتَك, قَلَّدَهُ نِعَمَهُ‬ ۹ —cf. the phrases ‫در گُردنِم قِلاده‬
‫طَوْق‬, ‫قِلَادَةٌ فِی عُنُقِی‬ (Lane, under ‫قلد‬), and see note on
II. ٦.

For Ṣalāḥu 'ddīn see II. ١٤, note.

XLI.

٢ زخمهٔ چو آتش با—زخمه is the Arabic مِضراب, the
Roman plectrum.

٣ پردهٔ عِراقی—this musical mode, like the Dorian
measure, has a solemn and grave character suitable to
war and religion.

مقصود باده بودش الخ—he sang 'as mortal lovers do,'
but there was a deeper meaning in his words. Wine is
an emblem of the Divinity. Cf. 'Omar Khayyām, Quatrain 287:

چه کُفر و چه اِسلام چه طاعت چه کُناه
مقصود توئی بهانه بر دار از پیش

٥ آب—آبِ رز here.

زندِ زبانه—literally, 'darts a tongue of flame.'

٦ از بهرِ عاشقانرا—را is redundant in this construction,
which is not uncommon.

٧ از آن پَی—most of the 'nominal' prepositions may
be thus used, e.g. از آن پس.

٨ چشمِ بدرا—xxv. ١١, note.

٩ شمسُ الحقِ جهانم—iv. ٨, note.

XLII.

١ همرنكِ جماعت شَو—the interpretation of these
words is doubtful. (1) جماعت means 'the community
or brotherhood of saints and spiritual men.' Cf. *Nafaḥātu*

'*l Uns*, p. 206, l. 5 : 'Associate with God, or if ye cannot,
with those who are the associates of God, in order that the
blessing of their society may lead you to him.'　Jalāl'uddīn
gives the same advice in the *Maṣnavī* (22. 4 ; Redhouse,
p. 53, l. 412) :

يك زمانى صُحبتى با اوليا

بِهتر از صد ساله طاعت بى رِيا

گر تو سنگِ خاره و مرمر شَوى

چون بصاحِب‌دل رسى گَوهر شَوى

مِهرِ پاكان در ميانِ جان نِشان

دل مده اِلّا بمِهرِ دلخَوشان

كوىِ نَوميدى مَرو اُمّيدهاست

سوىِ تاريكى مَرو خَورشيدهاست

دل تُرا در كوىِ اهلِ دل كشيد

تن تُرا در حبسِ آب و گِل كشيد

هين غِذاىِ دل بِده از همدِلى

رَو بجو اِقبالِ‌را از مُقبِلى

(2) جماعت is used mystically = divine unity, the All.　Cf.
'Aṭṭār, *Manṭiqu 'ṭṭair*, 1315 :

هر كه او همرنگِ يارِ خويش نيست

عشقِ او جُز رنگِ و بوئى بيش نيست

Whoever is not of one essence with his Beloved,
His love is no better than colour and perfume.

<hr>

[1] The text has بُوى.

For the جماعت of Mohammedan Theology = 'consensus of opinion in the Church,' see Dozy, *Supplément aux Dictionnaires Arabes*, under جمع. Naturally Jalālu'ddīn, in his condemnation of schism, is not speaking as one of the orthodox.

كوي خرابات—the tavern signifies God. Cf. *Gulshani Raz*, 839 seq.

دُردكشان—like بادهنوشان (XL. ٤), those who drain to the lees the cup of celestial love.

٢ هل تا نشَوی—cave ne fias. هل and هله (XXXIV. ٤) are lightened (مُخفّف) forms of هلا.

چشمِ نِهان—see XI. ٥, note.

٣ بِكشاي دو دستِ خَود—this may also mean: 'be open-handed, sacrifice all that you have.' Cf. note on جانبخشی (XXIX. ٥).

بِشكن بُتِ خاكیرا الخ—destroy 'self,' which veils you from God.

٤ از بهرِ عجوزیرا—for this construction see XLI. ٦, note, and for the meaning of عجوز, XIII. ٦, note.

چندین چه كشی كابین—why do you consent to pay so heavy a price? By Mohammedan law the dowry is paid to the wife (see Lane's *Arabian Nights*, Vol. I. p. 321; *Modern Egyptians*, Vol. I. p. 202). Cf. Ḥāfiz, I. 438. 5:

خَوش عروسیست جهان از رهِ صورت لیكن

هر كه پَیوَست بدو عُمرِ خَوش كابین داد

The world is a fair bride as to outward looks,
But he who weds with her gives his life's joy in exchange.

So 'Omar Khayyām, Quatrain 59 :

كُفتمِ بِعروسِ دهرِ كابينِ تو چيست

كُفتا دلِ خُرّمِ تو كابينِ من است

To Destiny, my bride, I said: ' What is thy dowry?'
' My dowry,' she answered, ' is thy heart's happiness.'

سِه نان —cf. XVI. ٧, note.

خشخاش ٥ — Virgil's 'soporiferum papaver.'

طعمِ دهان —the fragrant lips of the Beloved.　Food
and sleep produce spiritual lethargy.

ساقی ٦ —cf. III. ٧, note.

دَور—در مجلسِ او دَوری, like circulus in Latin, denotes
any company for social and convivial intercourse.　Here
it may refer to the mystic dance (سماع).　Cf. Brown's
Dervishes, p. 225: ' They (the Mevlevees) commence by
forming a circle, seated on sheep-skins spread on the floor
at equal distances from each other ; they remain nearly
a half-hour in this position, the arms folded, the eyes
closed, the head inclined, and absorbed in profound
meditation.'

اينجاست ربا الخ ٧ —cf.

بتو كرِ جان دِهمِ باشد تِجارت　(T. 241. 9).

كه بِدهی بهرِ جانی صد جهانمِ

فُلانی —ترك فُلانی كُن ٨ is here an abstract noun.
The miṣrā' should be rendered :

Go, renounce personality, that you may regard the being
of the Person.

For فُلان used of God cf. VI. ٨.

أَلَمْ تَكُنْ أَرْضُ با—Kor. IV. 99 : وَسِعَتِ ارضِ ٱلله ١٠.

ٱللّٰهِ وَاسِعَةً فَتُهَاجِرُوا فِيهَا, Was not God's earth wide enough
that ye might take refuge therein? با = notwithstanding
(XI. ٣, note).

در حبس چه خُسپیدی—why are you fast asleep in the
chains of sense and worldly illusion? See note on XXXVI. ٥.

ز اندیشه گُرِه کَم زن—do not bewilder yourself by
useless thinking. Cf. XIII. ١٢, note. مزن = کَم زن. But
it seems probable that ز اندیشهٔ stands for ز اندیشه گُرِه
گُرِه (by اضافت فَلَک, XXV. ١٣, note), and that کَم زدن is
synonymous with ترك گُرِفتن. Translate :

Pass away from thought of the knot (problem), that you
may see the solution in Paradise.

This rendering brings out more clearly the double contrast
of گُرِه with شرح, and of اندیشه (opinion) with بینی
(actual vision).

سَكَتَ عَنِ خاموش شَو از كُفتن ١١—like the Arabic
ٱلْكَلَام.

XLIII.

قَمَریست رو نموده ٢—VII. ١, note.

رسد از كمانِ پنهان الخ ٣—Man is defenceless against
the shafts of divine love : he must die to the world.   Cf.

ای بهر هنگامه دامِ عشقِ تو هنگامه‌گیر

وَی چکیده خونِ ما بر راه رهرورا نشان

صد هزاران زخم بر سینه ز زخمِ تیرِ عشق

صد شکاری خسته و نه تیر پیدا نه کمان

(T. 52. 11ª).

O thou, the snare of whose love is eternally fascinating,
And O thou, who hast spilled our blood upon the way
　　for a sign to the wayfarer,
Innumerable are the wounds on the bosom pierced by
　　the arrow of love,
Many the wounded victims, but neither arrow nor bow
　　is to be seen.

مِس هستیَت الخ ٴ—cf. IV. ۷; XXVII. ۸; XXXIX. ۸. The
base phenomenal alloy, which enters into the composition
of every creature, is purified and spiritualised by love, as
was Moses, when God revealed himself in glory to Mt Sinai
and made it dust, and Moses fell in a swoon (Kor. VII. 139).

چو قارون—Qārūn (Korah) points to Mohammedans
the moral of riches that 'grow in hell' and pride that goeth
before destruction. See Kor. XXVIII. 76—81, with Sale's
notes.

بدرونِ تُست مِصری الخ ٥—within you is a divine
element producing sweetness and harmony and love, just
as the plantations of Egypt produce sugar-candy (نبات ;
see Rosenzweig's note on Hāfiz, I. 282. 5). شکّر and مصر
are often found together. Cf. T. 219. 6ª (VII. ۱, note), and
Masnavī, 122. 2:

چونکه ذو آلنُّون از غمش دیوانه شُد

مِصرِ جانرا همچو شکّرخانه شُد

When Dhū 'l Nūn grew wild with longing for it (the light of inspiration),

It became, as it were, a sugar-shop to the Egypt of the soul (it filled his soul with sweetness).

شُدهٔ غُلامِ صورت الخ ٦—your adoration is fixed on something external, whereas that which you seek is, in reality, your better self. Cf. the notes on XVII. ١١, XXVI. ١.

تو چو یوسُفی الخ—you are the mirror of divine beauty—and you turn away from the mirror! Cf. Whinfield's *Masnavī*, p. 48 seq.

شش فتیله ٩—eyes, ears, nose, and mouth.

آن شرور—'divinae particula aurae,' Eckhart's 'fünkelîn der sêle.' See Vaughan, *Hours with the Mystics*, Vol. I. p. 147.

بـکـعبهٔ دل ١٠—the soul, being the house of God (بَیْتُ آللّٰه), is the Ka'ba to which Sūfīs make their pilgrimage.

ز خری الخ—it is not helplessness, but stupid obstinacy, that prevents you from travelling towards the Truth.

سعادتِ حقّ بفرماید تا تُرا = بکشاندت سعادت ١١ بکشند. For this personal use of سعادت cf. Dozy, *Supplément aux Dictionnaires Arabes*, under سعد.

XLIV.

تو یارِ خلوَتِ نازی الخ ٢—the soul, before she entered

the world, enjoyed intimate union with God. See XVII. ١,
note.

سفری کُن —cf. XIX. ١—٦.

فی مَقْعَد —ندیمِ مجلسِ اُنسی —cf. Kor. LXIV. 55 : ۴

صِدق, (the pious shall dwell) in an assembly of Truth.
اُنس conveys the idea of perfect friendship and devotion.
It is defined by Junaid as 'freedom from shyness (اَلْحِشْمَهُ)
without loss of reverence' (اَلْهَیْبَهُ); by Dhū 'l Nūn as
'absence of reserve between lover and beloved' (اِنْبِسَاطُ
اَلْمُحِبّ إِلَی ٱلْمَحْبُوب); by Ruwaim (*Nafahātu 'l Uns*,
p. 107, l. 12 seq.), as 'holding aloof from all but God,
even from yourself'; and by Muḥiyyu' ddīn Ibnu 'l 'Arabī
(*Kitābu 'tta'rīfāt*, p. 287), as 'the effect produced in the
heart by contemplation of the divine beauty.'

که ره بری بنشانه الخ —in order to penetrate the
inmost sanctuary of Absolute Being the pilgrim must
brush aside all phenomenal illusions.

ببار اشك و چو مُشتاق گردرا بنشان

که روی ماه نه بینیم تا درین گردیم

(T. 259. 1).

Shed tears and lay the dust, like a passionate lover,
For while we are in this dust we cannot see the
Beloved's face.

Cf. *Gulshani Rāz*, 195 ; Hāfiz, I. 324. 6 ; and note on رویوشها,
IX. ١٤.

حواسّ پنج نماز است الخ ۱۰—the senses are to the heart as outward observance to deep spiritual faith. For the five daily prayers performed by Moslems see Sale's *Preliminary Discourse*, p. 147 seq.; Lane's *Arabian Nights*, Vol. I. p. 18 seq. The parallel between the five senses and the five prayers corresponds to that between the seven divisions of the heart (see Vullers under هفت خليفه) and the seven verses of Al Fātiḥa (note on VI. ۰; Nöldeke's *Sketches from Eastern History*, p. 38).

فرو خَورَد الخ ۱۱—the glimmering contingent universe melts away and vanishes in the full glory of Being.

سُهَيل جان—Canopus rises in the south; hence the allusion to

رُكِن يمانى—the south-west corner of the Kaʿba. Burckhardt says south-east, but this is a mistake (see the Plan in Burton's *Pilgrimage to El Medinah and Meccah*, Vol. III. p. 288).

سعادت ۱۲ is said to mean 'escaping from self by vision of God' (*Nafaḥātu'l Uns*, p. 472, l. 11).

حديث عشق الخ ۱۳—keep silence concerning the high mysteries of love, which are revealed only to those far advanced on the spiritual path (سالِكان = رهگُذران).

تو بندگىّ خُدا كُن—'do thou, who art less divinely gifted, learn obedience' (عُبوديّت). This is the first lesson, and also the last; therefore even the perfect man must not linger in the state of فنا, but throw off his intoxication and comply with the law. See *Gulshani Rāz*, 347—368.

XLV.

٢ نقد—the pure gold of the spirit.

٤ مشارق شادیست که—مشارق (plural of مَشرِق) sig-nifies 'the different points of the horizon, from whence the sun rises in the course of the year' (Sale's Kor'ān, Vol. II. p. 309, note).

٥ بخواب—the sleep of phenomenal existence. See XXXVI. ٥, note.

دیّار—دیّاری, literally, a dweller, is mostly used with a negative, and seldom occurs in Persian except in the phrase دیّار نیست, there is no one.

٦ چشمِ خرد—the 'intelligentiae oculus' described by Richard of St Victor (Vaughan's *Hours with the Mystics*, Vol. I. p. 128). Cf. XI. ٥, note.

نفس همچو خر اُفتاد الخ—the animal soul is driven blindly along by its ruling passion. Cf.

هوای نفس مهار است و خلق چون شُتُران

بغیرِ آن شُتُرِ مست‌را مهار مگیر

(T. 204. 5).

Sensual desire is a bridle, and men are as camels: Do not suppose that there is any bridle, except that, for the senseless camel (the soul of Man: cf. T. 140. 4, quoted in the note to XXXVII. ١٣. In other words, the body and its passions are the only obstacles to union with the Divinity).

V شیرین عقیدهٔ—عقیده probably عقیده here means 'honey'
(cf. یَعْقِد), or 'date-syrup' (رُبّ).   The name عقید is given
to a sort of dried curds, which the Arabs drink melted in
water, but this beverage, although 'cooling and refreshing'
is 'vile-tasted' and 'boasts few attractions to the stranger'
(Burton, *Pilgrimage to El Medinah and Meccah*, Vol. I.
p. 362).   The only meaning of عقیده recognised by the
dictionaries, viz. 'article of faith,' 'doctrine,' is inappropriate : the poet obviously contrasts عقیده with سرکه and
غوره, as the sweet fruits of the spirit with the bitter gall
of worldly lusts.

٨ طبیب—cf.

آمد عشق چاشتی شکلِ طبیب پیشِ من

دست نِهاد بر رگِم گُفت ضعیف شُد مَجَس

(T. 210. 12ᵃ).

Love came to me at morn in the guise of a physician ;
He laid his hand on my vein and said, ' The pulse is
　　　weak.'

٩ دستاری...سو—for this word-play cf. T. 247. 2 ; 251.
12.   From Prof. Cowell's MS. (C²) 1 quote the following
beyt, because it affords another example of عقیله (XXXVII.
١٣, note) : .

تو در عقیلهٔ ترتیبِ ریش و دستاری

چگونه رطلِ گِران خواررا بدست آری

You are in the bonds of (absorbed in) the arrangement
　　　of beard and turban :
How will you gain Him who quaffs the mighty flagon
　　　(of love)?

۱۰ سیاه—buried in the dark attributes of Not-being.
Cf. note on دینی, XXXVI. ۱۳.

۱۱ کجاست تاجرِ مسعود الخ—cf. XLII. ۵, and note.

مُشتری‌طالع—a compound adjective = 'born under a
happy star.' مُشتری means (a) the planet Jupiter, (b) pur-
chaser (خریدار).

کُرمدار—cf. Sa'dī, *Gulistān*, p. 23, fourth line from the
foot :

کُرمِ تا کی بماند این بازار

How long will this mart remain busy ?

کف—که کف ز بحرِ وَیَست ۱۲—I have rendered کف
by 'hand,' in order to show the symmetry of this line with
the two preceding it.

XLVI.

۱ سردان—such as dogmatic theologians and rational-
ising philosophers. Cf. XXXVI. ۱۱, note.

۲ صورت—see Whinfield's *Maṣnavī*, p. 70.

همرهِ همدرد—cf. Sa'dī, *Gulistān*, p. 114 :

Thou hast no pity. Then God send
A fellow-sufferer for my friend,
To mourn with me and ne'er have done ;
Two faggots higher blaze than one.

۳ ار بشکنی—if you destroy the earthly chrysalis.

۴ که تُرا = کت.

کی دُهِرِ فرد شَوی —each individual entity is finally
absorbed in the All. Perhaps, however, کُهَرِ فرد should
be translated 'a single pearl.' Cf.

بصَدَف مانِمِ و خندِمِ چو مرا در شِگَنَند

کارِ خامان بُوَد از فتح و ظفر خندیدن

(T. 275. 10ᵃ).

I am like a shell and laugh when they break me;
To laugh in triumph and victory is a trait of the inex-
    perienced.

(خندِمِ refers to the sound caused by crushing the shell.)

جاي تو صدر بُوَد ``—cf. Hāfiz, II. 254. 3 :

در جاهِ عشق و دَولتِ رِندانِ پاکباز

پَیوَسته صدرِ مَیگَدَها بود مسکنِمِ

جا بجا بر گُذَری ۷ —Man, during his phenomenal
extrusion, is a homeless vagabond in the world. Cf.
Gulshani Rāz, 281, and note.

عدد—عددِ نرد is either 'die' (as numerus in Latin
poetry), or 'piece,' which gives a better sense.

گُرد—در آن گُرد ۸ گُرد sometimes = گُردون, but here, I
think, = گُردِ آفتاب, the atoms floating in a sunbeam, with
an allusion to Shamsi Tabrīz.

XLVII.

اَلْعَطْفُ عَلَی شَیْءٍ = بِر سِرِ چیزی بودن—بر سرِ کینی ۲
to incline towards a thing. Cf. Surūrī's commentary on

تو بر سرِ قدرِ خویش میباش و وقار

(*Gulistān*, p. 27).

Attend to (be mindful of) your rank and dignity.

Similar phrases are سر در سرِ چیزی and سرِ چیزی داشتن
کردن.

سبب غَیرتِ تُست الخ ۳ —see notes on IV. ۲, XXIII. ۷.

و اگر پرده دری تو الخ ۴ —cf. *Maṣnavī*, 8. 2; Whinfield's *Maṣnavī*, p. 7:

پرده بر دار و برهنه گو که من
می نگنجم با صنم در پیرهن

گفتم ار عُریان شَوَد او در عیان
نی تو مانی نی کِنارت نی میان

سرِ ایمان به مَیَت خَوش ه —cf. سرخَوش = مست.

همه‌را گوش کشیدی —cf.

چونکه در آید بقُصورِ دماغ
اُفتد از بامِ نگون هوش هوش

چونکه کشد گوش خِرَد سويِ خَود
گوید از دردِ خِرَد گوش گوش

(T. 74. 12).

When he enters the chambers of the brain,
Reason falls headlong from the roof.
When he pulls the ear of Intelligence towards him,
It cries in pain, 'My ear, my ear!'

چه روی تو الخ ۷—cf. Shakespeare, Sonnet LXVII.:

> Why should poor beauty indirectly seek
> Roses of shadow, since his rose is true?

If تو is addressed to the reader, the change of person, though harsh, is not unexampled. It may, however, denote the Beloved, whom the poet upbraids for having forsaken him.

نفری کف ببریدند ۸—xv. ۱۲, note.

ز پلیدی و ز خوبی ۹—of flesh and spirit, Not-being and Real Being.

فَإِذَا سَوَّيْتُهُ—چو درو روح دمیدی ۱۰—Kor. xv. 29: وَنَفَخْتُ فِيهِ مِنْ رُوحِی فَقَعُوا لَهُ سَاجِدِينَ, (God said to the angels:) When therefore I shall have completed him (Adam) and breathed of my spirit into him, do ye fall and worship him. روح is probably used here of the reasonable soul (نفسِ ناطقه). See *Gulshani Rāz*, 318 and note, 493.

ز نومیدیِ اوّل الخ ۱۲—when Man reflects of what he was created, and what, by gradual evolution, he has become, can he doubt the ultimate reality of his deepest aspirations, wild and impracticable as they seem at present? See XII. ۶—۱۰, and note, XVIII. ۶, note, Whinfield's *Maṣnavī*, pp. 216, 231, *Gulshani Rāz*, 317—338.

کلید ۱۳—Greek κλείς (κλειδ-), Arabic إقلید. The 'key' is Love.

XLVIII.

قفص ‏٢‎—Latin capsa or capsus (Nöldeke, *Persische Studien*, p. 38; Fraenkel, *Die Aramäischen Fremdwörter*, p. 118). As *s* in loan-words may be represented either by س or ص, the form قفس is equally correct.

تو باز خاص بُدی الخ ‏٣‎—the story of the 'white falcon,' whose beak and claws were cut by a 'vile old woman' (گُوژ كمپیری), is told in the *Masnavī*, 362. 18 seq.; Whinfield's *Masnavī*, p. 203. For the allegory cf. x. ٧, note, XLII. ٤, note.

طبلِ باز—see notes on XVI. ٣, XXIX. ٣.

بُلبُلِ مستی میانۀ جُغدان ‏٤‎—I cannot find this in the *Masnavī*. But cf. the tale of the Falcon and the Owls (*ibid.* 126. 13; Whinfield's *Masnavī*, p. 76).

بسی خُمار كشیدی الخ ‏٥‎—XIII. ٨, note.
خراباتِ جاودان—XLII. ١, note.

تاجرا...آفتاب ‏٨‎—cf. IV. ٨. He who is eternally glorified by union with the source of all light, desires no earthly crown.

كمر...میان—one meaning of میان is 'waist.' از میان رفتن =e medio abire (to die).

دو چشمِ كُشته ‏٩‎—obliquis oculis, enviously.

سوی جان نِگری—you look back with regret on the life of your individual soul, which is now exalted above life.

خَرَجتُ أَبتَغی در شِكارِ شُكور ‏١٠‎—cf. the saying, رَیحَانَ ٱللَّه, I went forth to seek the bounty of God (Lane

under راح). شُكور is the plural of شُكر, which, as applied
to God, means 'requital,' 'recompense.' شَكور, the Giver of
rewards, is a possible reading.

با دو پر—i.e. with hope and fear. According to the
Sūfīs, اَلْخَوْفُ وَالرَّجَاءِ لِلْمَرْءِ كَالْجَنَاحَيْنِ لِلطَّائِرِ) (Būstān,
p. 31, last line).

دو پر—چو سِپَر is followed by سِپَر (suggesting سه پر),
which leads up to سِنان. These trifles would hardly be
worth notice, if they did not illustrate the artificial character even of the best Persian poetry.

جانِبِ سِنان رفتی—this strange metaphor may perhaps
allude to the sport of hunting the antelope with hawks.
'The buck is seldom taken. The Arabs, are, indeed,
afraid to fly their hawks at the latter, as these fine birds,
in pouncing, frequently impale themselves on its sharp
horns' (Malcolm, *Sketches of Persia*, p. 54).

كه پیشِ بادِ خِزانی الخ ١١—all things tremble and
flee before the wind of death; only the soul, conscious of
immortality, remains unmoved and triumphant.

خموش...از ١٣—see XLII. ١١, note.

رنج گُفت و گُوی—speech is finite, silence infinite.

مخسپ—the soul, waking from the dark night of the
world, enjoys eternal day in the bosom of God. Cf. XXXVI.
٥, note.

ADDITIONAL NOTES.

I. ١ (note). Cf. the ḥadīs: لَا أَنْظُرُ إِلَى صُوَرِكُمْ وَإِنَّمَا أَنْظُرُ إِلَى قُلُوبِكُمْ, I do not look at your outward forms, but only at your hearts.

I. ١٠. The variant نِگْين‌كُنى (L.) must be taken as a compound. Translate: If thou art the Bezel-maker's thrall, O master. So we find (T. 133. 7ᵃ):

با تو ز زیان چه باك داریم

ای سودکُنِ همه زیانها

With Thee how should we be afraid of loss,
O Thou, who turnest every loss to gain?

II. ١٣ (note). See also *Nafaḥātu 'l Uns*, p. 539.

IV. ١. Cf. *Nafaḥātu 'l Uns*, p. 422, l. 4: Shaikh Aḥmad Ghazzālī relates that his shaikh, i.e. Abū Bakr Nassāj, exclaimed in his prayers, "O God, with what design was I created?" Answer came: "The design was that I might behold myself in the mirror of thy soul, and plant my love in thy heart."

IV. ٧. كردست مسرا كيميا : 'has converted copper

into the Philosophers' Stone.' For the derivation of كيميا
see Dozy, *Supplément*, sub voc.

IV. ١١. Cf.

كردم از حَيرت سُجودى پيشِ او

كُفت بى ساجِد سُجودى خَوش برآر

آه بى ساجِد سُجودى چون بُوَد

كُفت بيچون باشد و بى خارخار

كُردنكرا پيش كردم كُفتمش

ساجِدىرا سر ببُر از ذو آلفِقار

تيغ تا او بيش زد سر بيش شُد

تا بُرُست از كُردنمر سر صد هزار

(T. 206. 6).

I prostrated myself in bewilderment before him:
He said, 'Perform joyfully the act of prostration without
    the agent.'
'Alas! how can there be an act of prostration without
    an agent?'
He said, ''Tis an act involving neither method nor per-
    plexity.'
I offered my neck and said to him,
'Sever the agent's head with <u>Dh</u>ū 'lfiqār' (XXVI. ٣, note).
The more he plied the sword, the more my head increased,
Till there grew from my neck innumerable heads.

(For the last couplet, cf. XVIII. ٤, note.)

According to Abū 'l 'Abbās Dīnavarī (*Nafaḥātu 'l Uns*,
p. 161, l. 18), "The first stage of prayer (الذِّكُر) is to

forget self, and the last stage is the effacement of the
worshipper in the act of worship without consciousness of
worship, and such absorption in the object of worship as
precludes return to the subject thereof; this is the state
of supreme annihilation " (فَنَاءُ ٱلْفَنَاءِ).

VI. ١ (note). Further definitions of فقر are found in
the *Nafaḥātu 'l Uns*, p. 10, ll. 18—23 ; p. 11, ll. 3, 5, 14 ;
p. 102, ll. 14—21 ; p. 242, l. 5 ; p. 301, l. 15 ; p. 303, l. 2.

VI. ٣ (note). The words مَا لَا عَيْنُ رَأَتْ وَلَا أُذْنُ
سَمِعَتْ وَلَا خَطَرَ عَلَى قَلْبِ بَشَرٍ, What eye hath not seen,
nor ear heard, nor hath it entered into the heart of man,
are quoted from an ḥadīs, which is a mere translation of
the passage in I. Corinthians.

VII. ٤. چون دیده پُر شَوَد, i.e. with tears.

VIII. ٣ (note). Cf. the saying of Ma'rūf Karkhī
(*Nafaḥātu 'l Uns*, p. 43, l. 1) : " Beware lest God behold
thee save in the garb of a beggar " (فِی زِیِّ مِسْکِینٍ).

IX. ٣ (note). Cf.

فرشته رُست بعلمِ و بهیمه رُست بجهل
درین میان به تنازُع بماند مردُمزاد
کهی همیکشدش علمِ سوي عِلّیّین
کهیش جهل به پستی که هرچه بادا باد

(T. 164. 8).

The angel grew with knowledge, the beast with ignorance ;
Man remained in dispute[1] between them.
Sometimes knowledge draws him to the seventh Heaven,
Sometimes ignorance drags him down, so that (he says),
   'Come what will !'

(T. reads مردمِ راد, but this is plainly an error.)

---

[1] i.e., an object of dispute.

IX. ١٣ (note). Shaikh Abū Saʿīd ibn Abī 'l Khair said : "The veil between man and God is not earth or heaven, not the empyrean (عرش) or the throne (كُرسى); the veil is thy conceit and egoism ; when they are removed, thou hast arrived at God" (*Nafaḥātu 'l Uns*, p. 345, l. 15). See also ibid. p. 147, l. 3, p. 212, l. 21, p. 304, l. 6.

IX. ١٩٠. كوزهٔ ادراكها : the expression, كوزهٔ ادراك, occurs in a speech attributed to Jalālu 'ddīn (*Nafaḥātu 'l Uns*, p. 537, l. 15).

X. ٢. The longing for immediate vision of the divine beauty is illustrated by Shuʿaib, to whom, 'when his cries and wailing and dewy tears passed beyond measure, there came at dawn a voice from Heaven' :

گر مُجرمى بخشيدمت در جُرم آمُرزيدمت

فِردَوس خواهى دادمت خامُش رهٔ كُن اين دُعا

كُفتهٔ نه اين خواهم نه آن ديدارِ حقّ خواهمِ عيان

گر هفت بحرِ آتش شَوَد من در شَوَمِ بهرِ لقا

گر راندهٔ از منظرم رانده شَوَد چشمِ سرم

من در جحيمِ اولَىٰ‌ترم جنّت نشايد مر مرا

جنّت مرا بىِ روىِ او همِ دوزخست و همِ عدو

من سوختمِ زين 'رنگِ و بو كو فرّ انوارِ لقا

كُفتند ²بارى كمِ گِرى تا كُم نگردد مبصرى

كاين چشمِ نابينا شَوَد چون بگذرد از حدِّ بُكا

¹ See XXXIX. ٥, note.   ² يارى (T.).

كُفت ار دو چشم عاقبت خواهند ديدن روي او

هر جُزوِ من چشمی شَوَد کی غم خَورم من از عمی

(T. 12. 11ᵃ).

XI. ۳. دهانِ باز: دهان‌باز, with omitted preposition, may be the correct reading.

XI. ۸. The following definition of مُرید is ascribed to Mansūr Hallāj: هُوَ ٱلرَّامِی بِأَوَّلِ قَصْدِهِ إِلَى ٱللَّهِ سُبْحَانَهُ فَلَا يَعْرُجُ حَتَّى يَصِلُ, i.e., as Jāmī paraphrases it, 'The murīd is he who from the first makes Almighty God the goal of his efforts, and is never satisfied or engrossed by anything until he attains it' (*Nafaḥātu 'l Uns*, p. 174, l. 3).

XIII. ۱۵ (note). تميز = 'clean' in Turkish.

XIV. ۱۰ (note). زُهد: cf. *Nafaḥātu 'l Uns*, p. 131, ll. 20—22.

XIV. ۱۱ (note). استقامت: cf. *Nafaḥātu 'l Uns*, p. 131, ll. 7—11; p. 158, last line.

XV. ۱۶ (note). بيشهٔ شيران: cf. Dante, *Inferno*, Canto I. According to Boccacio, the 'selva selvaggia,' where the poet lost his way, represents the path of contemplative life: the wild beasts are the sensual passions. But possibly بيشهٔ شيران here = the World of Ideas (cf. Rosen's *Maṣnavī*, p. 154, note 533). Giordano Bruno, allegorising the story of Actaeon, describes Actaeon (the intellect) as letting loose his dogs (thoughts) 'upon the track of savage beasts in forests wild.' These 'savage beasts,' he continues, are 'the intelligible kinds of ideal conceptions, which are occult, followed by few, visited but rarely, and which do not disclose themselves to all those who seek them' (*The Heroic Enthusiasts*, translated by

Williams, Vol. I. p. 91). If this explanation be accepted, we must read with V. مزن in beyt ١٨.

XVI. ٩. آوارگيّ کوه الخ: cf. the saying, Gnostics (اهلِ معرفت) are the wild beasts of God: in the world they do not associate with mankind (*Nafaḥātu 'l Uns*, p. 62, l. 8).

XVI. ١٦. Cf. *Nafaḥātu 'l Uns*, p. 181, l. 1: 'The ways to God are more than the number of the stars in heaven, yet I desire one of them and cannot find it'; and again, 'Be content with the pain of search: what have you to do with finding?' (ibid. p. 422, l. 2); 'He is not to be found by search, but the seeker finds him and does not seek until he finds him' (ibid. p. 83, l. 13).

XVI. ١٨ (note). Phaedrus (III. 19) tells this anecdote of Esop:

> 'Et quidam e turba garrulus,
> Aesope, medio sole, quid cum lumine?
> Hominem, inquit, quaero, et abiit festinans domum.'

In the *Maṣnavī* the heading is: حکايتِ آن راهب الخ. Lévêque (*Les Mythes et les Légendes de l'Inde et la Perse*, p. 586) quotes from the Avadānas a very similar tale, of which a Brahman is the hero.

XVI. ٢١. Khwāja Bahā' u'ddīn Naqshband defines ايمان as 'the fixed determination of the heart to deny all things, whether good or evil, in the pursuit of which (human) hearts are absorbed, except God' (*Nafaḥātu 'l Uns*, p. 442, l. 16). For another definition, which, however, is only verbally different, see XXXV. ٢, note (*Nafaḥātu 'l Uns*, p. 434, l. 10).

XVII. The gist of this poem occurs in a passage from

Heywood's *Hierarchy of the Blessed Angels* (*England's Anti-phon*, p. 135):

> I have wandered like a sheep that's lost,
> To find thee out in every coast:
> *Without* I have long seeking bin,
> Whilst thou, the while, abid'st *within*.
> Through every broad street and strait lane
> Of this world's city, but in vain,
> I have enquired. The reason why?
> I sought thee ill: for how could I
> Find thee *abroad*, when thou, mean space,
> Hadst made *within* thy dwelling-place?

XVII. ٨. جَعَلْنَا : cf. Kor. II. 119 : مقصد پیر و برنا
.ٱلْبَیْتَ مَثَابَةً لِلنَّاس

XVIII. ١. وَز بهرِ یکی جان الخ : cf. *Nafaḥātu 'l
Uns*, p. 107, ll. 2—5 : 'The Shaikhu 'l Islām (Abū Ismaʿīl
ʿAbdu 'llāh ibn Abī Manṣūr Muḥammad Al-Anṣārī) said :
"Spiritual sacrifice (بذلِ روح) does not consist in going
forth to war that you may be slain, but rather in not
disputing with God about your soul (که با ٱلله تعالی بهرِ
جانِ خَود مُنازعت در نَگیری), in devoting to him your
soul, body, and heart, while you still have them, and in
not complaining of any affliction that comes to you from
him."'

XIX. ٩. و نی بحر توان شُد : cf. VIII. ٥, note.

XX. ١ (note). Cf. the saying of Abū 'l Qāsim Naṣrā-
bādī (*Nafaḥātu 'l Uns*, p. 46, l. 16): جَذْبَةٌ مِنْ جَذَبَاتِ
ٱلْحَقِّ تُرْبِى عَلَى عَمَلِ ٱلثَّقَلَیْنِ, "one pull from God is

better than (all) the actions of men and jinn" (quoted again, p. 441, l. 15, with the substitution of تُوازِی for (تُوُرِبی عَلَی). For a discussion of the whole question see Whinfield's *Masnavi*, p. 18 seq. While he condemns those who busy themselves about worldly objects, Jalālu 'ddīn praises the divine aspiration, 'göttliche Bestrebung,' of the saints and prophets (Rosen's *Masnavi*, p. 133).

XX. ٣. It is related of Shamsi Tabrīz (*Nafaḥātu 'l Uns*, p. 536, l. 9) that when he arrived in the territory of Baghdād, he discovered Auḥadu 'ddīn Kirmānī, and asked him what he was doing. "I am beholding the moon," said he, "in a bowl of water." "Unless," replied Shamsu 'ddīn, "you have a boil on your neck, why do you not behold it in the sky?" The story is re-told p. 686, l. 17.

XXII. ٧. جانِ دُوُم : Plotinus, following Plato in the Timaeus, distinguishes the immortal soul, which is derived immediately from God (ἡ ἀρχὴ τῆς ψυχῆς) and the mortal soul, constructed by the offspring of God (ψυχῆς ἄλλο εἶδος), which is 'subject to terrible and irresistible affections.' Jalālu 'ddīn refers here to the former—τῇ ἑτέρᾳ ψυχῇ τῇ καθαρᾷ (Plotinus, *Enneades*, II. 3. 9 ; Jowett's Plato, Vol. III. p. 653).

XXII. ٩. The Arabic proverb is : كُلُّ شَیْءٍ یَرْجِعُ إِلَی أَصْلِهِ, Every thing returns to its source.

XXII. ١٠. This metaphor of a divine centre, round which the phenomenal universe revolves, is a favourite with Plotinus (e.g. *Enneades*, VI. 9. 8). See Rousselot, *Les Mystiques Espagnols*, p. 105 seq.

XXIII. ٥. Cf. the sayings : لَا یَعْرِفُهُ أَحَدٌ غَیْرُهُ, He is known by none save Himself, and اَلْعِلْمُ فِی ذَاتِ ٱللَّهِ تَعَالَی

جَهْل[1], the knowledge of God's essence is ignorance (*Nafa-ḥātu 'l Uns*, p. 243, ll. 11—12).

XXIII. ٦. آن چِراغ : the reference may be to Kor. XXIV. 35.

XXV. ١٦. از غَیرِ اهل بنهُفتمِ : *Nafaḥātu 'l Uns*, p. 140, l. 20 : He is no gnostic (عارِف), who utters the knowledge of divine cognition (علمِ مَعرِفت) before the worldly.

XXVI. ٩. سادهرنگِی : cf.

ندارد رنگ آن عالَمِ و لیک از تابهٔ دیده

جو نور از جامِ رنگآمیز این سُرخ و کبود آمد

(T. 187. ٩ᵃ).

That world is colourless, but from the reflexion of the
    eye,
Like the light from a cup of coloured glass, these red
    and blue (tints) arise.

So Plotinus describes the Soul, which all true lovers desire, as : ἀχρώματον μὲν αὐτήν, ἀχρώματον δὲ καὶ τὴν σωφροσύνην ἔχουσαν (*Enneades*, I. 6. 5).

XXVIII. ٧ (note). Cf. *Nafaḥātu 'l Uns*, p. 299, ll. 15—18 : God endows His servant with part of His own knowledge, and assigns to him suffering in proportion to the knowledge which He has bestowed, in order that he may support that suffering by virtue of knowledge. Cf. Plotinus, *Enneades*, III. 2. 4.

---

[1] عِلمِ فی for عِلمِ بِ is not classical Arabic. We might render, 'Knowledge, in comparison with God's essence, is ignorance,' but this, probably, was not the sense intended by Dhū 'l Nūn, to whom the saying is ascribed. Cf. *Nafaḥātu 'l Uns*, p. 37, l. 3, where we find اَلعِلْمُ for التَّفَكُّر.

XXVIII. ٨ (note). Cf. the saying : أَلنَّفْسُ هِيَ أُمُّ
ٱلْأَصْنَامِ, Self is the mother of idols.

XXIX. ٥ (note). In the first miṣrā' of the passage
quoted from the *Maṣnavī* read, with the Būlāq Edition,
سربخشی for سربازی.

XXXI. ٣ (note). Saqsīn is found again (T. 192. 8ª):

گُويند كه در سقسين تُركى دو كمان دارد

گُر زآن دو يكى كُمِ شُد مارا چه زِيان دارد

They say that in Saqsīn the Turkmān has two bows;
If one of those has been lost, how am I the loser
     thereby?

It seems likely, from the mention of Turkmāns, that the
city on the borders of China is here intended.

XXXI. ٨. The first miṣrā' is a quotation from Kor.
LVII. 3.

XXXII. ٣ (note). Cf. the saying, مِنَ ٱلْقَلْبِ إِلَى
ٱلْقَلْبِ رَوْزَنَة, there is a window from one heart to another.

XXXIV. ١ (note). Cf. *Nafaḥātu 'l Uns*, p. 687, ll.
10—20; Plotinus, *Enneades*, I. 3. 2, I. 6. 2 and 4. According to the proverb : ٱلْمَجَازُ قَنْطَرَةُ ٱلْحَقِيقَةِ, Illusion is the
bridge to Reality.

XXXVI. ٣ (note). So we find عجائب used adjectivally :

دلِ ما يافت ازين باده عجائب بوئى

(T. 253. 11).

XXXVI. ١٣. Cf.

كِيست در گُوش كه او ميشنَود آوازم

يا گُدامست سُخُن ميكُند اندر دهنم

كيست در ديده كه از ديده برون مينگرد

يا چه جانست نگوئى كه منش پيرهنم

(T. 256. 9).

Who is he in mine ear that hearkens to my voice,
Or who is he that utters words in my mouth?
Who is he in mine eye that looks out of mine eye,
Or what is the soul—wilt thou not say—of which I
  am the garment?

XXXVI. ۱۵ (note). Cf. Junaid's definition of Sūfiism:
كه ساعتى بنشينى بى تيمار, to sit for a while without
repining (*Nafaḥātu 'l Uns*, p. 90, l. 20), and the saying of
Shaikh ‘Abdu 'llāh Balyānī :

درويشى نرنجيدن است اگر اين حاصل كنى واصل گردى

(*ibid.* p. 295, l. 12).

XXXVI. ۱۶ (second miṣrā‘). Cf.

جان چو روز است و تن ما چو شب و ما بميان

واسطهٔ روز و شب خويش مثال سحريم

(T. 252. 12).

The soul resembles day and the body night, and we in
  the middle
Are like the dawn between our own day and night.

(The iẓāfat of واسطه is dropped in scansion.)

XXXVIII. ۱. Cf. the anecdote which is told of Shaikh
Mufarrij : He was seen by one of his companions on the
day of ‘Arafa (9th of Dhū 'l Ḥijja) at ‘Arafāt, and by
another, on the same day, in his own house, where they
spent the whole day together. When these individuals
met and communicated to each other what they had seen,
they began to quarrel. Said one, "On the day of ‘Arafa

he was at 'Arafāt," and confirmed it with the oath of
divorce. "He was at home all that day," retorted the
other; and he too took the oath of divorce. The dis-
putants went before Shaikh Mufarrij and told him what
had passed between them. "You are both in the right,"
said he, "and neither of you has divorced his wife." A
great personage relates: "I begged the Shaikh to explain
how this could be, since the asseveration of each party
seemed to involve the perjury of the other. The Shaikh
desired a number of learned men, who were present, to
speak on this point, and all did so, but none gave a final or
sufficient answer. In the meantime it dawned upon me
what the answer was, and, at the Shaikh's invitation, I
spoke as follows: When a saint grows perfect in saintship,
in the sense that his spirituality can be clothed in a visible
shape, his power becomes absolute: he can show himself
in many forms and in divers places simultaneously, just as
he wishes. Therefore he may really have been seen in one
form at 'Arafāt and in another form in his own house, and
neither party has violated his oath." Shaikh Mufarrij
said: "What you have spoken is the true answer"
(*Nafaḥātu 'l Uns*, p. 676, l. 17—p. 677, l. 14).

XXXIX. ١١. There is in this couplet an allusion to
the entry of Jesus into Jerusalem, riding upon an ass.
See IV. ٩, note.

XXXIX. ١٢. فنينه: see Kazimirski, *Dictionnaire
Arabe-Français*, under فن. Cf. the phrase, فَتَّة مِنَ ٱلدَّهْرِ.
a particular period of time.

APPENDIX I.

SOME ILLUSTRATIVE PASSAGES FROM THE DĪVĀN,
WITH A LIST OF THE HISTORICAL AND
AUTOBIOGRAPHICAL ALLUSIONS.

A. *The Mystical Union of the Soul with God.* **Cf.**
Emerson : 'There is one mind common to all individual
men. Who hath access to this universal mind is a party
to all that is or can be done, for this is the only sovereign
agent.'

١   با نُه پِدَر در هر فلك يكچند دَوران كرده ام

با اختران در بُرجها من سالها گُرديده ام

٢   يكچند ناپيدا بُدم با او بهم يكجا بُدم

در مُلكِ أوْ أَدْنَى بُدم ديدم هر آنچه ديده ام

٣   مانندِ طِفل اندر شِكم من پرَوَرِش دارم ز حق

يكبَار زايد آدمى من بارها زائيده ام

٤   در خِرقهٔ تن‌پارها بودم بسى در كَرها

وَز دستِ خَود اين خِرقه‌را بِسيار من بِدريده ام

٥   با زاهِدان در صَومَعه شبها بروز آورده ام

با كافِران در بُتكده پيش بُتان خُسپيده ام

٦ هم دُزدِ عیّاران منم هم رنجِ بیماران منم

همِ ابر و همِ باران منم در باغها باریده ام

٧ بر دامنِ گَردِ فنا نشست هرگِز ای گُدا

در باغ و بُستانِ بقا کُلها فراوان چیده ام

٨ از آب و آتش نیستم وَز بادِ سرکش نیستم

خاكِ مُنقش نیستم من بر همه خندیده ام

٩ من شمسِ تبریزی نَیم من نورِ پاكم ای پِسَر

زِنهار اگر بینی مرا با کس مگو من دیده ام

(T. 257. 11ª).

I have circled awhile with the nine Fathers[1] in each
   heaven,
For years I have revolved with the stars in their signs.
I was invisible awhile, I was united with Him,
I was in the kingdom of "*or nearer*[2]," I saw what I
   have seen.
I have my nourishment from God, like a child in the
   womb;
Man is born once, I have been born many times[3].
Clothed in the mantle of corporeal limbs, I have busied
   myself often with affairs,
And often I have rent this mantle[4] with my own hands.
I have passed nights with ascetics in the monastery,
I have slept with infidels before the idols in the pagoda.
I am the theft of rogues[5], I am the pain of the sick,
I am both cloud and rain, I have rained in the meadows.

---

[1] See *Gulshani Rāz*, 227 seq.   [2] XVII. ١٠, note.
[3] XVIII. ٢, note.   [4] cf. I. ١٠, and note.

[5] Prof. Bevan suggests دردِ غَیّاران, 'the pangs of the jealous'—
a very attractive emendation.

Never did the dust of annihilation settle on my skirt, O
    dervish !

I have gathered a wealth of roses in the meadow and
    garden of eternity.

I am not of water nor fire, I am not of the froward wind ;

I am not moulded clay : I have mocked (transcended)
    them all.

O son, I am not Shamsi Tabrīz, I am the pure Light ;

If thou seest me, beware ! Tell it not to any, that thou
    hast seen.

    B. *Traces of Neo-platonist influence.* In the Intro-
duction I have noticed the chief doctrines common to
Jalālu 'ddīn and Plotinus. The resemblance is often
obscured by metaphorical expression.

    (*a*) Emanation.

ز جان تا تن بسی راهست و در تن مینماید جان

چنین دان جانِ عالمرا کز او عالم جوانستی

ز شخصِ عالمِ ۱کُبرَی چنین پرگار بیجهانست

که چرخ ار بی‌روانستی بدُنیا بی‌روانستی

زمین و آسمانهارا مدد از عالمِ عقلست

که عقل اقلیمِ نورانی و پاک و دُرفشانستی

جهانِ عقلِ روشن‌را مددها از صِفَت آمد

صِفاتِ ذاتِ خلّاقی که شاه کُنْ فَکَانستی

                    (T. 58. 9ᵃ).

---

[1] We should expect أَكْبَر, but cf. *Maṣnavi* (Būlāq Ed.) Bk I.
p. 100, l. 5, where the Turkish translation reads عالمِ کُبراده.

'Tis a long way from soul to body, and yet soul appears
    in body :

Regard thus the soul of the world, whereby the world is
    young (quickened).

Such is the material circumference[1] (depending) from the
    Person[2] in the Greater World,

That, if the circle[3] (itself) were not endued with life, there
    would be no life in this world of ours.

To the earth and the heavens comes replenishment[4] from
    the world of Reason[5],

For Reason is a realm luminous[6] and pure and pearl-
    scattering.

To the world of bright Reason come succours from Attri-
    bute,

The Attributes of the Essence of the Creator, who is lord
    of "*Be and it was.*"

    (*b*)   Emanation and Ecstasy.

١   يك گُوهرى چو بَيضا جوشيد و كُشت دريا

   كف كرد و كف زمين شُد وَز دودِ او سما شُد

٢   الحق نِهان سِپاهى پوشيده پادشاهى

   هر لحظه حمله آورد آنگه باصل وا شُد

---

[1] The region of formless matter (Not-being), in which the phenomenal world is reflected.

[2] Absolute Being.

[3] The Neo-platonists represent God as a circle, but the poet may
be thinking of the centrifugal devolution by which Being is communicated (cf. Plotinus, *Enneades*, I. 7. 1).

[4] For مدد see VI. ١ ٢, note.

[5] The νοῦς of Plotinus, the λόγος of Philo.

[6] Cf. *Enneades*, III. 5. 9.

٣   گرچه ز ما نِهان شُد در عالمی روان شُد

تا نیستش نخوانی ۱گر از نظر جُدا شُد

۴   هر حالتی چو تیراست اندر کمانِ قالب

زد در نشانهٔ خویش گر از کمان رها شُد

۵   گرچه صَدَف ز ساحِل قطره رُبود و گُم شُد

در بحر جوید اورا غوّاص کآشنا شُد

٦   آنگه ز عالمِ جان آمد سپاهِ اِنسان

عقلش وزیر گشت و دل رفت و پادشا شُد

٧   تا بعد چند گاهی دل یادِ شهرِ جان کرد

وا گشت جُمله لشکر در عالمِ فنا شُد

٨   گوئی چگونه باشد آمد شُدِ معانی

اینك بوقتِ خُفتن بنگر گِرِهگُشا شُد

(T. 162. 4ᵃ).

The one Substance boiled, like an egg, and became the
     Sea[2];
It foamed, and the foam became Earth, and from its
     spray arose the Sky.
In truth, a hidden army with a viewless king
Continually makes an onset, and then returns to its home.
Tho' it be hidden from us, it moves in the world;
Do not call it non-existent, tho' it be out of sight.

---

[1] T. has از عالمی جُدا شُد, where عالمی seems to have come
from the line above. The reading in the text is that of B².

[2] XIX. V.

Every instant there is, so to speak, an arrow in the bow
of the body:

If it escapes from the bow, it strikes its mark.

Tho' the shell stole a drop from the shore[1] and vanished,

The diver that is a friend[2] (of God) seeks it in the sea.

Then from the spiritual world the army of Man descended,

Reason was its vizier, and the Soul went forth and
became king.

At last, after a while, the Soul remembered the spiritual
city:

The whole army turned back and entered the world of
death.

'How,' you may ask, 'is the coming and going of ideas?'

Lo, consider the time of sleep[3]—it solves the difficulty.

C.   The Sleep of Phenomenal Existence[4].

١   بجُنب بر خَور آخِر که چاشتگاه رسید

ازآنکه خُفته چو جُنبید خواب شُد مهجور

٢   مگو که خُفته نَیَم ناظِرم بصُنعِ خُدا

نظر بصُنع حِجابست از چنان منظور

٣   روانِ خُفته اگر داندی که در خوابست

از آنچه دیدی نی خَوش شُدی و نی رنجور

(T. 32. 2).

---

[1] VIII. ٥, note.

[2] For the double meaning of آشنا (friend, swimmer or swimming)
cf. x. ٣, note.

[3] XXXIX. ٩, note.   [4] Cf. XXXVI. ٥, note.

[5] T. reads خَود. But چاشتگاه points to خَور, and خَورشید
occurs in the preceding couplet.

Come, move towards the Sun, for morning has arrived,
Because, when the sleeper moves, sleep is banished.
Do not say, 'I am not asleep, I am regarding the work
  of God':
Viewing the work is a veil over the Object of vision.
If the sleeping spirit knew itself to be asleep,
Whatever it might see, it would feel neither joy nor
  sorrow.

D. *The Theory of Ideas.*

زاده از اندیشهایِ خوبِ تو وِلدان و حور

زاده از اندیشهایِ زِشتِ تو دیوِ کلان

سِرّ و اندیشه مُهَندِس بین شُده قصر و سرا

سِرّ تقدیرِ ازلرا بین شُده چندین جهان

(T. 53. 5ª).

From thy good thoughts are born the boys of Paradise
  and the houris,
From thy evil thoughts is born the great demon (Iblīs)[2].
See how the secret thought of the geometrician has become
  a castle or a palace,
See how the hidden Providence without beginning has
  become this mighty universe.

E. *The Strife of the Elements towards Unity*[3].

هر چار عُنصُرند درین دیگ همر بجوش

نه خاک بر قرار و نه نار و نمر و هوا

---

[1] For اندیشهٔ by اضافت فِک.

[2] It is well known that, according to Zoroaster, the souls of the
pious after death are met by their own good thoughts, good words,
and good deeds in the form of a beautiful maiden, whereas a vile and
hideous woman represents to the souls of the wicked their evil
thoughts, evil words, and evil deeds. This notion occurs repeatedly
in Zoroastrian literature. See e.g. *The Book of Ardā Virāf*, pp. 167
and 311.   [3] Cf. *Maṣnavi*, 290, 8 seqq.

که خاک در لِباسِ کِیا رفته از هَوَس

که آب خَود هوا شُده از بهرِ این ولا

از راهِ اِتّحاد شُده آب آتشی

آتش شُده ز عشق هوا هم درین فضا

ارکان بِخانه خانه بِگشته چو بَیدقی

از بهرِ عشقِ شاه نه از لهو چون شُما

ای بیخبر بِرو که تُرا آبِ رَوشنی است

تا وا رهد ز آب و کُلت صفوَتِ صفا

زیراکه طالِبِ صِفَتِ صفوَتست آب

و آن نیست جُز وِصالِ تو با قُلزُمِ ضیا

(T. 10. 6ᵃ).

All the four elements are seething in this caldron (the
       world),
None is at rest, neither earth nor fire nor water nor air.
Now earth takes the form of grass, on account of desire,
Now water becomes air, for the sake of this affinity.
By way of unity water becomes fire,
Fire also becomes air in this expanse, by reason of love.
The elements wander from place to place, like a pawn,
For the sake of the King's love, not, like you, for pastime.
Go, ignorant one, for thine is a bright water (a divine
       principle),
That the quintessence of purity (the soul) may escape from
       thy water and clay (thy body);
Because the water seeks the quality of quintessence,
Which is nought but thy union with the sea of Light.

F. *Historical and Autobiographical allusions.* As one might expect, these are very few. The following list, though not absolutely complete, contains the most important. I should say that in compiling it I have used only the Tabrīz edition of the Dīvān.

(a) به یاد و بودِ مُحمّد نِگر که چون باقی است

ز بعدِ ششصد و پنجاه سخت‌بُنیادست

(T. 138. 3).

Behold, how enduring is the memory and existence of
　　Mohammed!
He is firmly stablished after six hundred and fifty years[1].

(b) مرا واجِب کُند کُر من بِرون آیم چو کُل از تن

که عُمرِم شُد بِشصت و من چو شین و سین درین شستم

(T. 242. 8ᵃ).

It behoves me to come forth, like a rose, from the body,
For my years are at sixty, and I am as 'shīn' and 'sīn' in
　　this 'shast[2].'

(c) باندیشه فرو بُرد مرا عقل چهل سال

بشصت و دو شُدم صَید و ز تدبیر بجستم

(T. 244. 1).

Forty years did Reason plunge me in care,
At three score and two I was made a prey and eschewed
　　(worldly) meditation[3].

---

[1] Either 650 A.H. or 661 A.H., according as we reckon from the Prophet's flight (Hijra) or from his death.

[2] Probably the meaning is: 'I am entangled (alluding to the shape of the letters شی and س) in this net (the phenomenal world).'

[3] This couplet is discussed in the Introduction.

(d)

خاقان اُردو خان اگر از جان نگردد ایلِ من

من پادشاهِ کِشوَرم بر خَیل و بر اُردو زنم

(T. 255. 9ᵃ).

Unless Khāqān Urdū Khān[1] becomes my devoted subject,
I am sovereign of the land, I will charge on (his) cavalry
and camp.

(e)

بر رافِضی چگونه ز بنی قُحافه لافم

بر خارِجی چگونه غمِ بو تُراب گویم

(T. 260. 7).

How should I boast of the Banū Kuḥāfa[2] to a Shī'ite?
How should I relate the woes of Bū Turāb ('Alī) to a
Khārijite[3]?

(f)

تو بدآن خُدای بِنگر که صد اِعتقاد بخشد

ز چه سُنّی است مروی ز چه رافِضی است قُنبی

(T. 355. 7).

Look thou on the God who bestows a hundred forms of
creed:
Why is the man of Marv a Sunnī, why is the man of
Kum[4] a Shī'ite?

---

[1] Probably the reference is to Halākū Khān, who overthrew the
Caliphate (656 A.H.). For اُردو see Herbelot, *Bibliothèque Orientale*,
Vol. IV. p. 296 seq.

[2] The mention of this tribe recalls Abū Bekr, whose father was
Abū Kuḥāfa. As is well known, the Shī'ites do not acknowledge the
first three Caliphs.

[3] The original Khārijites rebelled against 'Alī in the year 37 A.H.
(Mure, *Annals of the Early Caliphate*, Ch. XL.). Afterwards, the
name was given to a number of sects.

[4] Kum lies half-way between Teherān and Kāshān. Its inhabi-
tants, Shī'ites almost without exception, were regarded as desperately
fanatical. See Barbier de Meynard, *Dictionnaire de la Perse*, p. 459.

Of the famous Sūfīs who lived before him Jalālu'ddīn mentions Manṣūr Ḥallāj and Bāyazīd frequently; also Ibn Adham (T. 28. 2[a]). Among the poets Niẓāmī (T. 136. 6[a]), Sanā'ī (T. 175. 3[a]), and Ḥarīrī (T. 337. 9[a]). Other celebrated names are Abū Ḥanīfa and Shāfi'ī (T. 139. 9[a]), Akhfash (T. 216. 3), Kisā'ī (T. 109. 7[a]), and Plato (T. 303. 7; 349. 9). For 'Alī see XVI. ١١, note.

In T. 93. 10 we find a proverbial expression = 'carrying coals to Newcastle':

بصره چون کشم خُرما بکِرمان چون برم زیره

How should I take a load of dates to Baṣra or bring cumin to Kirmān?

APPENDIX II.

Translations in Verse. My aim has been, without departing from the sense, to reproduce, as far as possible, the passion and melody of the Persian. The arrangement of the rhymes in (c) and (d) corresponds to that of the original: a closer imitation could not be attempted, owing to fundamental differences of metrical system.

(a) VII.

He comes, a moon whose like the sky ne'er saw, awake or
    dreaming,
Crowned with eternal flame no flood can lay.
Lo, from the flagon of thy love, O Lord, my soul is
    swimming,
And ruined all my body's house of clay!

When first the Giver of the grape my lonely heart be-
    friended,
Wine fired my bosom and my veins filled up,
But when his image all mine eye possessed, a voice
    descended:
'Well done, O sovereign Wine and peerless Cup!'

Love's mighty arm from roof to base each dark abode is
    hewing
Where chinks reluctant catch a golden ray.
My heart, when Love's sea of a sudden burst into its
    viewing,
Leaped headlong in, with 'Find me now who may!'

    As, the sun moving, clouds behind him run,
    All hearts attend thee, O Tabríz's Sun!

(b) XII.

Poor copies out of heaven's original,
Pale earthly pictures mouldering to decay,
What care altho' your beauties break and fall,
When that which gave them life endures for aye?

O never vex thine heart with idle woes:
All high discourse enchanting the rapt ear,
All gilded landscapes and brave glistering shows
Fade—perish, but it is not as we fear.

While far away the living fountains ply,
Each petty brook goes brimful to the main.
Since brook nor fountain can forever die,
Thy fears how foolish, thy lament how vain!

What is this fountain, wouldst thou rightly know?
The Soul whence issue all created things.
Doubtless the rivers shall not cease to flow,
Till silenced are the everlasting springs.

Farewell to sorrow, and with quiet mind
Drink long and deep: let others fondly deem
The channel empty they perchance may find,
Or fathom that unfathomable stream.

The moment thou to this low world wast given,
A ladder stood whereby thou mightst aspire;
And first thy steps, which upward still have striven,
From mineral mounted to the plant: then higher

To animal existence: next, the Man,
With knowledge, reason, faith. O wondrous goal!
This body, which a crumb of dust began—
How fairly fashioned the consummate whole!

Yet stay not here thy journey: thou shalt grow
An angel bright and home far off in heaven.
Plod on, plunge last in the great Sea, that so
Thy little drop make oceans seven times seven.

'The Son of God!' Nay, leave that word unsaid,
Say, 'God is One, the pure, the single Truth.'
What tho' thy frame be withered, old, and dead,
If the soul save her fresh immortal youth?

(c) XXXI. ١—٦.

Lo, for I to myself am unknown, now in God's name
    what must I do?
I adore not the Cross nor the Crescent, I am not a
    Giaour nor a Jew.
East nor West, land nor sea is my home, I have kin nor
    with angel nor gnome,
I am wrought not of fire nor of foam, I am shaped not
    of dust nor of dew.
I was born not in China afar, not in Saqsīn and not in
    Bulghār;
Not in India, where five rivers are, nor 'Irāq nor Khorāsān
    I grew.
Not in this world nor that world I dwell, not in Paradise,
    neither in Hell;
Not from Eden and Riẓwān I fell, not from Adam my
    lineage I drew.
In a place beyond uttermost Place, in a tract without
    shadow of trace,
Soul and body transcending, I live in the soul of my
    Loved One anew!

(d) XXXVI. ١—٦.

Up, O ye lovers, and away! 'Tis time to leave the world
    for aye.

Hark, loud and clear from heaven the drum of parting
  calls—let none delay !
The cameleer hath risen amain, made ready all the camel-
  train,
And quittance now desires to gain : why sleep ye, travellers, I pray ?
Behind us and before there swells the din of parting and
  of bells ;
To shoreless Space each moment sails a disembodied spirit
  away.
From yonder starry lights and through those curtain-
  awnings darkly blue
Mysterious figures float in view, all strange and secret
  things display.
From this orb, wheeling round its pole, a wondrous slumber
  o'er thee stole :
O weary life that weighest nought, O sleep that on my
  soul dost weigh !
O heart, toward thy heart's love wend, and O friend, fly
  toward the Friend,
Be wakeful, watchman, to the end : drowse seemingly
  no watchman may.

(e) XLIV. ı—v.

Why wilt thou dwell in mouldy cell, a captive, O my
  heart ?
Speed, speed the flight ! a nursling bright of yonder
  world thou art.
He bids thee rest upon his breast, he flings the veil away :
Thy home wherefore make evermore this mansion of decay ?
O contemplate thy true estate, enlarge thyself, and rove
From this dark world, thy prison, whirled to that celestial
  grove.

O honoured guest in Love's high feast, O bird of the
    angel-sphere,
'Tis cause to weep, if thou wilt keep thy habitation here.
A voice at morn to thee is borne—God whispers to the
    soul—
'If on the way the dust thou lay, thou soon wilt gain
    the goal.'
That road be thine toward the Shrine! and lo, in bush
    and briar,
The many slain by love and pain in flower of young desire,
Who on the track fell wounded back and saw not, ere
    the end,
A ray of bliss, a touch, a kiss, a token of the Friend!

APPENDIX III.

TABLE SHOWING WHERE THE SELECTED POEMS OCCUR IN OTHER EDITIONS OF THE DĪVĀN.

The first number refers to the page, the second to the couplet with which the poem commences. When 'a' is affixed, it denotes that the couplet in question is printed in the margin of the text. Thus T. 7. 12ᵃ is the twelfth couplet, counted from the top, in the margin of page 7 of the Tabrīz Edition.

Number of the poem	Tabriz Edition	Lakhnau Edition	Rosen-zweig's Auswahl
I.	T. 7. 12ᵃ	Lakh. 24. 17ᵃ	
II.	113. 9	14. 8	
III.	126. 9ᵃ	8. 3ᵃ	
IV.		4. 3	
V.	119. 7ᵃ	21. 8	
VI.	134. 5		
VII.	20. 9ᵃ	25. 12ᵃ	
VIII.		28. 2	22
IX.	143. 5	41. 6	
X.	136. 9		
XI.	22. 2ᵃ		
XII.			32
XIII.	146. 3ᵃ	34. 10ᵃ	
XIV.		47. 4	
XV.	148. 6	30. 12ᵃ	
XVI.	146. 6	32. 1ᵃ	
XVII.			58
XVIII.	159. 3		

Number of the poem	Tabriz Edition	Lakhnau Edition	Rosen-zweig's Auswahl
XIX.	T. 199. 3	Lakh. 53. 7[a]	
XX.	171. 3		
XXI.	157. 11[a]	81. 12	
XXII.	175. 3[a]		
XXIII.	178. 9[a]	55. 10[a]	
XXIV.	171. 9	93. 14	
XXV.	33. 9	107. 10[a]	
XXVI.		97. 10	
XXVII.	33. 11[a]		
XXVIII.	40. 12[a]		
XXIX.	38. 11[a]		
XXX.		152. 10	
XXXI.	257. 5		
XXXII.	250. 4	161. 14	
XXXIII.	262. 11	160. 15[a]	
XXXIV.	247. 8		
XXXV.	267. 8		
XXXVI.	45. 7[a]		
XXXVII.		171. 16	
XXXVIII.	290. 9[a]		
XXXIX.	288. 12		
XL.	301. 6	214. 13[a]	
XLI.	300. 7	216. 5	
XLII.	319. 6	234. 14	
XLIII.	320. 5		
XLIV.	349. 12		
XLV.		242. 15	
XLVI.	347. 9		
XLVII.	326. 1[a]		
XLVIII.		220. 4	

APPENDIX IV.

COMPARATIVE TABLE OF PASSAGES QUOTED FROM THE MAṢNAVĪ.

The references given in the Notes are to the Bombay Ed. (1280 A.H.), of which the Lakhnau Ed. (1282 and 1291 A.H.) is a facsimile. The slight discrepancies shown below are due to defective pagination in the former. Both these editions are inferior to the text with Turkish translation published at Būlāq (1268 A.H.).

Quoted in the Notes	Bombay Edition		Lakhnau Edition		Būlāq Edition		
page	page	line	page	line	Book	page	line
202 (II. ١)	4,	7	4,	7	I.	2,	13
210 (IV. ١ ١)	7,	23	7,	23	omitted		
219 (VII. ٧)	8,	19	8,	19	I.	8,	25
223 (IX. ٣)	336,	5	336,	5	IV.	59,	3
229 (XI. ٨)	232,	23	231,	23	III.	72,	9
230 (XI. ٨)	233,	3	232,	3	III.	72,	13
231 (XII. ١)	32,	7	32,	7	.I.	47,	4
231 (XII. ٧)	278,	8	278,	8	III.	149,	6
235 (XIII. ١ ٥)	5,	8	5,	8	I.	3,	20
237 (XIV. ١ .)	541,	5	539,	5	VI.	79,	20
240 (XV. ١ ٧)	37,	4	38,	4	I.	56,	7
240 (XV. ١ ٧)	37,	12	38,	12	I.	56,	22
241 (XV. ١ ٧)	6,	8	6,	8	I.	5,	4
245 (XVI. ١ ٨)	459,	15	459,	14	V.	118,	1
245 (XVI. ٣ .)	118,	5	117,	5	II.	29,	10

Quoted in the Notes	Bombay Edition		Lakhnau Edition		Būlāq Edition		
page	page	line	page	line	Book	page	line
247 (XVI. ٢٢)	121,	11	120,	11	II.	34,	19
261 (XXII. ٨)	11,	18	11,	17	I.	13,	11
264 (XXIII. ٦)	21,	1	21,	1	I.	28,	10
267 (XXV. ١١)	12,	14	12,	14	I.	14,	22
268 (XXV. ١٢)	439,	2	439,	2	V.	82,	3
270 (XXV. ١٧)	542,	16	540,	16	VI.	82,	1
272 (XXVI. ٨)	21,	5	21,	5	I.	28,	15
278 (XXIX. ٥)	370,	13	370,	13	IV.	114,	8
290 (XXXVI. ٥)	385,	22	385,	22	IV.	140,	4
293 (XXXVI. ١٣)	176,	9	175,	9	II.	123,	11
294 (XXXVII. ١٣)	60,	10	60,	10	I.	93,	12
299 (XXXIX. ٩)	14,	4	14,	4	I.	17,	6
300 (XL. ٣٤)	12,	7	12,	7	I.	14,	10
303 (XLII. ١)	22,	4	22,	4	I.	30, 6[1]	
308 (XLIII. ٥)	122,	2	121,	2	omitted		
315 (XLVII. ٣٤)	8,	2	8,	2	I.	7,	25
317 (XLVIII. ٣)	362,	18	362,	18	IV.	101,	25
317 (XLVIII. ٣٤)	126,	13	125,	13	II.	42,	8

[1] The first line of this passage, يك زمانى الخ, is omitted.

INDEX TO THE NOTES.

I. PERSIAN AND ARABIC.

١

آشکارصنعت, xvi. ٢٠

آشنا, x. ٣

اطلس, xxii. ٩

آفت, xiv. ١١

افزوید, xviii. ٥

اقمر, xi. ١٥

اَلَسْت, ix. ٩

اَللّٰهُ اَكْبَر, xi. ٤

امان, vi. ١١

امکان, ii. ٧

اَنَا اَلْحَقّ, vi. ١٢

اِنتظار, xiii. ٩

اندیشه, xiii. ١٢, xlii. ١٠

اُنس, xliv. ٤

اهل, xxv. ١٦

عَو = او, vi. ١٣

اوانی, vi. ١٠

١

آبِ حیات, xxi. ٦

ابن سینا, xvii. ٩

اِتِّحاد, xxv. ١٢

عشق = آتش, vii. ١, xxxii. ٢

احوَلی, xxv. ١١

ادب, xxxii. ١٠

اِرجِعُوا, xxxix. ٨

اِرْجِعِی, xxix. ٣

از آن پَی, xli. ٧

از بهرِ چیزی را, xli. ٦, xlii. ٣

از میان رفتن, xlviii. ٨

اِستقامت, xiv. ١١, Add. Notes, ibid.

آستین, xxx. ٩

اِشتقاق, i. ٣

ایمان, xxxv. ٢, Add. Notes, xvi. ٢١

این و ان, xx. ٦

ب

با = notwithstanding, xlii. ١٠

با این همه, xi. ٣

باد دادن, xl. ٨

باده, xxxii. ٦, xli. ٣

بادهنوش, xl. ٤

باری, xxi. ٢

ناز, ii. ٩, xvi. ٣, xlviii. ٣, ٤

باغبان, xxxix. ٣

بافر, xi. ١

بُت, xxxiv. ١

بتر, x. ٢

بُتخانه, xvii. ٥

بجل, xxviii. ٤

بدل, xii. ٢

بر, بر, xiii. ٣

بُرد, xxii. ٩

بر دوختن, xxi. ١

بر سرِ (چیزی بودن), xlvii. ٢

بُریده سر, ii. ٣

بقا, iv. ١٠

بلا, x. ٨

بُلغار, xxxi. ٤

بندگی, xliv. ١٣

بو لهب, xxxii. ٢

به, with participle, xiii. ١

بیان, xxiii. ٧

بی پای, xxxv. ١٠

بی ز, xxxiii. ٤

بیسری, xxxvii. ١٦

بیشهٔ شیران, xv. ١٦, Add. Notes, ibid.

بیقرار, v. ٤

پ

پاسبان, xxxvi. ٦

پاك, xxxix. ٦

پایگاه, xxxvii. ٧

پای ماچان, xxix. ٧

پذیرا, xxvii. ٧

پُر, vi. ١٣

پرده دریدن, xlvii. ٤

پردهٔ عراقی, xli. ٣

پروانه, xxi. ٤

پریشان, ii. ٨

پستی, i. ٩

پنج و چار, XXVI. ٧

پياده, XL. ٧

پياله, VII. ۴

پير, I. ١٠, XXIX. ٧

ت

تافتن, XX. ٨

تبريز, VI. ١٥

تجنيسِ اشتقاق, I. ٣

تردامن, XIV. ٥

تُرك, XXVIII. ٦

تلخى, VI. ١

تماشا, IX. ١

تميز, XIII. ١٥, Add. Notes, ibid.

تو, XXV. ١٣

توبه شكستن, XXXVI. ١٠

ج

جادوئى, XXI. ١

جان, XXVIII. ١

جان‌بخشى, XXIX. ٥

جانِ جانان, XXXI. ٦

جانِ جهان, VI. ١٢

جان دادن, IX. ٥; cf. Add. Notes, XVIII. ١

جانِ نُوم, XXII. ٧, Add. Notes, ibid.

جانِ كُل, XXII. ٥, ٧

جرح, XIV. ٥

جماعت, XLII. ١

جَنان, XXIV. ۴

جَوّ, XXIV. ٩

جواب و سُؤال, XIV. ١

جُوال, XXIX. ١١

جوان, IX. ٥

جوشيدن, XIV. ٢

جَوف, XXIV. ٩

جَولان, II. ١١

جَيب, XXX. ٩

چ

چاكرنوازى, XI. ٦

چراغ, XXIII. ٦, Add. Notes, ibid.

چشمِ بدِ, XXV. ١١

چشمِ خِرَد, XLV. ٦

چشم داشتن, XXXIII. ٢

چشمِ كُشته, XLVIII. ٩

چشمِ نِهان, XLII. ٢

چغانه, XV. ١

چِثْل, XXVIII. ٢

چلیپا, XVII. ٤

چمن, v. ١

چنبر شُدن, XXI. ٥.

چه—چه, II. ٩

ح

حال, v. ٤, IX. ١٢—١٣, XIV. ١١

حقّ, II. ٧

حقیقت, XVI. ١٥

حقیقی, XIII. ٥

حلالی خواستن, XXXVI. ٢

حلقه بگوش, XIII. ١٠.

حُلول, XXV. ١٢

حوادث, x. ٣

حواسّ, XLIV. ١٠.

حیا, I. ١

خ

خاك بر سر, x. ٦

خام, x. ٨

خاموش (شُدن از چیزی), XLII. ١١

خانهٔ آب و گل, XXXIV. ٦, XXXV. ٨

خانهٔ صُنع, XXXV. ٩

خراب, VII. ٢

خرابات, XLII. ١

خشخاش, XLII. ٥

خُمر, XXX. ٦

خُمار, III. ٧

خمّاره, III. ٧

خندان, XXVI. ٣

خندق, XXV. ١٤

خواب, XXXVI. ٥, XXXIX. ٩

خواندن, XXXII. ١٠.

خون‌خواره, III. ٣

خویش, XXVI. ١

خیال, XV. ١٧

د

دُر, VIII. ٥

دُردکش, XLII. ١

دریا, I. ٨

دریچه, XXXII. ٣

دُزدیده, XXXVII. ٣

دست, XXVI. ٥

دستان, II. ١٣, XVI. ١١, XXXI. ١٢

دست بر سر, XI. ١٠.

دست دادن, XXXI. ١١

دُعا, IV. ١١, v. ٥

دغل‌فروش, XL. ۴

دفع كُفتن, XVI. ٥

دل, XXVIII. ۱

دم زدن, II. ۸

دِه, XXXVI. ۱۱

دُهُل زيرِ گُليم, I. ۱۳

دو ديده, XXXII. ٥

دَور, XLII. ٦

دوغ, XXIV. ۳

دوگانه, XV. ۱٥

دولابى, XXXVI. ٥

دَيّار, XLV. ٥

ديده, XVI. ۲۰

دَير, XVII. ٥

ديك, XXXVI. ۱۳

ديوان, I. ۷

ذ

ذو آلفقار, XXVI. ۳

ر

رازى, XXII. ۸

رأسُ آلحِمَارِ, XXXIX. ۱۱

رايتِ منصور, XXV. ۱۷

رُبا, XLII. ۷

رباب, XVI. ۲۲

ربابى, XVI. ۲۲

رَبَّیَ آلأَعْلَى, I. ٥

رُخ, X. ٥, XVII. ۷

رخت, XVIII. ٥

رخنه‌چه, XXXVI. ۱۱

رسن‌بازى, XXI. ٥

رِضوان, XXXI. ٥

رقص, XVI. ۱۰

رُكنِ يمانى, XLIV. ۱۱

رِندى, XXXI. ۱۲

رنگ, XXX. ۲

رنگ و بو, XXXIX. ٥

رهگُذر, XLIV. ۱۳

روپوش, IX. ۱٥

رَوِش, I. ۲

روم, XXII. ۸

رَى, XXII. ۸

رَيحان, XVI. ٦, XLVIII. ۱۰

ريشخند, XXXVI. ۱۱

ز

زبانِ مُرغان, II. ٥, XXXV. ۷

زبانه زدن, XLI. ٥

زخمه, XLI. ۲

زر, opposed to مس, IV. ۷, XXXIX. ۸, XLIII. ۴

زُلف, II. ۳, XV. ۱۱, XXI. ۴, XXVIII. ۵

زُهـد, XIV. ۱۰, Add. Notes, ibid.

زهر چشیدن, I. ۴

زُهره, V. ۶

زو, XXI. ۵

زیان کردن, I. ۱۲

س

سادهرنگی, XXVI. ۹, Add. Notes, ibid.

سادهروی, XIII. ۱۳

ساقی, III. ۷

سُبْحَانی, VI. ۱۲

سپر کردن, XXXVII. ۶

سر خر, XXXIX. ۱۱

سرد, XLVI. ۱

سرِ رِشته, XXVIII. ۵

سرِ زُلف, XV. ۱۱, XVII. ۳

سرو, XXVI. ۳

سعادت, XLIII. ۱۱, XLIV. ۱۲

سفر, XIX. ۱—۴, XXII. ۸, XXVII. ۷

سقا, IX. ۱۹

سقسین, XXXI. ۴

سماع, II. ۱۱, III. ۴, XLII. ۶

سنائی, XXII. ۱

سُهیل, XLIV. ۱۱

سَوَادُ الْوَجهِ, VI. ۱

سودگن, Add. Notes, I. ۱۰

سیاه, XLV. ۱۰

ش

شایِستن, with participle, XXXVI. ۶

شبان, XXVIII. ۱

شرر, XLIII. ۹

شر و شور, XXV. ۱۰

شش جِهَت, XXXIX. ۹

شش فتیله, XLIII. ۹

شِعار, XIII. ۱

شکّر, XLIII. ۵

شُکوز, XLVIII. ۱۰

شکیفتن, XXI. ۶

شمعهانی سرنگون, XXXVI. ۴

شیرِ خُدا, XVI. ۱۱

ص

صبا, IV. ۹

صحرا, I. ۱۳

صفِّ نعال, XXIX. ٧

صُفّه, XXIII. ٤

صورت, II. ٢, XXV. ١٣, XXXIV. ١, XLVI. ٢

صوفى, XXIX. ٤

صَياد, IX. ١٩

ط

طبلِ باز, XVI. ٣, XXIX. ٣

طريقت, I. ٢

طلب, XXXII. ٩

طِلِسم, XV. ٤

طَوق, II. ٦

ظ

ظُلم, XVI. ١٥

ع

عالى رِكاب, VIII. ٩

عُثمان, XVI. ٢٢

عجائب, used adjectivally, Add. Notes, XXXVI. ٤

عجب, used adjectivally, XXXVI. ٤

عجم, XXXII. ٥

عجوز, XLII. ٤

عدد, XLVI. ٧

عدل, XIV. ٥

عَدَم, II. ٧, VIII. ٩

عذرا, I. ٧

عِراقَين, XXXI. ٤

عرش, II. ١٢

عروس, V. ٨

عشق, I. ١, IV. ١٠

عقل, IV. ١٠

عقلِ كُلّ, IX. ٥, ١٤; XXII. ٥, ٧

عقيد, XLV. ٧

عقيده, XLV. ٧

عقيق, XVI. ١٣

عقيله, XXXVII. ١٣, XLV. ٩

عُمان, XII. ١٠

عنقا, XVII. ٧

عيان, XXIII. ٧

عيسَى, IV. ٩, XII. ١١, Add. Notes, XXXIX. ١١

غ

غرامت, XIV. ٥

غريب, XXV. ٤, XXXVII. ٢

غم, V. ٧

غمّاز, XIII. ١٦, XXV. ١٥

غمّازخانه, XXV. ١٥

غيور, XXV. ١٢

ف

فاعِلِ حقیقی, XXVI. ٩

فتح, XXV. ١٧

فِردَوس, XXXI. ٥

فِرعَون, XVI. ١٥

فَریضه, XXXIX. ٢

فقر, VI. ١, Add. Notes, ibid.

فلکِ اِضافت, XXV. ١٣, XXXVII. ١٣ (footnote), XLII. ١٠.

فُلان, VI. ٨

فُلانی, XLII. ٨

فنا, I. ٤

فَنَآءِ الْفَنَآءِ, Add. Notes, IV. ١١

فنا گَشتن, XXIII. ٥

فنینه, Add. Notes, XXXIX. ١٢

فَیض, IV. ٨

ق

قابَ قَوْسَیْن, XVII. ١٠

قارون, VI. ١, XLIII. ٤

قاف, XVII. ٧

قبا, I. ١٥

قبا کَردن, XXIII. ٨

قِبله, VI. ٢

قطّاره, XXXVI. ٢

قفس, قفس, XXIX. ٦, XLVIII. ٣

قِلاده, XL. ٩

قِلّاشی, XXXI. ١٢

قلب, XIII. ١٠

قَیصر, XIV. ٨

ک

کابین, XLII. ٤

کارخانه, XXXV. ٨

کارگه, XVI. ٢٠

کافر, XVI. ١٠

کاه, IV. ٤, ٧

کبک, II. ٩

کت, XLVI. ٤

کُجا—کُجا, IX. ٤

کعبه, XLIII. ١٠

کف, XIX. ٧, XXVI. ٥, XLV. ١٤

کفشکن, XXIX. ٧

کلید, XLVII. ١٣

کم زدن, XLII. ١٠

کِنار, XIII. ٦

کندن و پَیوَستن, XXXV. ٢

کِه, XVI. ١٨

کُهِستان, II. ٩

کهتِل, IV. ٤

کَوثر, XI. ٩

كوچ كردن, XXXVI. ١

كوچه, XXXV. ٥

كودكى, XXIX. ١٠

كوره, XXXVII. ١٠

كوزهٔ ادراك, Add. Notes, IX. ١٩

كيميا, IV. ٧, XLIII. ٤; Add. Notes, IV. ٧

كيوان, II. ١٠

گ

گبر, XXXI. ١

گر چنانكه, XXXVII. ١٧

گرد, XLVI. ٨

گر زآنكه, XXVII. ١٧

گرمدار, XLV. ١١

گل, XIII. ٨

گنيد خضرا, I. ١٤

گنج, XXVI. ٧

گنج در خراب, VIII. ٢

گنج روان, VI. ١

گنج نهان, IV. ٢

گهر فرد, XLVI. ٤

گوش كشيدن, XLVII. ٥

گوشوار, XIII. ١٠

ل

لحد, XXIV. ٦

لرزان, XVI. ١٣

لعل, XXVII. ٧

مـ

ماه, مه, VII. ١

ماهى, XXXIX. ٥

مثانى, VI. ٥, XLIV. ١٠

مجاز, XIII. ٥

مجذوب مطلق, VI. ١٢

مجنون, I. ٣

محرم, XXVIII. ٤

مدد, VI. ١٢

مرد, XXII. ٩

مرد خدا, VIII. ١

مرغ, X. ٧

مرغزى, XXII. ٨

مروزى, XXII. ٨

مرو الرود, XXII. ٨

مرو الشاهجان, XXII. ٨

مريد, Add. Notes, XI. ٨

مس, IV. ٧, XXXIX. ٨, XLIII. ٤

مستعار, XIII. ٥

مستى, I. ٩

مُسجّع, IX. ١٣

مشارق, XLV. ٤

مُشتری طالِع, XLV. ١١

مشك, IX. ١٩

مِصر, XLIII. ٥

مُصطَفَی, IX. ٥

معنی, II. ٢

مقام, XIV. ١١

ملامت, XIV. ٩

مندیش, XII. ٥

مَوج, IX. ١١

میان, XLVIII. ٨

ن

ناطِقِ اخرس, XXXVI. ١٧

ناموس, I. ٢

نبات, XLIII. ٥

نتانی, XX. ٨

نِثار, V. ١

ندا, VII. ٤

نظّاره, XXIII. ٥

نظامی, X. ١٠

نغمهٔ عُثمان, XVI. ٢٢

نفخهٔ صور, XXV. ٨

نفسِ کُل, IX. ١٠

نقّاش, XXXIV. ١

نقد, XLV. ٢

نُقطه, XXII. ١٠

نُقطهگویا, XXII. ١٠

نِثار, V. ٨

نِگین, I. ١٠

نِگین کُن, Add. Notes, I. ١٠

نماز, VI. ٥, XLIV. ١٠

نهنك, XVI. ٧

ه

هُدهُد, II. ٦

هستی, XXVI. ٣

هل, XLII. ٢

همرنك, XXXIV. ٥, XLII. ١

همی, XXXI. ١١

هوا, II. ١٢, X. ٧, etc.

هیج, VI. ١١

و

وَالضُّحَی, IX. ٦, XXIII. ٧

وامِق, I. ٧

وُجود, XXXVII. ٧

وَردِ احمر, XI. ١٢

وَلَد, XII. ١١

وَیسه, I. ٧

ى

يافته = يافت, XVI. ١٦

يا من هو, XXXI. ٨

يا هو, XXXI. ٨

ياي فاعِل, XVI. ٢٢

ياي وَحدت, XVI. ٢٢

يثرب, XXVII. ٦

يقين, XX. ٥

يوسُف, XV. ١ ٢, XVI. ٨, XLIII. ٦

II. ENGLISH.

Abū Lahab, XXXII. ٢

Adept, the Ṣūfī, above law, VIII. ٨

'Adhrā, I. ٧

Adjective, used as noun, II. ٨, IV. ١١, XVI. ١٣; formed by prepositions, XI. ١

'Alī, XVI. ١١

Anāhīd, V. ٦

Asceticism, XIV. ١٠

Assonance, I. ٣, XXV. ١٣

Avicenna, I. ٦, XVII. ٩

Bāb, I. ٥

Bāyazīd, VI. ١٢

Beloved, the cruelty of, III. ٣; likened to a rose, XI. ١٢

Bilqīs, II. ٦

Birds, the language of, II. ٥, XXXV. ٧

Blue and green, varieties of the same colour, I. ١٣

Body, conscious of the soul's superiority, VI. ١٣; composed of four elements, VIII. ١٣; compared to an ass, IV. ٩; to a camel, XLIII. ١٠

Bulghār, XXXI. ١٣

Canopus, XLIV. ١١

Chigil, XXVIII. ٢

Christianity, allusions to, VI. ١٣, XII. ١١, XXV. ١٢, XXXI. ١٠

Contingent Being, II. ٧

Cup-bearer, III. ٧

Dance, the mystic, II. ١١, III. ١٣, XLII. ٦

Death, a spiritual resurrection, XXV. ٦

Dervish, a king in disguise, VIII. ٣

Desert, of Absolute Being, I. ١٣; of Love, II. ١

Diogenes, the Cynic, XVI. ١٨

Director, the spiritual, I. ١٠, XXIX. ٧

Dualism, XXIII. ٦·—٧, XXV. ١١

Ecstasy, I. ٩, IX. ١٢—١٣

Egoism, XXVIII. ٨

Egypt, XLIII. ٥

Elements, the four, V. ١١, VIII. ١٣

Emanation, II. ٢, IV. ٨, VI. ١٢, IX. ١١, XIX. ٦

Evolution, XI. ٩—١٠, XXXVI.
  ٨, XLVII. ١٢
Existence, a disgrace, IV. ١١,
  XIII. ١
Eye, the inward, XI. ٥; the
  evil, XXV. ١١

Fakhru'ddīn Jurjānī, I. ٧
Fasting, VIII. ١
Forms, educative value of,
  XXXIV. ١, Add. Notes, ibid.
Fountain of Life, XXI. ٩
Freewill, = absence of self-will,
  XIII. ٣

God, the Beloved *par excellence*, I. ٣; compared to
  the bezel on a ring, I. ١٠;
  addressed as Bride, V. ٨;
  dwells in the soul, XVII. ١١;
  unattainable by human ex-
  ertion, XX. ١, Add. Notes,
  ibid.; desired to display his
  beauty, IV. ٣, XXIII. ٧; the
  only real agent, XXVI. ٩;
  transcends and pervades
  the universe, XXXVII. ٣;
  centre of the universe, Add.
  Notes, XXII. ١٠; unknow-
  able save by himself, XXIII.
  ٥, Add. Notes, ibid.
Grace, ebbs and flows in the
  soul, XVIII. ١

Hātifī, I. ٣
Headlessness, = self-annihila-
  tion, II. ٣, XXXVII. ١٦
Heaven, an obstacle to union,
  II. ١٣
Henna, V. ٨
Hidden saints, VIII. ١٠
Hidden treasure, VIII. ٣; in a
  mystical sense, IV. ٣
Hoopoe, II. ٦
Hope and Fear, the two wings
  of, XLVIII. ١٠
Humility, I. ٩

Ideas, the Platonic theory of,
  XII. ١
Illumination, IV. ١٠
Imagination, directs all human
  actions, XV. ١٧
Incarnation, XXV. ١٣
Intoxication, = ecstasy, I. ٩
'Irāqi 'Ajamī, XXXI. ١٤
'Irāqi 'Arabī, XXXI. ١٤
Izāfat, VII. ٧, X. ٨, XXVIII. ٧,
  XXIX. ١; dropped, XXV. ١٣,
  XXXVII. ١٣ (footnote), XLII.
  ١٠.

Jacob, XVI. ٨
Jāmī, I. ٣
Jealousy, of God, V. ٧, XXV.
  ١٣
Jesus, IV. ٩, XII. ١١, Add.
  Notes, XXXIX. ١١

Joseph, xv. ١٢, xvi. ٨, ٢٢,
    xliii. ٦
Journey, the mystic's, xix.
    ١—٤, xxvii. ٧

Kauṣar, xi. ٩
Kor'ān, quoted or referred to,
    I. ٣, ٥, ٦ ; II. ٥, ٦ ; IV. ٦,
    ٩ ; V. ٦, VI. ١٣, IX. ٩, XIII.
    ١٣, xv. ١٢, xvi. ٦, ٨ ;
    XVII. ١, ١٠ ; XXIII. ٦, ٧ ;
    XXIV. ٨, XXV. ٨, ١٢ ; XXVI.
    ١, XXIX. ٣, ١٢ ; XXXII. ٢,
    XXXIX. ٨, ٩ (footnote); XL.
    ٣, XLII. ١, ١٠ ; XLIII. ٥,
    XLIV. ٥, XLVII. ١٠ ; Add.
    Notes, XVII. ٨, XXIII. ٦,
    XXXI. ٨
Korah, VI. ١, XLIII. ٥

Lailā, I. ٣, X. ١٠
Learning, useless in love, VIII.
    ٧
Love, implies loss of selfhood,
    I. ١ ; opposed to Reason, IV.
    ١٠, IX. ١٩, XXXVII. ١٣ ;
    expressed in music, xv. ٥ ;
    compared to a player on the
    rebeck, XVI. ٢٢ ; does not
    admit of cure, XXXIII. ٥ ;
    transforms the earthly na-
    ture, XLIII. ٥
Lunacy, a mark of divine
    favour, I. ٣

Magianism, VI. ١٣
Majnūn, I. ٣
Man, the final cause of crea-
    tion, I. ١٠, XVII. ٢ ; above
    the angels, IX. ٣ ; the mi-
    crocosm, II. ٢, IV. ٣ ; com-
    pounded of Being and Not-
    being, II. ٧. IV. ٣ ; XLVII.
    ٩ ; must die to the world,
    I. ٥, II. ٢ ; a plaything of
    Deity, XI. ٦ ; compared to
    a lute, XVI. ٢٢ ; his worth
    dependent on his ideal, XVIII.
    ٦ ; the meeting-point of two
    worlds, XXXVI. ١٦ ; homeless
    in the world, XLVI. ٧ ; half
    angel, half beast, Add.
    Notes, IX. ٣
Manṣūr Ḥallāj, VI. ١٢, XVII.
    ١, XXV. ١٧, XXXVIII. ١
Merv, XXII. ٨
Metre, I. ٦, VIII. ٧, XI. ٥, ١٥ ;
    XXII. ٥, XXXIX. ٥
Mohammed, his night-journey
    to heaven, I. ٦ ; identified
    with Universal Reason, IX. ٥
Moon, a frequent metaphor
    for the Beloved, VII. ١ ;
    splitting of the moon, IX.
    ٧—٨
Moses, II. ٥, XVI. ١٥, XLIII. ٥
Moth and Candle, XXI. ٥
Mount Qāf, XVII. ٧
Music, xv. ٥, XLI. ٣

Najmu'ddīn Kubrā, XVI. ١.
Nīmfatha, XI. ١ᶜ
Nizāmī, I. ٣, X. ١.
Nizāmī 'Arūzī, I. ٧
Nominativus pendens, VII. ٧
Not-being, reflects the quali-
ties of Being, II. ٧, XL. ٦
Obedience, XLIV. ١٣
'Omān, sea of, XII. ١.
'Othmān, XVI. ٣٣
Outward form, an illusion,
XIX. ٨
Pain, synonymous with love,
III. ٣; inflicted as a proba-
tion, v. ٧, XXVIII. ٧
Partridge, hunted by the fal-
con, II. ٩
Passions, compared to lions,
XV. ١٦
Pearls, legend as to the origin
of, VIII. ٥
Persian oaths, XV. ٨
Pharaoh, XVI. ١٥
Phenomena, intoxicated with
the wine of love, I. ١٥; de-
rive their existence from
the Ideal, IX. ١٦; com-
pared to the tresses of the
Beloved, XV. ١١, XVI. ١.
Plurality, a phantom, XXVI. ٨
Poverty, spiritual, VI. ١
Prayer, IV. ١١, v. ٥, VI. ٥

Pre-existence of the soul, XVII.
١
Prepositions, doubled, IX. ١١;
omitted, XXII. ٩, XXVI. ٣,
Add. Notes, XI. ١ᶜ
Present Conditional, XXV. ١١ᶜ
Procrastination, XIII. ٩
Pronoun repeated, VI. ١ᶜ, ١.;
XXXVI. ٥
Prosody, XXI. ٣
Proverbs, Arabic, I. ٩, XIII.
٩, XIV. ١., ١٣; XVIII. ٦,
XXVIII. ٨; Add. Notes, XXII.
٩, XXVIII. ٨, XXXII. ٣

Quietism, XI. ٨, XXXVI. ١٥;
Add. Notes, ibid.

Rabāb (rebeck), XVI. ٣٣
Rai, XXII. ٨
Rāmīn, I. ٧
Reason, opposed to love, IV.
١., IX. ١٩, XXXVII. ١٣;
annihilated in union, XL. ٨
Religions indifferent, VIII. ٨,
XV. ٣
Reserve, doctrine of, XXV. ١٦,
Add. Notes, ibid.
Rizvān, XXXI. ٥
Roc, XVII. ٧
Rose, the celestial, XIII. ٨
Rubies, coloured by the sun,
XXVII. ٧

Rūm, XXII. ٨
Rustam, XVI. ١١

Sa'dī, IX. ١
Saints, advantage of associating with, XLII. ١; unrecognised, VIII. ١٠
Ṣalāḥu'ddīn Zarkūb, II. ١٣
Sanā'ī, XXII. ١
Saqsīn, XXXI. ١٣, Add. Notes, ibid.
Saturn, II. ١٠
Sea, of divine love, I. ٨; of Absolute Being, VIII. ٥, IX. ١٠, ١١
Self, the true, XXVI. ١
Self-annihilation, I. ١٣, II. ٣, IV. ١١, VI. ١, VII. ٢, XXVII. ٨, XLII. ٣
Silence, I. ١٨, XXVI. ٩, XXXVI. ١٧
Sīmurgh, XVII. ٧
Slavery, the badge of, XIII. ١٠
Sleep, of phenomenal existence, XXXVI. ٥
Solomon, II. ٥—٧
Sorcery, XXI. ١
Soul, entangled in the Beloved's tresses, XXI. ١٣, XXVIII. ٥; identical with God, XVII. ١١; reluctant to enter the world, XXXV. ١٠; obscured by pride, XXXVI. ١٣; suffers tribulation, v; cannot reveal divine mysteries, XIII. ١٦; remembers her heavenly origin, XVII. ١, XXXIX. ٥; soul of the world, VI. ١٢; compared to a child in the cradle, III. ١٣; to a bird, X. ٧, XVI. ٣, XXIX. ٧, etc.; to a mirror, XI. ٧, XIII. ١٥, XXVIII. ٢; to a window, XXXII. ٣; to a frenzied camel, XXXVII. ١٣, XLV. ٧; to the Ka'ba, XLIII. ١٠; to Jesus, IV. ٩
Sūfī, XXIX. ١٣; must live in the present, XIII. ٩
Sūfiism, definition of, Add. Notes, XXXVI. ١٥
Sulaimān Khān, the Bābī, XVI. ١٠

Tabrīz, VI. ١٥
Talismans, XV. ١٣
Tashdīd, VIII. ٩, IX. ١٩, XVI. ٧, XXIII. ٥, XXXVI. ٢, XL. ٥
Traditions, of the Prophet, I. ١, ١٣; IV. ٢, VI. ١, VIII. ١, ١٠; IX. ٣, XI. ٩, XV. ٣, XVII. ٢, ١١; XVIII. ٧, XXV. ١٢, XXVII. ٧, XXX. ٢, XXXV. ٨; Add. Notes, I. ١, VI. ٢
Trinity, the Christian, VI. ١٣

Union, beyond the reach of intellect, XIX. ٩; involves

identification of subject and object, xxv. ٩

Unity, of creeds, viii. ٨, xv. ٢; of lover and Beloved, xxxviii. ١; a sea of blood, xxxiv. ٥

'Unṣurī, i. ٧

Veils, ix. ١٣, Add. Notes, ibid.

Waisa, i. ٧
Wāmiq, i. ٧
Wine, an emblem of the Divinity, xli. ٣

World, the phenomenal, viii. ٩; within the eye, xxxv. ٣; regarded as a cube, xxxix. ٩; compared to a dead mistress, xiii. ٧; to a dyeing-vat, xxx. ٧; to a mirror, xl. ٧; to an old woman, xlii. ١٣

Yellow, = pale, xxxvii. ١.

Zāl, xvi. ١١
Zuhra, v. ٧